MENTAL HEALTH AND PUNISHMENTS

How might we best manage those who have offended but have mental vulnerabilities? How are risks identified, managed and minimised? What are ideological differences of care and control, punishment and therapy negotiated in practice? These questions are just some which are debated in the eleven chapters of this book. Each with their focus on a given area, authors raise the challenges, controversies, dilemmas and concerns attached to this particular context of delivering justice.

Taking insights on imprisonment, community punishments and forensic services, this book provides a broad analysis of environments. But it also casts a critical light on how punishment of the mentally vulnerable sits within public attitudes and ideas, policy discourses, and the ways in which those seen to present as risky and dangerous are imagined.

Written in a clear and direct style, this book serves as a valuable resource for those studying, working or researching at the intersections of healthcare and criminal justice domains. This book is essential reading for students and practitioners within the fields of criminology and criminal justice, social work, forensic psychology, forensic psychiatry, mental health nursing and probation.

Paul Taylor is Head of the Department of Social and Political Science at the University of Chester, UK. His research is interdisciplinary, drawing together areas of criminology with the more general concerns of culture within public service/armed forces occupations. Further, he writes and researches on a range of substantive issues relating to biography, including: mentally vulnerable individuals and the criminal justice process; ageing, welfare and punishment; and criminal justice practitioner well-being.

Sharon Morley is a Senior Lecturer at the University of Chester, UK. Her research and publications have focused on a wide range of criminological topics. Her main research has focused on narrative accounts of young women and their everyday experiences of violence; dating violence; precautionary strategies; and gender, space and self-regulation. More recently her research is concerned with female offenders who have mental health issues, particularly the punishment of women offenders who have mental health issues. Sharon's books include the Companions in Criminology and Criminal Justice series, such as the *Companion to State Power, Liberties and Rights* (Policy Press). Her publications also include articles on mental health, victimisation and injustice.

Jason Powell is Professor of Social Gerontology and Associate Dean of Health and Social Care at The University of Staffordshire. He is an elected Academician of The Academy of Urbanism. Dr. Powell has interests in interdisciplinary research focusing on ageing, Foucault and social policy. He has held many research and knowledge exchange grants in the UK, EU and Asia and disseminated his research globally with many publications, including 72 academic books and top ranked refereed journal articles. These include The Journal of Applied Gerontology; Journal of Health Politics, Policy and Law; and The Scandinavian Journal of Caring Sciences. Dr. Powell is Editor-in-Chief of Illness, Crisis & Loss (SAGE).

MENTAL HEALTH AND PUNISHMENTS

Critical Perspectives in Theory and Practice

Edited by Paul Taylor, Sharon Morley and Jason Powell

LONDON AND NEW YORK

First published 2021
by Routledge
2 Park Square, Milton Park, Abingdon, Oxon OX14 4RN

and by Routledge
52 Vanderbilt Avenue, New York, NY 10017

Routledge is an imprint of the Taylor & Francis Group, an informa business

© 2021 selection and editorial matter, Paul Taylor, Sharon Morley and Jason Powell; individual chapters, the contributors

The right of Paul Taylor, Sharon Morley and Jason Powell to be identified as the authors of the editorial material, and of the authors for their individual chapters, has been asserted in accordance with sections 77 and 78 of the Copyright, Designs and Patents Act 1988.

All rights reserved. No part of this book may be reprinted or reproduced or utilised in any form or by any electronic, mechanical, or other means, now known or hereafter invented, including photocopying and recording, or in any information storage or retrieval system, without permission in writing from the publishers.

Trademark notice: Product or corporate names may be trademarks or registered trademarks, and are used only for identification and explanation without intent to infringe.

British Library Cataloguing-in-Publication Data
A catalogue record for this book is available from the British Library

Library of Congress Cataloging-in-Publication Data
Names: Taylor, Paul, 1981– editor. | Morley, Sharon, editor. | Powell, Jason L., 1971– editor.
Title: Mental health and punishments: critical perspectives in theory and practice / edited by Paul Taylor, Sharon Morley and Jason Powell.
Description: Abingdon, Oxon; New York, NY: Routledge, 2020. | Includes bibliographical references and index. |
Identifiers: LCCN 2020006077 | ISBN 9780815375142 (hbk) | ISBN 9780815375159 (pbk) | ISBN 9781351240611 (ebk)
Subjects: LCSH: Mentally ill offenders. | People with mental disabilities and crime. | Prisoners—Mental health services. | Criminal justice, Administration of.
Classification: LCC HV6133 .M44 2020 | DDC 364.3/8—dc23
LC record available at https://lccn.loc.gov/2020006077

ISBN: 978-0-8153-7514-2 (hbk)
ISBN: 978-0-8153-7515-9 (pbk)
ISBN: 978-1-351-24061-1 (ebk)

Typeset in Bembo
by codeMantra

CONTENTS

List of contributors   *vii*
Preface   *x*

     Introduction   1
     Paul Taylor and Andrew Reeves

1   The rise of psychiatry: mental illness/disorder and social control   6
     Barbara McNamara and Jason Powell

2   Mental health and the criminal courts: fitness to plead, culpability and the defence of insanity   19
     Rajan (Taj) Nathan

3   Causal relationships or casual associations? Assessing the nature and character of mental illness/disorder and crime   33
     Ian Cummins

4   Containing them, liberating us: the *shadow* side of criminal psychopathy   45
     Leon McRae

5   Community punishment and mental illness and disorder   71
     Lol Burke

6 Uneasy bedfellows: imprisonment, mental health and
 public service austerity 87
 Jane Senior

7 Continuity and change in penal policy towards personality
 disordered offenders 107
 Ailbhe O'Loughlin

8 The therapeutic management of child sex offenders 129
 Karen Harrison

9 Mental health, young people and punishments 143
 Gillian Buck and Sean Creaney

10 'Securing' treatment for female prisoners with
 mental health issues 159
 Sharon Morley

11 Intellectual disability and punishments 173
 Andrew Lovell

Index *189*

CONTRIBUTORS

Dr Gillian Buck is Senior Lecturer in Social Work at the University of Chester, UK. Her research interests include peer-led services, criminal justice, youth justice and the voluntary sector. Before working in research and teaching, Gill worked as a Social Worker in a youth offending team.

Prof Lol Burke is Professor in Criminal Justice at Liverpool John Moores University, UK, and specialises in the areas of probation research, policy and practice. He has a particular interest in the way that occupational culture acts out in probation settings, the dynamics of supervision and resettlement provision for released prisoners.

Sean Creaney is a Lecturer in Psychosocial Analysis of Offending Behaviour at Edge Hill University, UK. He is currently an advisory board member at empathy-led charity Peer Power. His research interests include peer mentoring, risk-based practices and children's involvement in the design and delivery of services. Sean's PhD thesis was a Bourdieusian analysis of children's participation in decision making in youth justice.

Dr Ian Cummins is a Senior Lecturer and Head of Social Policy in the School of Health and Society at the University of Salford, UK. He initially qualified as a probation officer and then also worked as a mental health social worker. His research interests reflect this practice experience and focus on mental health issues in the CJS and the history of community care.

Prof Karen Harrison is a Professor in Law and Penal Justice at the University of Lincoln, UK. Over the last 20 years, she has established a national and international profile in sentencing and penal policy. She has written extensively on the

viii Contributors

legal and ethical implications of risk reduction and management strategies with high-risk sex offenders and has recently completed an empirical project looking at why British South Asian women fail to report sexual abuse.

Prof Andrew Lovell has been Professor in Learning Disabilities in the Department of Mental Health and Learning Disabilities, Faculty of Health & Social Care at the University of Chester, UK since 2012. Andy received his PhD in 2004 from the department of sociology at the University of Liverpool, which explored, within a social constructionist framework, the role of self-injury over the life course of a group of individuals with learning disabilities. He has a clinical background working as a nurse with people with learning disabilities, mental health difficulties and a background of offending and violent behaviour.

Dr Barbara McNamara joined the BSc (Hons) Health, Wellbeing and Social Care course team at the University of Bradford, UK in 2014. She is a Lecturer in Health and WellBeing. Barbara has worked as a Lecturer in higher education since obtaining a BA (Hons) in Sociology and Social Policy in 2006 and an MA in Research methods in 2007 at the University of Liverpool. In 2012 Dr McNamara completed her PhD at the University of Liverpool and her thesis (from a Feminist Foucauldian stance) explored women's experiences of self/body and identity work in Commercial Weight loss organisations.

Dr Leon McRae is a legal academic, who has taught criminal law, criminology and mental health law at Keele University, UK; Birmingham University, UK; and King's College London, UK. He is currently an external examiner on the LLM programme at the LSE (Mental health law: The criminal context). Leon researches in the field of mental health law (mainly the criminal context), criminal law, critical criminology, medical law and, increasingly, speaks psychoanalytic concepts to legal decision-making and criminal responsibility.

Prof Rajan (Taj) Nathan (MBBCh, MMedSc, MRCPsych, DipFSc, MD) is a Consultant Forensic Psychiatrist and Director of Research and Effectiveness with Cheshire Wirral Partnership NHS Foundation Trust, UK, an Honorary Senior Research Fellow at the University of Liverpool, a Visiting Professor at the University of Chester and an Adjunct Professor at Liverpool John Moores University, UK. He has over 20 years' experience of working in a range of forensic clinical settings (including secure hospitals, prisons and community forensic services) and medico-legal contexts (including the regular provision of independent expert opinion in criminal and family proceedings). He has published extensively with a particular focus on violence, offending and personality disorder.

Dr Ailbhe O'Loughlin is a Lecturer at York Law School, University of York, UK. Ailbhe holds an LLB in Law and French from Trinity College Dublin and an MSc in Criminology and Criminal Justice from the University of Oxford. She completed her PhD studies in law at the London School of Economics in 2016. Her research explores the role of law, policy and practice at the intersections between the criminal justice system and the forensic mental health system.

Dr Andrew Reeves is an Associate Professor in the Counselling Professions and Mental Health at the University of Chester, UK. He is a BACP Senior Accredited Counsellor/Psychotherapist, and a Fellow of BACP and the Higher Education Academy. His practice experience, over 30 years, has been with children and families and in adult mental health settings. He has written extensively on working with risk in therapeutic contexts. He is Chair of the British Association for Counselling and Psychotherapy, Director of Colleges and Universities for the Charlie Waller Memorial Trust and an independent practitioner, specialising in working with risk and men's mental health.

Dr Jane Senior qualified as a mental health nurse in 1990 and worked clinically in a variety of acute, forensic, community and prison settings for over ten years. She was fortunate to receive funding from the NHS to undertake a PhD at the University of Manchester examining models of mental healthcare delivery in prisons. She is still at the University of Manchester, working as a Senior Lecturer (Research & Teaching) in forensic mental health. Her research interests include prison mental health, suicide and self-harm, liaison and diversion and the role of police and policing in mental health issues.

PREFACE

The very beginnings of this book came after a tutorial between Paul, then a lecturer in Criminology, and an undergraduate student enrolled on his mental health and crime module of study. They debated ways in which those interested in criminology, but new to the topic of mental illness and disorder, could be or become more familiar with the intersections of crime, justice and the mentally vulnerable. It takes a great deal of practice to navigate the social science and health literature, Paul's Bachelor Degree students would remark, and finding those sources that critically question institutions, practices and the law even more so. The works of Jill Peay and Herschel Prins had always been mainstays, along with the progressive literature in journals that navigate multiple disciplinary fields of sociology, health studies, political science, psychology and law. However, there is still more room to contribute to this fascinating interdisciplinary field, and thus this text evolved.

This collection of chapters written by experts in their respective fields takes an approach that provides critical insights into the discursive, legal, policy and practice dimensions of contemporary punishments. Its focus is on how, and in what ways, systems of punishments and sanction are delivered to those deemed to suffer or endure mental illness or disorder. The terrain of the converging disciplines of medicine and criminal justice (specifically punishments) is complex, and the web of governance broad-reaching, and this text aims to illuminate on this in a sophisticated, yet accessible way. The text does have a UK-focus bias, but this should not deter readers from considering critical issues elsewhere. The examples in focus in each chapter inform the reader with technical detail of the form and function of practice and procedure; however, throughout a critical lens of interpretation is applied insofar that discussions take place that question the efficacy of practices and potential (un)intended outcomes. Indeed, this edited collection approaches the analyses of the subject matter in a way that not only examines issues of public protection, but also the rights and liberties of those subject to legal and administrative controls.

A key strength of this text is that it deals with interventions across the secure estate as well as those that operate outside of it. This book provides a developed understanding of the nature of risk management, the delivery of 'justice' and the means by which punishment should or could be delivered. Thus, within the disciplines of criminal justice and medicine, and within the services themselves, the concepts of care and control often come together. Therefore, a book that addresses, brings together and deliberately demystifies these seemingly disparate yet fundamentally interconnected areas is highly practical to students, scholars and practitioners.

In its presentation of materials, this book generates viewpoints emerging from the perspectives of key writers and experts from the academic domain as well as practitioners in the field of mental health and offender management. There is a logical progression of critical enquiry throughout each chapter and brings attention towards unique issues where the not-so disparate worlds of care and punishment converge.

The journey of the mentally disordered suspect, defendant and/or offender is a complex one; this can be further complicated by innovations in management strategies, political imperatives and operational/practical obstacles and dilemmas. Moreover, diagnosis, policy and legislation in this area are a changing and changeable landscape. In the UK and elsewhere, there is evidence of an increasing expedience to shape, diagnose, label, classify, target and alter behaviour. A therapeutic optimism is becoming increasingly evident among the management of offender groups such as sex offenders and offenders diagnosed with a personality disorder. Within the contemporary crime control agenda, mental health services have an active role, and some critics would argue that the benevolent character of healthcare remains at risk because of a preoccupation by governments to manage risk through clinical and actuarial risk assessment.

The editors hope that readers find the chapters here informative, but more than that, that this book arouses the curiosity of its readership and allows them to think more deeply about the experience of those involved.

INTRODUCTION

Paul Taylor and Andrew Reeves

As we embark on the second decade of the twenty-first century, our consciousness towards risk, danger and dominant discourses of protectionism and security continue. Be they in respect of, for example, the limitations of legal controls to maintain safety against domestic and international terrorism, and the legislative restrictions on gun ownership, to name but a few. Central to much of the public and political debate, though, are four core questions: who are seen to pose a substantial risk to the community; what those threats or risks may be; how might those risks be exercised; and what is the likely impact. This type of analysis can be applied to all manner of academic enquiries into crime, harm and society, but the answers to these questions debated in political, legal and scientific domains will shape the trajectory of criminal justice policy, and its responses, in turn, will shape the public view on this kind of offending.

The reason that we begin this introduction in this way is to draw attention, in particular, to the first of the four questions, the 'who' question. Associating the alleged and convicted perpetrators of risks, crimes and harms with social groups often results in enhanced measures to surveil, manage, legally control, monitor or punish. The resultant effect is public awareness of the risks of a 'group' are manufactured or heightened. We are privy to some excellent criminological analyses on the wider effects of criminal justice and penal policy on social groups, immigrants, those from lower socio-economic groups or followers of particular religions. Public fear of particular social groups, and their exercising prejudice and discrimination, is not a latent phenomenon; on the contrary, it is something which evolves through historical periods, uses the actions of state actors and institutions as a reference point and listens to 'expert' voices on the topic. This coupled with the production and distribution of pejorative stereotypes based on social characteristics leads to a palpable fear among large swathes of the public who then demand heightened restrictions to be applied to those deemed dangerous.

One social group that has shouldered much of the burden of public suspicion and concern has been those experiencing mental health problems, often referred to as those with a 'mental illness'. Assimilating illness with risk and dangerousness has been an intransigent discourse for several centuries, but where do these concepts come from? We cannot simply blame news media for malicious or disparaging headline language such as 'crazies', 'psychos', 'nutters', 'loonies' and 'madmen'. We must look more closely at the discursive, legal and administrative control of madness and mental illness.

History is littered with cases of the mentally disordered perpetrating violent offences. These can often be unprovoked, randomised attacks, sexual in nature, extremely violent, predatory, cases of multiple murder or targeted on the vulnerable such as children. Cases such as that of Ian Brady, who was convicted of the murder of three children (and admitted to a further two) in the 1960s, represent the epitome of the dangerous mentally ill. Cases such as this act as cultural reference points and a marker for society of the possible threats that exist. The public narrative on crime and dangerous offending, in instances such as this, can become firmly locked on the mentally ill as a collective, which distorts the true facts that these are atypical rather than commonplace.

The penal landscape for the mentally disordered offender continues to evolve based on the influences of legislative, criminal justice and expert opinion, and undoubtedly is shaped by the public view to some extent. Evolution and revolution in the area of control around such a group is particularly complex given that they fall between two stools of penal and health policy and practice. Many academic commentators have issued concern over proportionality, effective 'treatment' and the stigmatising effects of the duality of being labelled as a 'mentally', 'disordered' offender. To this end, development of punishments and controls for those who experience mental vulnerability, illness or disorder need to establish an approach that is sensitive to the multifarious issues at work – public protection, promotion of desistance from crime, welfare of the offender and the health needs that may present. Dangers exist where one of these may take precedent at the expense of the others; something campaigners, academics and advocates raise caution over as can be seen in this text.

Each chapter of this edited collection gives readers valuable insights into the historical and contemporaneous developments in specific areas. This covers not just the law and policy, but also attitudes and the nomenclature that surround the mentally disordered offender. This book is an invitation to examine the convergence of punishment and control on those in receipt of expert-applied diagnosis. But as readers engage with each chapter, we insist that each area of analysis is understood in a broader and context. What follows here are a series of points that readers should reflect on as they journey through this book. They are important considerations, questions and debates – many of which are not resigned to history, but rather continue to be rehearsed decade after decade. Others are new phenomena that present themselves because of the introduction of new policy, new legislation, or new ideas on the most appropriate way to manage those who have offended with a mental illness or disorder.

Consider the language that surrounds the mentally disordered offender. How do terms such as 'dangerousness' become used and applied in this context. Terminology may become widely used, but at the same time carry with it little specificity. When it comes to diagnosis, readers should critically reflect on its origins, the powerful influencers involved in their development, the gendered application, their popularity of use in different periods, the divisions between mental illness and mental disorder, questions of treatability of diagnosis and effectiveness, and any lasting implications of diagnostic labels on the person.

When considering appropriate punishments and controls for the mentally disordered offender, consider the basis of justifications for outcomes. Reflect on the decisions of security and therapy, care and control. How are risk judgements formed? In criminal justice and mental healthcare practice, risk assessment and risk management strategies prevail. They utilise processes of 'testing', 'calculating' and 'identification' to formulate management plans. A paradigm of risk pervades contemporary approaches and manifests itself in the use of law, targeting of controls, determines lengths of containment, informs the necessity for programmes of behavioural adaptation and assists in the decision-making of the prescription of pharmaceuticals. But in the quest to getting risk management 'right', who's interests prevail, and what do outcomes look like – for society, and for the offender? In this process there is no exact science and critics have argued of the risks associated with attempts to objectively calculate the future by assessing the past and the present. It is not my intention here to suggest that alleviating risks of harm in the future is a bad thing; rather in securing the future, what are the costs for those in the present? When thinking about those detained by the State, we must recognise their vulnerability and limited voice amidst powerful rhetoric on enhanced surveillance, stricter containment, elaborate controls, retribution and dangerous identities.

About the chapters

The conceptualisation and critical engagement with these challenges in this text have been structured across several thematic ideas: the psychiatrisation of crime and the criminalisation of mental illness and disorder; punishing the mentally ill and disordered; critical debates and contemporary concerns around punishment; and critical explorations in mental health and punishments. McNamara and Powel, in their chapter, *The rise of psychiatry: mental illness/disorder and social control*, consider the origins and development of the links between the problematisation of 'madness' in the context of deviance and social order, and how certain 'mental illnesses' have been positioned within a narrative of threat. Finally, they offer a challenge to the power of psychiatry and how, in its 'unmasking', both the treaters and the treated might find opportunity to rethink the future of (forensic) psychiatry.

Rajan (Taj) Nathan explores the role of the criminal justice process through court procedures to critically reflect on whether mentally ill people, or mentally disordered offenders, are being fairly treated in this context in his chapter, *Mental health and the criminal courts: Fitness to plead, culpability and the defence of insanity*. The capacity to participate in proceedings, whether criminal or civil, is a critical issue here in the process of fair justice.

Ian Cummins, in his chapter, *Causal relationships or casual associations? Assessing the nature and character of mental illness/disorder and crime*, explores the polarities of the argument between the positioning of the 'mentally ill' as a violent group, or not. The deconstruction of this argument centres on how the mentally ill have been responded to over time: through imprisonment, or through the deinstitutionalistion of the structures that offered both care and containment in the context of a developing social policy.

The place of the 'psychopath' in our current construction of mental disorder and the continuum of mental health on which it is argued we all have a place is explored from several different perspectives by Leon McRae in the chapter *Containing them, liberating us: The shadow side of criminal psychopathy*. The relationship between society and the psychopath, ranging from fascination, attraction, fear and loathing, is carefully deconstructed by McRae and, therefore, critical questions emerge: the expectation of 'treatment' and recovery; the place of 'treatment' as a mechanism of separation; and why the notion of psychopath is positioned by society as it is, and the service that positioning then is afforded.

Lol Burke, in the chapter *Community Punishment and mental illness and disorder*, reflects on the long-standing concern of the place of those with mental health difficulties in the criminal justice system. Mechanisms for diversion away from criminal processes often fail to prevent those who would be served better in mental health services still finding themselves in court and prisons. Burke further considers the development of Mental Health Treatment Requirement and the Offender Personality Disorder Pathway as ways in which mental health needs might be better served.

Jane Senior develops these ideas further in her chapter, *Uneasy bedfellows: Imprisonment, mental health and public service austerity*, and critically considers the development, and current state, of mental health care in the prison context.

Continuity and Change in Penal Policy towards Personality Disordered Offenders, by Ailbhe O'Loughlin, considers the Dangerous and Severe Personality Disorder concept, established in 2001, to "test treatment, management and risk assessment techniques for individuals thought to pose a high risk of serious harm to the public stemming from a severe form of personality disorder". In that context, the subsequent decommissioning of these units in 2011 and development of the re-titled Offender Personality Disorder Pathway (OPDP) are critically evaluated, specifically as to whether the OPDP has the capacity to meet what O'Loughlin describes as the "conflicting aims" of public protection, the safe management of a challenging group in an institutional setting and the broader aim of improving health outcomes for offenders.

Karen Harrison tracks the development of the public's perception of the child sex offender – often synonymously known as a paedophile – and the subsequent treatment programmes typically located within mental health services. Her chapter, *The therapeutic management of child sex offenders*, asserts that mental health route is not an appropriate context for the delivery of treatment to child sex offenders and instead offers three ways in which child sex offenders might be therapeutically managed.

Mental health, young people and punishments, by Gillian Buck and Sean Creaney, offers a critical introduction into the ways in which the behaviour and mental health of young people in the criminal justice system have been constructed. Following their analysis, they present an argument for an approach to young people that nurtures well-being and relationships, and that the development of services should be young person informed.

Sharon Morley, in *'Securing' treatment for female prisoners with mental health issues*, begins with the stark assertion of prison as a "brutalising and inhumane environment", and states this is particularly so for women prisoners. In acknowledging that will be times where prison for violent female offenders is required, suggestions are made as to how such units might more appropriately meet their needs

Finally, Andrew Lovell considers the relationship between concepts of punishment and intellectual disability. Contemporary applications for our understanding are framed within an historical positioning, and several good practice developments are carefully outlined.

Taken as a whole, the chapters together offer a compelling and critical account of the relationship between mental health and punishment, across groups and cultures, and, drawing on best evidence, offer important links to both theoretical development and practice. There is no doubt that the needs of the most vulnerable in our society often fall through the gap between the public's need for a sense of punishment, and the treatment opportunities that often struggle to deliver what is needed in the face of social, political and policy demands.

1

THE RISE OF PSYCHIATRY

Mental illness/disorder and social control

Barbara McNamara and Jason Powell

This chapter is a focus on the rise and consolidation of psychiatric power and its control of individuals and populations who have become problematised and classified as mentally ill and madness throughout a long and enduring history of the present. For example, Michel Foucault (1982) describes how the patient and madness are socially constructed through disciplinarian techniques, such as the 'medical gaze' – the use and abuse of surveillance to control societal ills and give credibility to medical institutions and professional power as the instigator as the truthful arbiter of labelling mental illness (Porter, 1990). The key aim of Foucault's point here has been "to create a history of the different modes by which, in our culture human beings are made subjects" (1982, p. 208). The history of how people are classified as subjects as having a medical disorder or mental illness is about revealing how psychiatry became embedded in the occidental culture in particular to have the legitimacy and power to define people as problems of scientific knowledge sanctioned by its truth claims that were rarely contested (Scull, 1993).

Indeed, in path-breaking work such as *Madness and Civilization* (1965), Foucault traces changes in the ways in which madness and mental illness were discussed which has obvious implications for psychiatry and the management of disorder and mental illness. Foucault utilises the distinctive methodology of archaeology for these studies that aim to provide a "history of statements that claim the status of truth" (Davidson, 1986, p. 221).

In order to trace the emergence of legitimacy of professions of psychiatry, one has to understand the contextual backdrop of how its knowledge formation was legitimised by science so any attempt to sanction the definition, management and control of madness and mental illness was never challenged as if science was seen as the master narrative of 'truth', who can challenge or resist it? Once science becomes absorbed into professions, it moulds what those professions become, and the people who come into interaction with psychiatry, in particular, has found it difficult to resist the power and control of its profession and subsequent classification practices and processes of medicalisation (Foucault, 1965; Scull, 1993).

This is unashamedly a critical theory of psychiatric power and an understanding of how people become seen as a 'problem' which has consequences for those individuals who have been defined as mentally ill (Porter, 1990). The irony, of course, is in the rise of modernity, the more professions professed liberation and empowerment, the more they controlled. Furthermore, psychiatric power as Sim (1990) has eloquently claimed, the more 'humane' it claims as its truth status, the more it controls and constructs the conditions of mental illness for powerless individuals and subjugated populations.

It becomes a surveillance technique used to classify and monitor the behaviour of 'mental disorder' of patients which uses deviancy conceptual dualities of normality/abnormality to simplistically characterise human behaviour which is more complex and open to historical and contemporary interpretation (Sim, 1990). The chapter traces the historical emergence of asylums, Bedlam and the devastating implications it had in terms of treatment of individuals. We then explore psychiatric power and its relationship to mental illness which was seen as a subtle change to managing social and moral order. We move to evaluate some of the theoretical implications psychiatric power has if it is unchallenged in its hegemony of creating grand narratives of mental illness for powerless individuals and populations. We also track the current treatment structures of 'virtual asylums', hospitalisation and rise of community-based services framed by contemporary political debates and gendered issues of psychiatric units. We finally assess the possibilities and challenges of resisting psychiatric power through opportunities for self-determination, self-exploration and the rethinking of psychiatry itself.

Understanding the past is crucial in unravelling the emergent power of psychiatry in the present and implications and possibilities for the future in terms of resistance to dominant modes of power, surveillance and classification practices of mental illness and disorder and the consequences attached to it in terms of institutional confinement and the potential for meaningful human agency.

'Digging into the past': historical roots of psychiatric power

Tracing the historical development and consolidation of treatment of medical disorder and its relationship with its patients, uncovers the existence of a general consensus, that the treatment of the mentally ill has reflected how society conceptualised both mental illness and the mentally ill person at a biological and interpersonal level (Carron & Saad, 2012). According to these authors, there exists documented evidence depicting, on the one hand, cruel and inhumane acts, while on the other hand, the delivery of compassionate and benevolent care.

The origins of psychiatric services date back to 1247 when a monastic priory The Priory of St Mary of Bethlehem, shortened to Bedlam, was founded by the church in London (Symonds, 1995) and through its conversion to a hospital in 1357 became Europe's first insane asylum (Allderidge, 1997). Bedlam has been housing the mentally ill, as in those described by the Stow's Survey of London (1720) as raving and furious and capable of cure; or, if not yet, are likely to do mischief to themselves or others; and are poor and cannot otherwise be provided for (Allderidge, 1997).

However, for over 600 years, its inmates have survived in conditions of inconceivable abuse, and worst of all their suffering became a source of entertainment for the rest of London (Allderidge, 1997; Symonds, 1995). For example, to increase its funding, the historical hospital was open to the public and the inmates were put on display and their bizarre behaviour and cruel treatment was considered to be a form of theatre (ibid.). McMillan (1997) has demonstrated how patients, who suffered from illnesses now recognised as schizophrenia, dementia, depression, autism and epilepsy, to mention but a few, were confined in badly ventilated apartments and never discharged but by death.

As was true as much of medicine at this time, the treatment was rudimentary, often harsh and generally ineffective (ibid.). For example, 'the quiet', 'the noisy' and 'the violent' were all congregated together, a majority of which were chained to beds by their wrists or ankles and subjected to a range of treatments including immersion in icy water, starvation, bloodletting, purging, beating and spells in isolation (Clouette & DesLandes, 1997). Some received a treatment known as rotation therapy which involved spinning the patient in a chair suspended from the ceiling until they vomited (ibid.). Indeed, as McMillan (1997), Allderidge (1997) and Symonds (1995) note, many patients who may have survived their illness died from their therapy, and what became apparent for Davison and Neale (1997) was that the management of the 'insane' appeared more important than the medical procedures.

Linked to this, such increased medical treatment, therefore, was formed in the 'project of modernity' (Foucault, 1965, 1982) based on Enlightenment notions of progress and bringing social order to individuals' lives. In modernity, asylums as a form of social control were characterised by the processes of normalisation, discipline and surveillance (Foucault, 1977) originally linked with the development of the modern prison but increasingly reflected in diffuse use of surveillance via new forms of knowledge (Foucault, 1977).

However, within the early nineteenth-century concern for the wellbeing of patients who have mental illness gradually increased and at the recommendation of the House of Commons select committee, county asylums were set up in 1807 to probe into the state of lunatics (Hunter & MacAlpine, 1974). Further legislation followed, including the Wynn's Act of (1808) advocating for the better care and maintenance of lunatics, being paupers or criminals and the Shaftesbury Acts of (1845), arguing for the better regulation of the care and treatment of lunatics (Hunter & MacAlpine, 1974).

In an arguably more positive vein, Bendiner (1981) illuminated how Pinel's Treatise on insanity (1806) within a Parisian 'madhouse' known as the Menagerie recognised that the mentally ill were suffering from a disease requiring differential diagnosis, prognosis and therapy. Pinel's revolutionary diagnosis and treatment therefore, promoted the removal of chains and shackles in a bid to provide more affectionate and supportive care in a more therapeutic setting (ibid.). Importantly, Pinel's revolutionising work paved the way for recognising that the mentally ill was suffering an illness out of their control and by implementing the concept of 'moral treatment' a new philosophy emerged suggesting that mentally ill patients should be viewed with compassion and care and afforded their dignity as individual human beings (Davison & Neale, 1997).

Throughout the nineteenth century, most asylums were built on the outskirts of major cities and operated as self-sufficient communities with their own water supplies, farms, laundries and factories (Andrews et al., 1997). Consequently, they were isolated from the local community and the psychiatrists working with them were isolated from their own colleagues and those in other medical specialities (Ibid.). With the idea of self-sufficiency and emergence of 'moral therapy' around the turn of the nineteenth century, the idea of patient work became, according to Scull (1993, p. 102), "a major cornerstone" of treatment.

As described by Jeremy Bentham (as cited in Porter, 1990, p. 131) work was an economic necessity and the workhouse, for example, was: "a mill to grind rogues honest and idle men industrious". Alongside Pinel's Treatise on insanity (1806) The York Retreat emerged in Great Britain as the epitome of this kind of reformed regimen, whereby asylum superintendents and psychiatrists argued in favour of patient work to facilitate self-improvement through the patients acceptance of social morality, adoption of self-governance within a social community and retaining self-restraint during religious services (Carron & Saad, 2012). However, this philosophy was abandoned in the latter part of the nineteenth century when the moral era took a different 'medical' turn.

Re-framing the treatment of controlling mental illness: psychiatric benevolence or malevolence?

So far, as detailed above, it is possible to see that psychiatry was perceived progressively becoming more humane in its approach, as clinicians developed more effective treatments for the mentally ill (Beveridge, 2014). Nevertheless, this philosophy was abandoned in the latter part of the nineteenth century when the moral era conceded to a more medically based paradigm of treatment for the mentally ill and this transition paved the way for what is known as the modern asylum, which lasted until the 1950s (Digby, 1985).

In terms of admission criteria, and progression towards the establishment of a more modern asylum, the Lunacy Act (1890) set the parameters, providing a legal system in which a patient had to be certified as insane in order to be admitted to the asylum (Andrews et al., 1997). During this period no psychiatric opinion was sought before admission, and thus medical officers in mental hospitals had no control whatsoever over the selection of the patients they were expected to treat, nor was there any opportunity to follow up upon discharge into the community (Rollin, 1990).

There was no legislative provision for patients to be treated voluntarily in the asylum, yet, the situation remained somewhat different in registered hospitals such as the Bethlem where admissions continued to take place free from certification (Andrews et al., 1997). For example, by 1900, only 3% of the patients admitted to Bethlem were certified, compared with 97% of the asylum population (ibid.). Importantly, these differences in admission criteria contributed to an enormous rise in the asylum population, as demonstrated in the growth of the Colney Hatch Asylum, the largest in Europe, originally built to accommodate 1,250 patients yet, was enlarged within ten years to expand capacity to 2,000. In 1937 (when it was renamed Friern Hospital), there were more than 2,700 patients and the rise in population was due to a number of factors, including first, the admission of many severely disabled patients who could never be discharged; second, patients were admitted with an increasing number of inadequately understood and untreatable conditions presenting with psychiatric symptoms such as metabolic disorders, lead poisoning, syphilis and intracranial tumours (Hunter & MacAlpine, 1974).

As noted by these authors once admitted to the asylum, medical officers classified patients as either curable or incurable and took into account other factors including the duration of their illness and the manifestation of any other complications including epilepsy and paralysis (ibid.). In a bid to address the increase in the asylum population, the Mental Treatment Act (1930) was introduced to extend the voluntary admission procedure to asylums, which stimulated the establishment of outpatient departments. Here, applicants could be examined to ascertain their fitness for reception as voluntary patients into asylums, and by 1935 there were 162 outpatient departments compared to just 25 in 1925 (Hunter & MacAlpine, 1963). These were the origins of community psychiatric services that we have today (Andrews et al., 1997).

The establishment of the National Health Service (NHS, 1948), the introduction of phenothiazine drugs in the 1950s and the changing social and political climate around this time were all factors that influenced the gradual closure of the large Victorian institutions (Department of Health and Social Security (DHSS), 1957). Instead, it was envisaged that by keeping patients in hospital when they have recovered from the acute stage of illness, was an infringement of their human rights.

The Royal Commission (1957) on the Law Relating to Mental Illness and Mental Deficiency (DHSS, 1957) recommended that no patient should be retained as a hospital inpatient when he or she has reached the stage at which he or she could go home. Here, the Mental Health Act (1959) was heralded as the first piece of mental health legislation providing clarification as to why an individual might need to be admitted to hospital and treated against their will (Fenton et al., 1997). In doing so, this Act provided a distinction between voluntary and involuntary treatments and provided a much clearer pathway especially in the form of compulsory assessment and treatment for the mentally ill when a "failure of agency itself" is encountered (Greco, 1993, p. 357).

So far, according to Beveridge (2014), the history of psychiatry was written mainly *by* psychiatrists and was a rather benign progress facilitating change as brought about by the actions of eminent individuals at the expense of consideration afforded to explore the wider social, cultural and political context. Indeed, this kind of history was seen by non-medical people as complacent, self-congratulatory and serving to legitimise psychiatry's present. However, this rather rosy view of psychiatry's past and the institutionalisation of psychiatric patients and their receipt of poor standards of care and quality of life was challenged by those outside the psychiatric profession.

Critical interpretations of psychiatric power

Foucault (1965), using the York Retreat as an example, opened up the dialogue between the disciplines of psychiatry and philosophy to question if, and to what extent, psychiatrists of this period exerted power motivated by their compassion to work with disturbed and distressed patients with specific conditions, or, on the other hand, were agents of the state and as a means of social control aided society in ridding it its debris – the so called 'mad' (Scull, 1979).

In other words, Foucault (1965) argued that the mad enjoyed reasonable freedom until the arrival of the Enlightenment in the eighteenth century which saw the birth of psychiatry. Foucault (1965) called psychiatry the 'great confinement', which, as demonstrated above, saw vast numbers of the mentally disturbed herded into institutions. In doing so, for Foucault (1965) the voice of 'unreason' was silenced by the forces of 'reason', in the shape of the emerging lunacy profession, and thus psychiatrists helped manufacture madness within the asylum (Szasz, 1970).

Although the philosophy in the moral era allowed for the more humane treatment of the mentally ill, Foucault (1965) argued that the self-improvement through an acceptance of social morality, adoption of self-governance within a social community, retaining self-restraint during religious services and of having a desire to work (Carron & Saad, 2012), was highly repressive without losing sight of the potential of resistance. Foucault (1965) referred to this as 'constraining power', through which the patient was returned to "the order of God's commandments", succumbing "his liberty to the laws that are those of both morality and reality" (ibid., pp. 247–248).

Consequently, in *Psychiatric Power* (1973) and in a lecture entitled *The Punitive Society* (1973), Foucault declared that: "it is now time to talk about power", which in psychiatric power (1973, p. 4) was described as something that is not possessed but rather exists through "dispersion, relays, networks" and "reciprocal supports" that are "rife with struggle, war, tactics, strategies" and "microphysics" (ibid., p. 16). Techniques of surveillance are so sophisticated, argues Foucault, that "inspection functions ceaselessly. The gaze is everywhere" (1977, p. 195).

Foucault points here to the means through which power is exercised. He places the processes of discipline, surveillance, individualisation and normalisation at the centre of his analysis of psychiatry. These processes were part of a strategy that extended "control over minutiae of the conditions of life and conduct" (Cousins & Hussain, 1984, p. 146). Within this discourse, the psychiatrist became "the great advisor and expert" (Rabinow, 1984, pp. 283–284) in the utilisation of scientific-medico insights in constructing mental illness through its power.

For Foucault (1973), the history of psychiatric power as undoubtedly, one of struggle, of mastery and of the direction of others and as Foucault (1973, p. 174) asserts, the mantra as threaded out in the clinic or asylum is: "I direct, I praise, reward, reprimand, command, constrain, threaten, and punish every day".

Indeed, if we set psychiatric power and its relationship with the patient within a wider context and within the large public asylums of the late nineteenth and early twentieth centuries, we can locate evidence detailing institutional profiteering on the part of asylum staff, coercion of patients, withdrawal of food and rewards such as cigarettes or outings as punishment for noncompliance, intolerance to idleness and work as a default setting as opposed to choice for the purpose of self-improvement (Szasz, 1970).

Illustrating this point, Erving Goffman (1961) in his work on *Asylum* examines the social situation of hospitalised mental patients arguing that total institutions such as the hospital or asylum are spaces where immersion is complete, where inmate's roles are defined, where the culture inhibits relationships, and where its inhabitants become what the institution needs them to become.

Goffman (1961) speaks about the mortification of the self, encompassing how the self changes and how, over time, personal identity is substituted by organisational identity to the degree that a completely new role emerges, that is, the role of the patient. Eventually, for Goffman, after a period of time, post mortification, everyone within a total institution starts to submit to the definition of the self that the organisation enforces on them and thus the positive aspects of mental illness became somewhat forgotten. For example, through the usual range of physical treatments such as 'the carrot and the stick', patients begin speaking the language of the organisation, reiterating the goals of the organisation, and tolerating the authority and set rules of the organisation, as in being reprimanded for any misdemeanours and symptomatic behaviour, fixed with the ever surveying eye and placed under physical restraint (Freebody, 2016). In time, Goffman (1961) argues that the patients become aware that their very survival depends on understanding the political, the social, psychological and economic nuances of their environment and are thus compelled to construct a new self and a new vision focused on surviving and succeeding within the asylum.

Yet, what happens when patients leave an institution, as in the very place in which they have learned to survive and possibly thrive? Can those who have been admitted for too long, successfully move on when their sense of self has been totally defined by the institution and have become professional patients?

Revisiting Durkheim's work on the production of individuality Foucault (1973, p. 57) begs the question, is there any "individual beneath power relations who can be freed" when institutions impose a morel rule, a limitation of liberty, a submission to order, an engagement of responsibility in order to desalinate the mind? In other words, is it possible that both Foucault (1965) and Goffman (1961) have over-emphasised the repressive nature of treatments received within the asylum?

Is subordination to a routine, the acceptance of discipline and maintenance of concentration important in preparing the patient for re-entry outside the asylum? For Goffman the ideal situation for patients is to obtain these benefits of treatment and leave before they have lost a sense of self by becoming enmeshed in the asylum's culture and values (Goffman, 1961).

Contemporary issues in the hospitalisation of mental illness

At the beginning of the 1960s, the Conservative party supported the disbanding of the asylums and in 1962 the Hospital Plan for England and Wales projected closure of half of all mental beds by 1975 (Ministry of Health, 1962). From 1971 onwards there followed a dramatic change in the facilitation of psychiatric provision. A government paper on 'Hospital Services for the Mentally ill' (DHSS, 1971) proposed the complete abolition of the mental hospital system with all services being delivered by district general hospitals with close liaison with general practitioners and social services. This model promoted the re-organisation of psychiatric services mirroring other hospital disciplines, namely the inpatient and outpatient facilities within a hospital building (ibid.). As a result, outpatient clinics became a vital part of psychiatric service provision and moved from having a triage function to becoming a resource for both assessment and follow-up.

Alongside these developments, there was also a shift towards the provision of other community-based services for people with mental illnesses, such as day services, supported housing and community-based mental health nurses and social workers. This was referred to as community care and was supported by many government policies such as Better Services for the Mentally Ill (DHSS, 1975) Care in the Community (DHSS, 1981) and Community Care with Special Reference to Mentally Ill and Mentally Handicapped people (House of Commons Social Services Committee Department of Health and Social Security, 1985). However, the community service provision for individuals who had previously resided in an asylum has been subject to much debate over the last 40–50 years, particularly due to the reported incidences of inadequacies. For example, one of the accomplishments of community care has been the provision of a diversity of supported housing supplied by non-statutory organisations (Poole et al., 2002). Here, the majority of people who have transitioned from the asylum to the community, even with the most complex needs, have increased their social networks, gained independent living skills, improved their quality of life and have not required re-admission (Tanzman, 1993).

However, the private provision of long-term inpatient care for patients referred to by Mann and Cree (1976) as the 'new long stay' is more problematic due to the reduction in psychiatric inpatient beds since the 1950s. Indeed, Poole et al. (2002) have exposed how and why a sheer lack of NHS resources and associated costs for patients with more challenging behaviours or who have unusual psychiatric needs has provided a market opportunity for large and small businesses to exploit the situation.

Patients often arrive in the 'virtual asylum' when discharged from lengthy unproductive spells in acute psychiatric wards, from prisons, special hospitals, NHS secure units and some have been shunted from institution to institution since childhood (Poole et al., 2002). Many have a chequered reputation with local NHS services – who have lost the capacity to deal with them and thus, in the absence of any appropriate NHS provision, these patients are placed in the private sector (ibid.). Of course, a variability of care is widespread in the NHS, yet it is possible to measure the quality of care.

However, within the 'virtual asylum', lessons from our past continue to be ignored when the accruing evidence exposes how care tends to be basic, patients are subjected to little purposeful activity and depending on the size of the establishment, there is a disparity in terms of qualified staff available (Poole et al., 2002). Like Goffman's (1961) work in *Asylum* the inmates in the 'virtual asylum' are likely to receive rehabilitation, albeit this is once again focused on the absorption of the culture with little or no monitoring of the quality of individual care (Poole et al., 2002). Nursing home inspection teams coupled with the Mental Health Act Commission can monitor legal requirements, but fail to sufficiently supervise individual care within a 'virtual asylum' (ibid.). Reverting back to the 1970s, it is possible to see how incidents of moral panic concerning mental health patients have continued to govern the development of mental health policy in the UK. For example, concerns about the neglect and abuse in mental hospitals yielded to the perceived dangers associated with mentally ill people living in the community during the 1990s. For example, the high-profile case of a schizophrenic Christopher Clunis, who murdered Jonathan Zito in an unprovoked attack at Finsbury Park station in London (Ritchie et al., 1994), highlighted the potential for community patients living a transitory lifestyle to detach from mental health services possibly. Consequently, for Poole et al. (2002) this has produced some badly thought-out policies which have made the 'virtual asylum' vulnerable to a destructive moral panic, which predominantly apportions blame on service users, psychiatrists, clinicians and purchasers.

As Priebe et al. (2005) note, if the private sector provision of the 'virtual asylum' were to suffer from disrepute, the costs of reproviding services in the NHS would make the idea of reinstitutionalisation appear more lucrative, and this appears to be already taking place elsewhere in Europe. As this historical backcloth demonstrates, the main victims of this situation will inevitably be the patients and their families as opposed to the politicians and policymakers who unintentionally created the 'virtual asylum' (Poole et al., 2002). These authors suggest that what is required is the formation of a partnership between the public and private sector with receipt of clearly defined and agreed agenda's for the private sector so that there exist suitable systems to develop, manage and monitor the interface between both sectors. This takes time, reorganisation, better thought-out policy initiatives and more conjoined methods of thinking. As Poole et al. (2002, p. 350) strongly asserts:

> If these basic requirements cannot be achieved for mental health, with its long history of cooperation with non-statutory services, then an overarching NHS policy of public-private partnership has little credibility for other healthcare sectors.

Psychiatric units in the NHS are also gendered in the private-public healthcare landscape. Powell and Taylor (2015) have illustrated that women in secure psychiatric units lack any control over their own situations/lives and have few role models. They have pointed to psychiatric secure units as anti-therapeutic and as adding to the social control and disciplination to which women feel adding to powerlessness. As Powell and Taylor point out (2015, p. 141):

> Psychiatric secure units act as a structure of symbolic violence which is part of the system of domination of female patients, while at the same time a measure of its imperfection. If the hierarchy were actually legitimate, symbolic violence would not be necessary to maintain it.

If this stresses domination and power, as Foucault (1977) enquired, what of the potential of resistance?

Conclusion: the future of psychiatry – questions of resistance or rethinking psychiatry?

In those parts of the psychiatric establishment where care is most emphasised, rather than regimen and control, particularly in psychiatry, there seems to be a potential resistance on the provision of care based on a rigorous emphasis on the patient's own subjective experience outside of the medical gaze (Benner, 1994). In these patient care contexts, substantial attention has been devoted to the ethical implications of various medical definitions. Specifically, the discussion also focuses on how language shapes the response to illness, and to how definitions and paradigmatic models impact communication between psychiatric professionals and patients (Rosenberg & Golden, 1992).

Significant work has demonstrated how the *lived body* is experienced in altered form and how taken for granted routines are disrupted, invoking new action recipes (Rosenberg & Golden, 1992). Thus, an alternative approach to social control seeks to offer a corrective to the seeming dominant emphasis on bio-medical conceptualisations of mental illness; it excavates how we problematise disorder at a surface level by digging underneath such surfaces to reveal meanings and subjective sense of self that have been historically silenced by rigid historical models of psychiatric power. Hence, more qualitative methods that illuminate the human meanings of social life that brings to life issues associated with understanding their own identity rather than having it imposed on them is an important issue of self-governance and resistance to disciplination (Settersten, 1999). This is a difficult task given the cultural domination psychiatry. Yet, the opportunities for meaningful human agency should never be lost sight of without simultaneously never losing sight of the threats that power and social control can have for human beings with human rights.

This chapter has provided a historical and contemporary focus to how mental illness was treated by institutions and professions such as psychiatry (Foucault, 1965). Rethinking psychiatry is a huge task in modern society that illuminates an understanding of the relationship between states of individual mental health and classification practices and confinement. As an approach applied to understand mental illness, psychiatry could alternatively seek to reveal how human rights awareness is implicated in the production of *social* action, social situations and social worlds of people not as 'cases' but as person-centred.

Therefore, it is both inadequate and insensitive for psychiatrists to view *people* only as objects. People who interact with psychiatrists are subjects with sentient experience. Psychiatry could focus on the investigation of *social* products as humanly meaningful acts. The meaning contexts applied by the psychiatrist explicates the points of view of individuals. It also expresses their lifeworld and gives impetus that people with mental illness are people first which is a healthy corrective to the hegemony of psychiatric power.

References

Allderidge, P. (1997). *Bethlem hospital 1247–1997: A pictorial record.* Chichester: Phillimore & Co.

Andrews, J., Briggs, A., Porter, R., Tucker, P., and Waddington, K. (1997). *The History of Bethlem.* London: Routledge.

Bendiner, E. (1981). Philippe pinel: Reason for the unreasoning. *Hospital Practice (Office Ed.), 16*(6), 76E–76P.

Benner, P. (1994). *Interpretive phenomenology: Embodiment, caring, and ethics in health and illness.* Thousand Oaks, CA: SAGE Publications.

Beveridge, A. (2014) The history of psychiatry: Personal reflections in J. R. Coll Physicians Edinburgh 2014; 44, 78–84. doi: 10.4997/JRCPE.2014.118, accessed 15 August 2018

Carron, M., & Saad, H. (2012). Treatment of the mentally ill in the pre-moral and moral era: A brief report. *Jefferson Journal of Psychiatry, 24*(1). doi: 10.29046/JJP.024.1.001

Clouette, B., & Deslandes, P. (1997). The hartford retreat for the insane: An early example of the use of 'moral treatment' in America. *Connecticut Medicine, 61*(9), 521–527.

Cousins, M., & Hussain, A. (1984). *Michel Foucault.* New York: Palgrave Macmillan.

Davidson, A. (1986). Archaeology, genealogy, ethics. In Hoy, D. (Ed.), *Foucault: A critical reader* (pp. 221–234). Oxford: Hutchinson.

Davison, G. C., & Neale, J. M. (1997). *Abnormal psychology* (7th Ed.). New York: John Wiley & Sons.

Department of Health and Social Security (1957). *Royal commission on the law relating to mental illness and mental deficiency*. London: HMSO Cmnd. 169.

Department of Health and Social Security (1971). *Hospital services for the mentally ill*. London: HMSO.

Department of Health and Social Security (1975). *Better services for the mentally ill*. London: HMSO.

Department of Health and Social Security (1981). *Care in the community*. London: HMSO.

Digby, A. (1985). Moral treatment at the retreat, 1796–1846. In Bynum, W. F., Porter, R., Shepherd, M. (Eds.), *The anatomy of madness: Essays in the history of psychiatry* (p. 68). II. London, New York: Institutions and Society, Tavistock.

Fenton, W.S. & Blyler, Crystal & Heinssen, Robert. (1997). Determinants of medication compliance in Schizophrenia: Empirical and clinical findings. *Schizophrenia Bulletin*, 23, 637–651. doi: 10.1093/schbul/23.4.637

Foucault, M. (1965). *Madness and civilisation: A history of insanity in the age of reason*. Translator. Howard R; pp. 247–248, New York: Random House.

Foucault, M. (1973). *The birth of the clinic*. London: Tavistock.

Foucault, M. (1977). *Discipline and punish*. London: Tavistock.

Foucault, M. (1982). The subject and power. *Critical Inquiry*, 8(4), 777–795. Retrieved from JSTOR.

Freebody, J. (2016). *The role of work in late eighteenth- and early nineteenth-century treatises on moral treatment in France, Tuscany and Britain*. Retrieved from https://www.manchesterhive.com/view/9781526109255/9781526109255.00007.xml

Goffman, E. (1961). *Asylums: Essays on the social situation of mental patients and other inmates*. London: Penguin, Doubleday.

Greco, M. (1993). Psychosomatic subjects and the 'Duty to be Well': Personal agency within medical rationality. *Economy and Society*, 2(3), 357–372.

House of Commons Social Services Committee (1985) Community Care. Second Report from the Social Services Committee, House of Commons. HMSO: London cited in Goodwin, S. (1989). Community Care for the Mentally Ill in England and Wales: Myths, Assumptions and Reality. *Journal of Social Policy*, 18(1), 27–52. doi:10.1017/S0047279400017190.

Hunter, R. A., & Macalpine, I. (1963). *Three hundred years of psychiatry, 1535–1860: A history presented in selected English texts*. London: Oxford University Press.

Hunter, R. A., & Macalpine, I. (1974). *Psychiatry for the poor: 1851 Colney Hatch Asylum—Friern Hospital 1973 : A medical and social history*. Folkestone: Dawsons of Pall Mall.

Mann, S. A., & Cree, W. (1976). 'New' long-stay psychiatric patients: A national sample survey of fifteen mental hospitals in England and Wales 1972/3. *Psychological Medicine*, 6(4), 603–616. doi: 10.1017/s0033291700018249

McMillan, I. (1997). Insight into bedlam: One hospital's history. *Journal of Psychosocial Nursing and Mental Health Services*, 35(6), 28–34. doi: 10.3928/0279-3695-19970601-19

Ministry of Health (1962), *The hospital for England and Wales*: London: HMSO.

Porter, R. (1990). *English society in the eighteenth century* (Revised Ed.) London: Penguin Books.

Poole, R.,Ryan,T., & Pearsall, A. (2002) The NHS, The Private Sector, and the Virtual Asylum, *British Medical Journal*, 325, 349–350.

Powell, J. L., & Taylor, P. (2015). Gender, masculinity, contemporary history and the psychiatric secure estate: Back to the future? *World Scientific News*, 22, 145–156.

Priebe, S., Badesconyi, A., Fioritti, A., Hansson, L., Kilian, R., Torres-Gonzales, F., … Wiersma, D. (2005). Reinstitutionalisation in mental health care: Comparison of data on service provision from six European countries. *BMJ*, 330(7483), 123–126. doi: 10.1136/bmj.38296.611215.AE

Rabinow, P. (Ed.). (1984). *The Foucault reader*. New York: Peregrine.
Ritchie, J. H., Dick, D., & Lingham, R. (1994). *The report of the inquiry into the care and treatment of Christopher Clunis*. London: HMSO.
Rollin, H. R. (1990). *Festina Lente: A Psychiatric Odyssey*. London: British Medical Journal., Ch. 7, p. 59.
Rosenberg, C., & Golden J. (Eds.) (1992). *Framing disease: Studies in cultural history*. New Brunswick, NJ: Rutgers University Press.
Scull, A. (1993). *The most solitary of afflictions: Madness and society in Britain, 1700–1900*. New Haven, CT: Yale University Press.
Scull, A. (1979). *Museums of madness: The social organization of insanity in 19th century England*. New York: St. Martin's Press.
Settersten Jr., R. A. (1999). *Lives in time and place: The problems and promises of developmental science*. Amityville, NY: Baywood Publishing Co.
Sim, J. (1990). *Medical power in prisons: The prison medical service in England 1774–1989*. Milton Keynes: Open University Press.
Symonds, B. (1995). The origins of insane asylums in England during the 19th century: A brief sociological review. *Journal of Advanced Nursing, 22*(1), 94–100. doi: 10.1046/j.1365-2648.1995.22010094.x
Szasz, T. (1970) *The manufacture of madness*. London: Harper and Row.
Tanzman, B. (1993). An overview of surveys of mental health consumers' preferences for housing and support services. *Hospital & Community Psychiatry, 44*(5), 450–455. doi: 10.1176/ps.44.5.450

2

MENTAL HEALTH AND THE CRIMINAL COURTS

Fitness to plead, culpability and the defence of insanity

Rajan (Taj) Nathan

Recognising the potential vulnerabilities of defendants and those convicted during criminal court proceedings is critical in the delivery of justice in a way that is fair, just and humane. While measures in criminal proceedings in respect of the presence of mental vulnerabilities of the defendant are nothing new, distinguishing vulnerability may be more challenging. The question then, as has been asked by others (see for example, Cooper et al, 2015), is where criminal proceedings do engage parties with mental illness or disorder, how well our criminal courts ensure that such defendants are not unfairly disadvantaged. All who are charged with a criminal offence are to be presumed innocent until proven guilty, and indeed Article 6 of the European Convention on Human Rights and the Human Rights Act 1998 require this. Central, though, to concerns around the adjudication of guilt or innocence when the defendant displays mental vulnerabilities is the matter of participation in proceedings. This issue of participation will be explored as we proceed in this chapter. Court cases can be broadly divided into those that involve the prosecution of, and sentencing for, criminal offences (criminal proceedings) and those that involve a dispute between two parties about rights and properties (civil proceedings). Although mental health issues may arise in civil proceedings (e.g. with concerns about the effect of mental ill-health on parenting capacities in family proceedings), this chapter focuses on mental health and the criminal courts in England and Wales.

Magistrates' courts

The vast majority of criminal proceedings are dealt with in magistrates' courts. Magistrates, or justices of the peace, are unpaid lay people appointed by the Lord Chief Justice. They undergo training and receive guidance on points of law and procedure from a trained legal advisor. In adult criminal courts, magistrates sit in a bench of three, with one of the three approved as the chair who speaks in open court. Proceedings in magistrates' courts may also be presided over by a district judge (formerly known as a stipendiary magistrate) who is paid and legally qualified. A district judge sits alone and oversees more complex cases.

All criminal proceedings are heard initially in magistrates' courts. For the less serious 'summary' offences (such as road traffic offences or minor property damage), the proceedings can be dealt with in their entirety by the magistrates' court. Thus, in these cases, the magistrates determine guilt or innocence and pass sentence. However, some cases are passed on (or committed) to the Crown Court for trial. This is mandatory for serious, or 'indictable,' offences such as murder, rape or robbery. There are a group of offences which fall between summary and indictable, known as 'triable either way' (such as assault occasioning actual bodily harm) for which the defendant may choose to have the matter dealt with by magistrates or committed to Crown Court. Committal to Crown Court can also occur when a potential prison sentence is being considered that is over the threshold allowed in a magistrates' court (i.e. more than 6 months for one offence, or 12 months in total).

Crown court

The Crown Court is a single entity which sits in centres across England and Wales. Cases are heard before a judge and jury. In the Crown Court, the jury listens to the evidence and delivers a verdict on the defendant's guilt or innocence. The judge oversees the procedure, rules on matters of law and passes sentence.

Criminal proceedings

Pre-trial

In the pre-trial stage, the prosecution case is presented to the defence to allow the defendant, with support from his legal representatives, to decide whether to enter a guilty or not guilty plea to charges. If, in the case of summary or triable either way offences, the defendant enters a not guilty plea in a magistrate's court, a trial date is fixed. For those cases committed to the Crown Court, a Plea and Trial Preparation Hearing (PTPH) is held at which the indictment is read out and the defendant is asked if they plead guilty or not guilty. In the event of a not guilty plea, issues for the trial will be identified and the trial date set.

Trial

Determining whether the defendant is responsible for an offence relies on an adversarial process. Rather than having the explicit aim of identifying the truth, this process entails first the prosecution making its case and then the defence defending itself against the prosecution allegations. The prosecution has the 'burden of proof' meaning that it is required to make a case for conviction. Having heard both sides, the magistrates and the jury in Crown Court trials then must decide whether or not they accept the prosecution's case. They must be sure 'beyond all reasonable doubt' which is the 'standard of proof' required for a criminal conviction. However, for specific matters that may arise in the course of the proceedings, the burden of proof may switch to the defence and a lower standard of 'on the balance of probability' may apply. Examples of where this occurs are described in the sections below on fitness to plead, insanity and diminished responsibility.

For a defendant to receive a fair trial, he or she should be able to participate meaningfully. However, the defendant's ability to participate may be compromised by certain characteristics, including learning difficulties or mental health problems. As explained below the formal 'fitness to plead' procedure provides some safeguards. With the test for fitness to plead being so narrowly focused, vulnerable defendants often fall outside its provisions. In these cases, the court may agree to procedural adaptations to facilitate engagement (such as avoiding lengthy sessions and allowing for regular breaks). The extent to which adjustments are applied and the effect of any adjustments on engagement is largely unknown. Since vulnerabilities may not always be readily apparent, it follows that some vulnerable defendants will be disadvantaged with respect to their ability to properly engage in the criminal justice process.

Sentencing

Following a trial resulting in a conviction, the court may sentence immediately or delay sentencing to allow for reports to be prepared to assist the process of sentencing. Pre-sentence probation reports include an assessment of the risk of reoffending and provide assistance to the court in determining the most suitable sentence. At the sentencing hearing, the court decides the sentence on the basis of sentencing guidelines which take into account a range of factors such as the nature of the offence, aggravating factors (such as an offence committed whilst on bail for other offences) and mitigating factors (such as reduced mental illness or disability). However, with reference to mitigation by virtue of mental illness or disability, Peay (2016) highlights that "the Sentencing Guidelines are not specific about the extent of this reduction in culpability or how it is to be assessed in specific offenders."

Sentences for convicted offenders include discharges, fines, community sentences or prison sentences. A discharge is reserved for the least serious cases, where it is held that the experience of the proceedings in itself is enough of a punishment. The most common sentence is a fine. The amount is decided on the basis of the seriousness of the offence and the means of the offender.

Community sentences involve the imposition of one or more requirements from a list which includes unpaid work, participating in an offence-related programme (on an individual or group basis), prohibition from a defined activity, a curfew, supervision and a treatment-based requirement (i.e. drug rehabilitation, alcohol treatment and mental health treatment). Pursuant to section 207(1) of the amended Criminal Justice Act 2003, mental health treatment requirement "means a requirement that the offender must submit ... to treatment by or under the direction of a registered medical practitioner or a registered psychologist ... with a view to improvement of the offender's mental condition." The offender must have expressed a willingness to comply with such a requirement.

The commonest prison sentence is a determinate one, which sets a fixed term for the sentence. Offenders are released from prison once they have served half the term. Those sentenced to over two years are released at the halfway point and serve the remainder of the sentence in the community subject to licence conditions. A breach of licence conditions may result in recall to prison. Following release of an offender who committed the index offence on or after 1 February 2015 and who was sentenced to less than two years, he or she will be subject to (i) licence conditions for half the duration of the sentence, and then (ii) supervision for a period that when combined with the period of licence amounts to a total of 12 months following release. A breach of the terms of supervision may result in court proceedings and potential punishment for the breach.

Extended sentences are reserved for offenders who have a particular risk and offence history profile which indicates they present a significant risk to the public. Extended sentences comprise a custodial term and an extended period of licence. For sentences delivered on or after 13 April 2015, the offender is eligible for parole once they have served two-thirds of the custodial term. If released before the end of the custodial term they will be subject to licence conditions for the remainder of the custodial term and the extended period of licence. If they are not released before, then the offender is automatically released once the fixed term is served and then will be managed in the community under licence conditions for the extended period.

Life sentences are either mandatory (for all offenders convicted of murder) or discretionary (e.g. for certain offenders convicted of specified offences who pose a significant risk of serious harm). The judge specifies a minimum term that must be served before the offender is eligible to apply for parole. Following the release, the offender will remain subject to licence for life.

Appeals

If, following the conclusion of the proceedings, there is the case for arguing there may have been a procedural irregularity or there is new evidence that may have led to a different outcome, then the offender (who in this process is known as the appellant), can appeal against the conviction and/or sentence. The appeal is heard in the court next up in the hierarchy from the court where the proceedings were originally heard (i.e. the court of first instance). Thus appeals against a decision in a magistrate's courts are heard in the Crown Court, and Crown Court decisions are appealed to the Court of Appeal (Criminal Division). The next and final appeal court in England and Wales is the Supreme Court.

Diversion from custody

Mental disorder can cause the defendant to be particularly vulnerable to the adverse effects of being held in police or prison custody. Policy initiatives (such as those recommended by the 2009 Bradley report) and service developments (such as criminal justice liaison teams and prison mental health services) have been introduced to support the 'diversion' of offenders with mental health problems and learning difficulties to the appropriate support services. Despite improvements, many vulnerable offenders still find themselves detained in custodial environments without the appropriate level of support. A recent review by Birmingham et al. (2017) found that "in the main, though, the past decade and a half has been characterised by a lot of talk and a great deal of political rhetoric, which has not actually resulted in much change for the better." Even where the need for diversion from custody to hospital is identified, the pressure on available inpatient mental health services can lead to lengthy delays and time-limited admissions followed by a return to custody.

The role of expert opinion and reports

Particular issues may arise in some cases which require the input of specialists with expertise in the area pertinent to that issue.

Pre-trial issues

The most common pre-trial issue in cases of a defendant with mental health problems is fitness to plead which is explained in more detail below.

Pre-trial expert evidence may also inform decisions about whether an intermediary is required. Although the statutory provision of intermediaries applies to witnesses, the court may, in certain circumstances, allow the use of an intermediary to assist a defendant to ensure a fair trial. The intermediary's role includes giving advice on the arrangements for hearing evidence from the vulnerable witness (or defendant) and to assist in the communication with a witness (or defendant) whilst giving evidence. In addressing a question about the use of an intermediary, the expert should be mindful of the legal criteria for intermediaries for witnesses. The Youth Justice and Criminal Evidence Act 1999 mandated that a witness whose evidence is likely to be diminished as a consequence of a vulnerability (which includes a mental disorder, as that term is used in the Mental Health Act, 1983, or a significant impairment of intelligence or social functioning) is eligible for the assistance of an intermediary.

At trial

In criminal law, most offences are defined by both a forbidden act (actus reus or 'guilty act') and a certain state of mind (mens rea or 'guilty mind'). Where there has been a reason to question the defendant's mens rea, expert evidence may be sought to assist the court. Issues on which expert evidence relating to the defendant's mental functioning may be commissioned include the ability to form intent, insanity and diminished responsibility, which will be expanded on below.

At sentencing

Expert evidence relating to psychiatric or psychological issues may be requested to explore factors that could be presented to the court as mitigation to be taken into account when determining the appropriate sentence.

Additionally, if a mental disorder is suspected, or has already been identified in the course of the proceedings, expert evidence can be requested to address the question of appropriate treatment. In accordance with section 37 of the Mental Health Act 1983, where there is written evidence from two registered medical practitioners that a defendant is suffering from a mental disorder that is of a nature or degree for which hospital treatment is deemed necessary, the court may order admission to hospital.

Expert evidence

In criminal cases, expert witnesses may be instructed by the solicitors for the defendant, by the Crown Prosecution Service or by the court. In contrast to 'witnesses to fact,' who must confine themselves to what they have seen or heard in person, expert witnesses are permitted to present their opinions to the court. In most cases, the expert opinion is presented in the form of a written report, but on occasion, the expert is required to attend in person. For example, whilst a hospital order (under s. 37 of the Mental Health Act, 1983) can be made if the court has been furnished with reports from two doctors and the identified hospital, the court cannot add restrictions under s. 41 of the Act to the hospital order unless oral evidence from one of the doctors recommending the hospital order is heard. The expert may also be called to court if their evidence is contested, such as when a defence of insanity or diminished responsibility is not accepted by the prosecution.

Expert's assessment and opinion

The data on which the expert witness's opinions rely must be derived through an assessment process that is recognised by the relevant body of specialists and/or supported by scientific literature. Similarly, the way that data is formulated to arrive at the opinion should be recognisable to specialists in that field as acceptable practice and/or grounded in a body of academic work. Thus, a mental health clinician who provides expert evidence on diagnosis should elicit information using accepted clinical approaches (e.g. a clinical interview or an interview schedule) and make sense of that information using the recognised diagnostic approaches (e.g. ICD 10, World Health Organization, 1993; or DSM 5, American Psychiatric Association, 2013). The expert may deviate from commonly used approaches in occasional scenarios, such as an uncooperative patient refusing to engage in a clinical interview or where a rare condition is identified that is not described in the current diagnostic systems. In these scenarios, the expert must refer explicitly to deviation from generally accepted practice, the rationale for doing so, and any limitations to the opinion that the deviation causes.

The expert is independent and therefore his/her opinion should be impartial and uninfluenced by the party who instructs him/her. The expert should not offer an opinion on issues that are not within their area of expertise. If this applies to the instructions in their entirety, then the expert should not agree to accept them. In some cases, there may be elements of the case which fall within the experts' area and some that are outside it. For example, in a case of an elderly defendant who has been charged with murder, a forensic psychiatrist may be called on to assist the court on whether there are clinical issues that may form the basis of a diminished responsibility defence. If the forensic psychiatric assessment uncovers evidence of dementia, then unless the forensic psychiatrist has specialist expertise in this clinical area, he/she should be careful about providing definitive opinions about the specific nature of dementia. In this case, the forensic psychiatrist may recommend that a psychiatrist or psychologist with specialist expertise in dementia is also instructed to undertake an assessment. Experts need to continually reflect on the boundaries of their expertise and remain vigilant to the risk of overstepping those boundaries. As well as the boundary between one's own area of expertise and the areas of other specialists, the expert witness must be mindful of the additional risk of presenting an opinion on an issue which does not require expert opinion.

The sources of information that the expert evidence relating to psychiatric or psychological issues should routinely consider include the clinical assessment, documents arising from the proceedings, and the subject's medical records.

The clinical interview should follow the general format for clinical assessments, but some areas will require a more detailed assessment. In criminal cases, there should be a more in-depth inquiry into offending, particularly the index offence. However, there are certain cases in which the expert should avoid discussing the index offence allegations with the defendant. This may occur when the defendant's decision about what plea to enter depends on the issue of fitness to plead being resolved first. If the expert is left in doubt about the limits to their enquiries, they should seek clarification from the instructing party before undertaking the assessment. As well as the assessment being more detailed in some respects, the expert often needs to extend the assessment to areas that would not form part of the usual clinical assessment. These areas will depend on the questions the expert is instructed to address and may include fitness to plead, the capacity to form an intent, insanity, and – in homicide cases – diminished responsibility.

If available, the medical records should be studied to collate an account of previous mental health assessments (especially diagnostic assessments) and episodes of treatment. Particular attention should be paid to any recorded descriptions of the defendant's mental state around the time of the alleged offences. The documents from the criminal proceedings made available to the expert usually comprise a list of the charges, a summary of the key evidence and the police interviews of the defendant, prosecution witness statements, and a list of previous convictions. There may also be exhibits, such as photographs of the crime scene or transcripts of the text or social media communication. Studying these documents provides the expert with an understanding of the allegations, without which it can be difficult to properly interview the defendant about the alleged offence. The expert should also factor in witnesses' accounts of the defendant's behaviour and demeanour as this may provide indirect support for the presence or absence of mental state disturbance.

It may also be helpful to obtain information directly from others, such as treating clinicians or family members. In the latter example, the expert should liaise with the instructing solicitors as contact with family members may be problematic in certain circumstances, such as where family members are prosecution witnesses. The expert should list all sources of information and any other materials taken into account in the assessment and report preparation.

The extensive and ever-expanding literature exploring the relevance of advances in neurobiology on legal rules (i.e. neurolaw) has raised the prospect of allowing the results of neurobiological tests to be used to support a 'psychiatric defence.' As yet, the actual use of such results has been very limited. The empirical identification of neurobiological anomalies underpinning criminal and aggressive behaviour mostly relies on group-level analyses. It cannot be assumed that the identification of a predefined anomaly in an individual is causally related to a specific act by that individual.

Fitness to plead

Fitness to plead is a term that not only relates to the defendant's capacity to enter a plea, but it also extends to other elements of participating in the criminal proceedings. The European Court of Human Rights, in *SC v UK* (2004), offered the following direction on the meaning of 'effective participation':

> [It] presupposes that the accused has a broad understanding of the nature of the trial process and of what is at stake for him or her, including the significance of any penalty which may be imposed. It means that he or she, if necessary with the assistance of, for example, an interpreter, lawyer, social worker or friend, should be able to understand the general thrust of what is said in court. The defendant should be able to follow what is said by the prosecution witnesses and, if represented, to explain to his own lawyers his version of events, point out any statements with which he disagrees and make them aware of any facts which should be put forward in his defence.

Criteria

It is a long-established principle that before there can be a trial, the defendant must respond to the indictment with a plea of not guilty. Historically a response would be encouraged from reticent defendants by brutal means such as the use of increasingly heavy weights applied to the body. By the mid-nineteenth century, unresponsive defendants who were considered 'mute of malice' were tried as if they had entered a guilty plea. On the other hand, those found to be 'mute by visitation of God' were detained as criminal lunatics. Criteria for unfitness to plead were first articulated in the case of *R v Dyson* 1831 which involved a mute woman who was charged with murdering her child. Later the same decade, a case was heard in which the current test of fitness to plead was established. Pritchard, who was 'deaf and dumb,' had been indicted for bestiality. In 1836, the trial judge advised the jury to determine whether the defendant was

> of sufficient intellect to comprehend the course of proceedings in the trial so as to make a proper defence – to know that he might challenge any of you to whom he might object – and to comprehend the details of the evidence.

This test has been confirmed in subsequent cases and operationalised in more contemporary language in terms of the capacity to do the following: understand the charge, distinguish between a plea of guilty and not guilty, instruct one's solicitors, challenge a juror to whom one objects, follow evidence in court, and give evidence in one's defence.

The Law Commission's Unfitness to Plead report (2016) found problems with the current legal approach to testing fitness to plead, including the uncertainty about the formulation of the test due to the repeated revision of the 1836 *R v Pritchard* ruling, an undue focus on intellectual ability, and the lack of attention in the test to the accused's ability to make decisions in the proceedings. To address the identified problems, the Law Commission recommended reformulating the test of unfitness to plead in statute.

Process

Whereas if fitness to plead is raised by the prosecution, the 'beyond all reasonable doubt' standard remains – if the issue is raised by the defence it must be proved on the balance of probabilities.

In practice, if mental health or learning disability issues are suspected, particularly if they seem to interfere with discussions between the defendant and the defence solicitors, then a medical assessment of fitness to plead is commissioned. This is usually undertaken by a psychiatrist and should involve a full psychiatric evaluation supplemented by a specific assessment of the fitness to plead criteria. Fitness to plead does not require the individual to know in advance the relevant procedural rules, such as that a defendant can object to someone being a member of the jury. Rather, armed with this knowledge, the defendant should be able to implement it if necessary. If it appears to the clinician that the defendant may have some difficulties in relation to one or more of the fitness to plead criteria, then it does not necessarily lead to a conclusion that there is unfitness. The clinician should consider whether practicable steps can be taken to support the defendant to become fit to plead. Thus, if the attention levels of a defendant with attention deficit hyperactivity disorder are compromised to a degree that it would be difficult to follow what is said during a lengthy hearing, the expert could recommend introducing more regular breaks during which there are opportunities for the discussions between the defendant and the defence team. Alternatively, in the case of a defendant with autism spectrum disorder who struggles to understand idioms and expressions involving inferences about the minds of others, it would be reasonable to advise that language used by officials (either with the defendant or the proceedings which are had in court with the defendant present) avoids the use of such abstractions wherever possible.

If the defendant is found to be fit to plead, then the proceedings continue in the normal way. However, in the event of a medical assessment suggesting unfitness, then a specific process is activated involving three steps. First, the judge scrutinises the evidence, including the medical evidence, to rule on whether or not the defendant is unfit to plead. Second, if it is held that the defendant is unfit to plead, then a jury is empanelled for a trial of the facts. The difference between this and a standard trial is that the defendant does not participate. Without participation, the defendant cannot be found guilty and therefore the objective is to determine whether or not 'the facts are found.' Third, in the scenario in which both (i) the defendant is deemed to be unfit to plead and (ii) the facts are found, then the sentencing options available to the court are limited to a hospital order, a supervision order or an absolute discharge. A hospital order may be with or without restrictions pursuant to section 41 of the Mental Health Act. For an offence, the sentence for which is fixed by law (i.e. murder), the court must make a hospital order and restriction order. In the event of a hospital order, a mental health problem that may have been the basis of the unfitness to plead could respond to treatment and as a result the defendant may become fit to plead. If this occurs, then the matter can be returned to court for trial.

Mens rea

For behaviour to be deemed a criminal offence, the law is not only concerned with the physical act or failure to act (actus reus). It is also necessary to be satisfied that there was a particular state of mind (mens rea). The particular nature of the required state of mind to be guilty depends on the specific offence.

To be convicted of an offence of specific intent, the jury needs to agree that beyond all reasonable doubt that, as well as committing the act, the defendant possessed the intent to commit the act. For example, section 18 of the Offences Against the Person Act 1861, which carries a potential for a life sentence, requires the prosecution to demonstrate that the defendant's actions causing significant injury were accompanied by an intent to cause those injuries. On the other hand, the lesser offence of section 20 of the Offences Against the Person Act 1861, the sentence for which is limited to a maximum of five years, does not require specific intent. In most cases, the services of a psychiatric expert are not required to assist in the resolution of these issues. In some, however, the nature of the offence or the presentation of a defendant accused of section 18 wounding may lead the solicitors to consider instructing a psychiatric expert to explore whether the mens rea was compromised by psychiatric issues. The question of whether or not the perpetrator of the attack had the intent to cause the injuries is properly a matter for the jury to decide having heard the evidence. The expert must confine his/her opinion on the impact of any psychiatric issues on the capacity to form the necessary intent. In practice, though, this is often a false distinction, since opinion on the capacity to form intent is critically informed by an assessment of the evidence relating to whether or not the defendant possessed the intent.

M'Naghton rules – defence of insanity

A call for clarity about how the courts test a defence of insanity arose in response to outrage about the perceived message sent out to criminals by the finding in 1843 that Daniel M'Naghton, who had been charged with murder, was insane and therefore not guilty. He was a Scottish craftsman who had become overwhelmed by beliefs that he was being persecuted by the ruling Tory party. He had been seen in acting suspiciously in the vicinity of Whitehall in the months before he shot Edward Drummond, the personal secretary to Prime Minister Robert Peel. The defence amassed medical evidence to support the contention that Daniel M'Naghton acted under the influence of delusions and therefore was not guilty by reason of insanity. Unsurprisingly, given the strength of the case and the rather lame rebuttal by the prosecution, the defence was accepted. Queen Victoria was amongst those who expressed their dismay at the outcome of the trial. The House of Lords responded by posing a series of questions to a panel of Queen's Bench judges. Within their responses was a legal definition of insanity which has endured in England and Wales and had a significant influence in some other jurisdictions.

The following introduction to the rules makes it clear that there is a presumption of sanity:

> the jurors ought to be told in all cases that every man is to be presumed to be sane and to possess a sufficient degree of reason to be held responsible for his crimes until the contrary be proved to their satisfaction.

To establish a defence of insanity

> it must be clearly proved that, at the time of the committing the act, the party accused was labouring under such a defect of reason, from disease of

the mind, as not to know the nature and quality of the act he was doing; or if he did know it, that he did not know he was doing what was wrong.

Thus to prove insanity, it is not sufficient that there was a serious mental illness at the time of the offence or the defendant's criminal actions were strongly influenced by symptoms of the mental illness. It is necessary to specifically demonstrate that a defect of reason due to the mental illness was present to the extent that the defendant's understanding of his actions (or his understanding that he was acting in contravention of the law) was absent. These rules set a high bar for a finding of insanity and it has been argued that if they had been in place earlier, Daniel M'Naghton's was unlikely to have benefitted from the defence. In the event, M'Naghton was sent to Bethlem Hospital and then, shortly after its opening, he was transferred to the Broadmoor Criminal Lunatic Asylum, where he remained until his death in 1865.

As with fitness to plead the standard of proof is 'on the balance of probabilities' if raised by the defence and 'beyond all reasonable doubt' if raised by the prosecution. The sentencing options are the same as a finding of unfitness to plead.

Partial defences to murder – diminished responsibility

A conviction for murder results in a mandatory life sentence. Diminished responsibility is a partial defence to a charge of murder and if successful results in a conviction for the lesser offence of manslaughter for which the Court has sentencing discretion. The defence of diminished responsibility was introduced by the Homicide Act 1957. It is for the defence to raise and the case must be made to at least the standard of a balance of probabilities.

The Coroner's and Justice Act (CJA) 2009 amended the 1957 Act to bring the defence more in line with the contemporary understanding of mental processes. The defence can be separated into four elements. First, it must be shown that the defendant was suffering from an abnormality of mental functioning. Second, this abnormality must have arisen from a recognised medical disorder. Thus, if there is a history of mental problems, the psychiatric expert must attempt to elucidate whether, at the time of the killing, there was clinically significant mental state disturbance due to diagnosable condition. Third, the abnormality must have substantially impaired the defendant's ability to do one or more of three things, namely understand his conduct, to form a rational judgement or to exercise self-control. To comment on this, the psychiatrist needs to assess whether or not any identified mental state disturbance was such that it is likely to have caused an impairment of these mental processes and if so the extent of that impairment. Four, the abnormality of mental functioning must be held to have provided an explanation for the defendant's acts and omissions in relation to their involvement in the killing.

MacKay (2018) commented on the changes to the law of diminished responsibility in the following terms:

The new diminished responsibility plea was introduced for the twin purposes of clarification and modernisation. However, while the latter may have been achieved it is open to doubt as to whether the new provision achieves the goal of "clarification" insofar as the impairment factors are concerned. ... [The impairment factors] are not purely medical or psychiatric matters but are rather medicolegal concepts which require careful analysis not only from a medical but also from a legal perspective.

In the event of a successful defence of diminished responsibility, a hospital order with or without restrictions may be considered. However, the criteria may not be met for a hospital order and the court can consider other sentences including a prison sentence.

Conclusion

This chapter has provided a comprehensive overview of criminal proceedings in relation to defendants who have mental vulnerabilities, illnesses and disorders. At the heart of criminal justice practice is the maintenance of safeguards and the pursuit of justice in a fair and just way. Procedural aspects and outcomes are, of course, predicated on the way that they are administered. There are consequently risks to the appropriate delivery of justice if recognition and action over vulnerabilities of the defendant are not adequately supported. For the defendant, the avoidance of being unfairly disadvantaged because of the presence on a mental illness, disorder or some other vulnerability is critical – and this being the responsibility of the courts to facilitate. To this end, we should be encouraged by developments in our processes, but at the same time monitor how well provisions adequately recognise vulnerabilities, protect and safeguard the defendant's right to a fair trial.

References

American Psychiatric Association (2013). *Diagnostic and statistical manual of mental disorders (DSM-5®)*. American Psychiatric Pub.

Birmingham, L., Awonogun, O., & Ryland, H. (2017). Diversion from custody: An update. *BJPsych Advances*, 23(6), 375–384. doi: 10.1192/apt.bp.116.016113

Cooper, P., Backen, P., & Marchant, R. (2015). Getting to grips with ground rules hearings: A checklist for judges, advocates and intermediaries to promote the fair treatment of vulnerable people in court. *Criminal Law Review*, 6, 417–432.

Department of Health. (2009). The Bradley report: Lord Bradley's review of people with mental health problems or learning disabilities in the criminal justice system.

Law Commission (2016). *Unfitness to plead*. Stationery Office (Great Britain).

Mackay, R. (2018). The impairment factors in the new diminished responsibility plea. *Criminal Law Review*, 6, 457–466.

Peay, J. (2016). Responsibility, culpability and the sentencing of mentally disordered offenders: Objectives in conflict. *Criminal Law Review*, 3, 152–164.

World Health Organization (1993). *The ICD-10 classification of mental and behavioural disorders: Diagnostic criteria for research*. World Health Organization.

Further reading

Badger, D., Vaughan, P., Woodward, M., & Williams, P. (1999). Planning to meet the needs of offenders with mental disorders in the United Kingdom. *Psychiatric Services*, *50*(12), 1624–1627. doi: 10.1176/ps.50.12.1624

Catley, P., & Claydon, L. (2015). The use of neuroscientific evidence in the courtroom by those accused of criminal offenses in England and Wales. *Journal of Law and the Biosciences*, *2*(3), 510–549. doi: 10.1093/jlb/lsv025

Dixon, J. (2015). Treatment, deterrence or labelling: Mentally disordered offenders' perspectives on social control. *Sociology of Health & Illness*, *37*(8), 1299–1313. doi: 10.1111/1467-9566.12313

James, D. V. (2010). Diversion of mentally disordered people from the criminal justice system in England and Wales: An overview. *International Journal of Law and Psychiatry*, *33*(4), 241–248. doi: 10.1016/j.ijlp.2010.06.006

McKenzie, J. G. (2016). *Guilt: Its meaning and significance*. Routledge. doi: 10.4324/9781315559674

Weare, S. (2017). Bad, mad or sad? Legal language, narratives, and identity constructions of women who kill their children in England and Wales. *International Journal for the Semiotics of Law – Revue Internationale de Sémiotique Juridique*, *30*(2), 201–222. doi: 10.1007/s11196-016-9480-y

Legislation cited

Coroners and Justice Act 2009.
Criminal Justice Act 2003.
Homicide Act 1957.
Human Rights Act 1998.
Offences Against the Person Act 1861.
Youth Justice and Criminal Evidence Act 1999.

3

CAUSAL RELATIONSHIPS OR CASUAL ASSOCIATIONS? ASSESSING THE NATURE AND CHARACTER OF MENTAL ILLNESS/DISORDER AND CRIME

Ian Cummins

The link between mental illness, violence and other offending remains an area of controversy. The debate can become polarised around two extremes: that no such link exists or the mentally ill as a group are violent. This chapter will place these debates within the context of the development of two interrelated policies – the expansion of the use of imprisonment and deinstitutionalisation. One of the most startling features of social policy development over the past 30 years is the expansion of the use of imprisonment. In the 1970s, criminologists were seriously considering how the prison as an institution was on the verge of disappearing and pondering how it would be replaced as the central penal mechanism in liberal democracies. The overlap between mental health and the criminal justice system is a well-established one. The criminal justice system has become a default provider of mental health care in many instances. The chapter will conclude with a brief discussion of Penrose's hypothesis, which identified a hydraulic relationship between the use of imprisonment and the use of institutionalised forms of care for mental illness.

Mental health issues in the criminal justice system

There is a tendency to view the criminal justice system and mental health systems as distinct entities that occasionally overlap – for example, in forensic mental health provision. This is misleading. The boundaries between the two are much more porous than is generally acknowledged (Seddon, 2007). It is a combination of factors that lead to some individuals in the criminal justice system being recognised as having a mental health problem. It is important to acknowledge here that the overwhelming majority of professionals working the criminal justice system do not have formal mental health qualifications. Mental health problems can be masked by drug and alcohol misuse. These combined with the nature of the environment in police custody suites, the Courts and prisons mean that offenders with mental health problems may not have their needs identified or addressed adequately. Foucault (2012) emphasised that the prison as an institution has always been used to accommodate a variety of individuals labelled as deviant by the wider society.

There is a danger of presentism in all areas of social policy. This is particularly the case in the fields of mental health and its intersection with the criminal justice system. In 1780, John Howard carried out his famous inspection of the state of the prisons in England. As well as describing the appalling physical conditions that led to disease and hunger, the corruption amongst warders, Howard noted that the prisons were housing more, what he termed 'idiots' and 'lunatics'. Also, Howard indicated that the increases in the number of what we might now term 'mentally disordered offenders' meant that the prison regime was unable to meet their needs. This had a detrimental effect on the prison regime for all those in prisons. Similar observations have been at regular intervals since. However, the recent expansion in the use of imprisonment has occurred during the period when the impact of deinstitutionalisation has been most clearly felt. The combination has exacerbated these problems. The criminal justice system has become something of a default provider of mental health care. This is the case across all the stages of the criminal justice system. The result is that more criminal justice system professionals are being asked to take on roles or tasks that involve responding to individuals experiencing mental distress.

A problem of definition?

One of the most fundamental issues that debate in this field raise is, what is the definition of the term *mentally disordered offender?* At its narrowest, the term might only be used for those convicted of offences and sentenced under the provisions of the Mental Health Act (1983). This is a very small group, and it also does not cover those who people with mental health problems who are in contact with the police or in police contact. At its broadest, it could include anyone in contact with the criminal justice system who has mental health problems. This is a very wide definition and includes groups with varying needs. It will thus include acutely unwell individuals who might be admitted to a mental health unit but also those who would be treated as an outpatient. This definition acknowledges the porous nature of the boundaries between the criminal justice system and mental health systems. The use of the term *'offender'* is more problematic. For example, if someone is detained under section 136 MHA by a police officer, they have not committed any offence but they have been drawn into the criminal justice system by virtue of their contact with the police. The limited research that explores the experiences of people detained under section 136 indicates that they see it as a punitive rather than therapeutic intervention. Law and policy allow the mental health of an individual can and should be a consideration in decisions at every stage of the criminal justice system. This is the case from potential contact with a police officer on the street, through custody, charging and sentencing. The police, courts and prisons can be viewed as a series of filters (Cummins, 2016a).

Policing and mental illness

The role of the police in responding to people who are experiencing some form of mental health crisis has come under increasing scrutiny. There are concerns from the police that they are being increasingly called upon because of the gaps in community mental health services. The Police have considerable discretion in terms of their response but have always had a role in responding to those experiencing mental distress. The general police role of maintaining public order will inevitably include what we might term welfare work – looking for missing people, for example. The police role is thus a combination of preventing crime, detecting and apprehending those who have committed offences and a more general one (Bittner, 1967). This has always been the case since the establishment of the modern police force. However, it is clear that the pressures have increased since the development of deinstitutionalisation and the policies of austerity adopted since 2010 (Cummins, 2013). Lord Adebowale (2013) described mental health as a 'core business' for the police. His study confirmed earlier work by the Sainsbury Centre (2008) which had concluded that between 15 and 20% of police work relates to mental health issues. A very significant proportion of this work involves dealing with cases where people with mental health problems are victims of crime. To this must be added, cases where people with mental health problems have committed crimes, mental health emergencies and section 136 MHA, supporting community mental health services and ensuring that people in custody are safe.

Mental disorder and offending

The above forms the policy context which creates the environment in which mental health and criminal justice system professionals work. As outlined above, there is considerable overlap between the two groups, who are often responding to very similar situations. Cummins (2013) outlined that the thrust of policy has been to divert individuals with mental health problems from the criminal justice system at the earliest opportunities. The current difficulties in both prisons and mental health services illustrate that diversion, if it is achievable, requires robust and well-funded community mental services.

The problem of defining the term 'mentally ordered offender' contains within it two difficulties – what do we mean by mental disorder and who is considered an offender. Both terms cover a huge range of behaviour. Both fields a number of ethical and philosophical issues. Eastman and Starling (2006) note a purely biomedical model of illness cannot be transferred easily to mental health. We see mental illness, if we accept the term at all in the impact it has on an individual's behaviour, thoughts and language. The reason why we think people are ill is that they are 'behaving oddly'. It is a very powerful cultural trope that sees mental illness, particularly the most serious forms, as changing the character or personality of an individual. This is reinforced in cultural representations of mental illness (Cross, 2010). The existence and impact of mental illness have huge implications in the criminal justice system field. In particular, it forces us to consider the key questions of autonomy and responsibility are being considered. Psychiatric diagnosis has a role to play in the criminal justice system. This means that the Courts can be the site of debates about diagnosis and the impact on responsibility. Legal and policy changes have an impact on the way that these debates are constructed. The reform of the Mental Health Act (2007) has seen the creation of the term 'dangerous and severe personality disorder'. This term is, in effect, a legal categorisation cloaked in terms of psychiatric discourse.

One of the core notions of the Anglo-American legal tradition is individual autonomy. Individuals are free to act or are autonomous. The individual is not coerced into committing an offence. An individual must have been in a position, in which they could make a choice. This model has important implications for the legal treatment of mentally disordered offenders. Nagel (1978) suggests that behaviour is intentional if the individual acts on a belief or desire. These must be independent and pass what he terms "critical scrutiny". An individual who is forced or coerced to take part in a criminal enterprise could argue that they were not responsible. The final leg of Nagel's schema is that the beliefs and desires that are the spring for action will pass critical scrutiny. Lipkin (1990) uses the example of John Hinckley. Hinckley's shooting of President Reagan was the result of a delusional belief system, in which not only did the President approve of his actions but also they would lead to Jodie Foster entering into a relationship with him . Both ideas are so bizarre that they could not pass any critical scrutiny. Therefore, Hinckley's mental illness and the delusional beliefs he held were the cause of his attempt to assassinate the President of the United States. He should be viewed differently to someone who murders in the course of a robbery. This is a rare and highly unusual example. However, it demonstrates the fundamental principles that need consideration.

Punishment is based on the notion that the offender took a conscious, rational decision to ignore or break the law. They were not coerced. Thus an offender can only be punished if they deserve it because they have committed the offence and there is a positive outcome for society. This is usually justified by reducing offending by both: that individual and the wider deterrent effect. Offenders are viewed as moral agents, who have chosen a particular course of action. Becker's (1968) influential Rational Choice Theory of offending is the clearest exposition of this approach. It argues that offenders essentially carry out a form of cost-benefit analysis before deciding to commit an offence. In this analysis, they consider the chances that they will be caught, the possible punishment and the rewards of the crime.

Mental disorder has impacts on thinking and how we view the world. A fundamental question is the extent, if any, that mental disorder can be said to lead to an offence. A legal defence of insanity is based on the idea that mental disorders affect reasoning and decision making (Morse, 2003). There is a further complication herein that the links between mental illness and offending are not as straightforward as this line of argument suggests. The Hinckley case is very unusual. The defence could demonstrate a clear link between the delusional ideas and the shooting of Ronald Reagan. The majority of cases are not like this. However, leaving aside the issue of substance misuse and addiction, it is largely agreed that individuals are not responsible for the symptoms of mental illness and that such symptoms can affect the individual's ability to act as a moral agent.

Eastman and Starling (2006) strongly argue that mental illness is an issue for the criminal justice system because of its effects on individual autonomy. It is a matter of degree that is altered by not only the nature and severity of the mental disorder but other factors such as the efficacy of a particular course of treatment. It is important to note that mental disorder cannot be used to explain all offending. It can only be used to excuse or be part of mitigation for those offences where the disorder affected the reasoning that led to the commission of that crime. There is an inherent danger that the portrayal of the effects of mental disorder is to turn those experiencing mental distress into machines. As well as being philosophically problematic, Morse (2003) suggests that such accounts are inaccurate. He argues that a hallucinating person retains the ability to act intentionally, to act for reasons. John Hinckley and Chapman both had clear reasons for acting in the way they did. The issue for the Criminal Justice system is to what extent the delusional basis of those reasons should be seen as a mitigating factor.

The issues of autonomy, responsibility and the extent to which mental illness should be seen as a mitigating factor are played out in the Courts. The case can become not about whether an individual carried out an act. The questions under consideration are more concerned with the existence and any potential impact of mental illness on the defendant. The trial of Peter Sutcliffe the so-called Yorkshire Ripper is a high profile example of this. He entered a plea of guilty to manslaughter on the grounds of diminished responsibility. This was initially accepted but then rejected by the Crown. The trial then, in essence, became a debate about whether Sutcliffe was 'mad'. It involved psychiatrists for both the defence and the prosecution arguing their positions. It was for the jury, not the mental health professionals, to settle the question ultimately. Sutcliffe was found guilty and sentenced to life for the brutal murders of 13 women and 7 further cases of attempted murder (Bilton, 2003). Sutcliffe was transferred to forensic mental health services in 1984. He spent 32 years there before being transferred back to a maximum-security prison in 2016.

Imprisonment

One of the most significant features of social and public policy in the United Kingdom in the past 35 years has been the consistent rise in the number of people in prison. The United Kingdom has not been alone in developing what has come to be termed a penal state (Cummins, 2016b). There are four nations of the United Kingdom, with differing legal and sentencing systems. The focus here will be on England and Wales. The United States has seen the greatest increase in the use of imprisonment. There are over 10.2 million people in prison. Around 2.4 million of those are in prison in the United States. Three countries, the United States, Russia (0.68 million) and China (1.64 million), hold roughly a quarter of the world's prisoners (Walmsley, 2013). Walmsley (2013) concludes that prison populations have continued to grow across the five continents since the turn of the century. The standard comparative measure for imprisonment is the rate per 100, 000 of the population. Since 1999, the overall world prison population rate has increased from 136 per 100, 000 to 144 per 100, 000. The United States remains at the top of this incarceration league with a rate of 716 per 100,000.

The United States should be viewed not only as an outlier in terms of penal policy, but also, I would argue, a warning of the damage that mass incarceration can do to individuals, communities and the wider social fabric. In his analysis of the development of mass incarceration, Simon (2014) highlights three key drivers. Fear of crime and the political fallout from being seen as weak on the issues leads to a ratcheting up in sentencing. Custodial sentences replace community penalties or supervision. Custodial sentences become longer – driven by the perceived need to be tough on crime. In the United States, this was driven by the war on drugs. Finally, mandatory and or indeterminate sentences are introduced (Simon, 2007). These factors combine to produce a perfect storm. All these factors are present to a greater or less degree in the British context. Progressive parties have been unable or unwilling to shift the terms of the debate for fear of being seen as soft on crime. The impact of imprisonment is not limited to individuals who are sentenced by the Courts. In the United States, these impacts have to be viewed through the prism of race. There is a significant body of research that demonstrates the wider damage that has been done to the African-American community (Drucker, 2013). Many US states prevent ex-prisoners from voting, accessing social housing or completing educational programmes. This serves to create a new "caste" of disenfranchised and marginalised young black men (Alexander, 2012).

England and Wales is the jurisdiction in Europe that has seen the most dramatic rise in the use of imprisonment. This increase and its impact have not been, until relatively recently, the centre of any concentrated political debate. In 2018/2019 statements by the then Prisons Minister, Rory Stewart and the Justice Secretary, David Gauke have indicated a shift in approach. They have highlighted the need for a more constructive prison regime, questioned the effectiveness of short sentences and recognised the impact of drug and substance misuse on prison regimes. These statements have to be viewed in the context of the development of a prison regime that has seen the number of prisoners rise, while there have been significant cuts in the number of prison officers. There were 64,000 people in prison in 2000, and this rose by a third to over 86,000 in 2012.

On average it costs around £38,000 per year to imprison someone and one has to ask whether these huge sums of money represent the best use of public funds. Recidivism rates are poor with 73% of those aged under 18 years sentenced to custody reoffending within six months of release. Also, serious questions are now being asked about how safe prisons are, with 88 suicides in prisons in England and Wales in 2015. Put this bleak figure alongside reports of violence towards staff, bullying and lack of constructive activities and the result is a toxic mix (HM Chief Inspector of Prisons for England and Wales, 2015).

Mental health care in the prison setting

One of the key contemporary policy concerns is that the criminal justice system is being increasingly asked to provide mental health care. The Trencin statement (World Health Organization, 2008) commits governments to provide the same level of health care to prisoners as the general population. It states that:

> Prisoners shall have access to the health services available in the country without discrimination on the grounds of their legal situation.

This is an important moral and ethical statement. It is an aim that many governments have failed consistently to achieve. The expansion in the use of imprisonment and the overcrowding that often accompanies it makes it difficult to provide appropriate ongoing care. Those sentenced to imprisonment do not represent a cross-section of the population. They come from overwhelming poor, marginalised and urban communities. Marmot (2010) has demonstrated the impact of social inequalities on health – both physical and mental. There is a clear gradient in health. Karban (2017) has highlighted the need for a health inequalities approach to tackle the most deeply engrained mental health issues. These problems have been exacerbated by the impact of austerity (Cummins, 2018). Cuts in public services inevitability have the greatest impact on those most in need of services. There is a pincer effect here – demand for services increases at the time when the services are under the greatest pressure. The health care needs of prisoners are much higher than those of the general population. These reflect the socio-economic background of the prison population but also the impact of other factors such as alcohol and drug abuse.

There are additional problems providing mental health services within a prison environment or across the criminal justice system. The starting point is a statement of the obvious fact that a police or prison cell is not and can never realistically hope to provide a therapeutic environment. In addition, security and other organisational needs will mean that prisoners might be moved at short notice and so on making it difficult to provide consistent care. Prisons can be brutalising environment, so may create or exacerbate mental health problems. The impact of mass incarceration was demonstrated in the case of *Brown v. Plata* in the United States (Simon, 2014). Prisoners sued the state of California – and won – on the basis that the state had failed to provide adequate health care. This included mental health care. The case went to the Supreme Court which found 5-4 in favour of the prisoners. In writing the majority decision, Justice Kennedy emphasised that prisoners retained the essence of human dignity. Any prison regime that provided such inadequate care violated this fundamental concept.

One of the major concerns of academics, policymakers and campaigners, who seek to reduce the numbers in prison, is that many prisoners experience mental illness. Also, there are concerns that this group of prisoners do not receive appropriate care and treatment. Singleton et al. (2003) is now 20 years old but remains the benchmark study in the United Kingdom of the mental health needs of prisoners. Fazel and Seewald (2012) carried out a meta-analysis of studies of prisoners' mental health. Prisoners experience higher rates of mental illness. Surveys estimate that one in seven prisoners are diagnosed with depression or psychosis. These figures appear to have remained unchanged for over a decade

Research has also consistently demonstrated high rates of comorbidity between mental illness and substance misuse. This combination has profound health and social implications. Treatments are not as effective and reoffending rates are higher. Rates of psychiatric disorders and drug dependence are much higher amongst female prisoners. The poor mental and physical health of women in prisons (and the need for alternatives to imprisonment) was outlined in the Corston Inquiry (Corston, 2007)

Fazel and Seewald (2012) study indicate that prisoners are a particularly at-risk group for suicide and self-harm. In male prisoners, the rates are 3–6 times higher and for female prisoners, the rate is six times higher than the wider community. It should be noted that the risk factors for self-harm and suicide such as drug and substance misuse problems, the experience of abuse and/or sexual violence are all higher amongst men and women in prison. There are differential patterns identified here, including lower rates of suicide and self-harm experienced by black, Asian and mixed-race prisoners.

Fazel and Seewald (2012) also examine violence and victimisation. People with mental health problems are more likely than other groups in the general population to be subject to violence. Violence is almost taken as a given of daily prison life but there is little research that examines its prevalence. Studies indicate that physical assault is 13–27 times more common in prison than in the community. The prison culture makes it difficult to carry out work in this area as assaults are likely to be under-reported, mostly because of the possible consequences of being seen as an informer. Fazel and Seewald (2012) concluded that both male and female prisoners experiencing mental health problems were more vulnerable to sexual violence and physical assault.

This detailed piece of work demonstrates that the rates of mental disorder are higher amongst prisoners than the wider community. This is particularly the case for serious mental disorders such as psychosis and depression. In addition, about 20% of prisoners have a substance misuse problem. Features of the prison environment (higher levels of violence, bullying and intimidation alongside the availability of new psychoactive substances such as spice) increase the risks to mental health.

Fazel and Seewald (2012) argue that there is a need for a robust and systematic assessment of prisoners for mental health problems, alongside acute detox services on arrival at all prisons. These recommendations are calling for the current best practice in community mental health to be applied to the prison setting.

The prison and the asylum are two of the key institutions of modern welfare states (Foucault, 2003; 2012). They can be regarded as separate and distinct regimes – one punitive the other therapeutic. This is a very limited analysis that does not take account of the symbolic and functional roles that they both had in the management of social deviance. There is an argument that the failure of community care has seen the distinctions between them become even more blurred and confusing. As we have seen above, the debates about the nature of mental illness and its potential links with offending behaviour continued to be played out in Courts and other settings. This not to suggest that people with mental health problems are more likely than others to commit a crime. It is rather an acknowledgement that in some, if not, the majority of cases, it can be difficult if not impossible to establish conclusive causal links between specific symptoms of mental illness and the commission of offences. Even where this is the case, it is still possible to argue that the offender should be punished.

Penrose (1939 and 1943) put forward the intriguing hypothesis that there is a fluid relationship between the use of psychiatric inpatient beds and the use of custodial sentences. The 1939 paper was based on the analysis of statistics from European countries and argued that there was an inverse relationship between the provision of mental hospitals and the rate of serious crime in the countries studied – as one increases, the other decreases. The 1943 paper was a study of the rates of hospital admission in different states in the USA and the numbers in state prisons. Later in his work, he argued that a measurable index of the state of development of a country could be obtained by dividing the total number of people in mental hospitals and similar institutions by the number of people in prison. The policies of deinstitutionalisation and the development of the penal state appear to support the main thrust of Penrose's argument. He suggested that society responds to deviance in one of two ways, either by medicalising it or punishing it.

Penrose's hypothesis could be criticised for equating mental illness with criminality. I would suggest that this is not his intention. He was rather arguing that we should not criminalise the mentally ill. He supported more therapeutic interventions and approaches. The development of community-based mental health services is based on both moral and clinical arguments. Its main proponents, for example, Basaglia in Italy, saw the institutionalised treatment of the mentally ill as a political issue – one of human rights (Foot, 2015). Community-based services, it was argued, would be by definition more humane. Those who argued for community-based mental health services did not envisage that asylums would be replaced by police and prison cells. Deinstitutionalisation, a progressive policy aimed at reducing the civic and social isolation of the mentally ill, has not achieved its aims. Wolff (2005) and Moon (2000) argue that asylums have been replaced by a fragmented and dislocated world of bedsits, housing projects, day centres or increasingly, prisons and the criminal justice system. This shift has been termed 'transinstitutionalisation'.

The policy of deinstitutionalisation is followed across the world. At the same time, there has been a clear shift towards a more punitive prison policy. As Wacquant (2009) argues, throughout the industrialised world, there has been a large prison-building programme and investment in the criminal justice system. Gunn (2000) and Kelly (2007) found that the reduction in the number of psychiatric beds in the United Kingdom occurred at the same time as the rise in the prison population, as Penrose predicted. The clash of the two policies outlined above – deinstitutionalisation and mass incarceration – seems to provide evidence to support Penrose's original hypothesis. Large and Nielessen (2009) undertook a review of Penrose's original hypothesis using data from 158 countries. They suggest one of the main features of Penrose's argument is that there is an unchanging proportion of any population that will need, or be deemed to need, some form of institutional control. They concluded that though there was a positive correlation between prison and psychiatric populations in low- and middle-income countries, there was no such relationship in high-income countries.

Penrose's hypothesis can be seen as a statistical argument – the examination of the relationship between two major institutions: prison custody and psychiatric care. There are several problems that arise here. Such an approach equates crime and mental illness. Also, it fails to explore the reasons behind the changes in patterns of use of the two institutions. The increase in the use of prison continues despite the general reduction in the crime rate (Garland, 2001). Therefore, it is part of a wider change in society and government attitudes rather than simply a response to crime. The changes in the use of institutional psychiatric care are the result of a combination of social attitudes, improved medical and treatment approaches, recognition of the cost of in-patient treatment and recognition that citizens should not lose their civic and human rights because of mental ill-health.

Conclusion

As outlined above, there is a danger that 'mad' or 'bad' limits our understanding of the causality of offending while at the same stigmatising mental illness. There is a further danger that it will fail to recognise that the term 'mentally disordered offender' or any variation thereof will include a wide range of individual experiences. If it is only used in circumstances where the defence makes clear links between symptoms of mental illness and offending, then it will be used increasingly rarely. There is a further danger that the conclusion of the 'mad' / 'bad' debate is that we see the options as either treatment or punishment. This would constitute a clear breach of the Trencin statement. We need to reaffirm that the criminal justice system should be based on the fundamental principle of a recognition of the dignity of all involved.

References

Adebowale, L. V. (2013). *Independent commission on mental health and policing.* London: House of Lords.

Alexander, M. (2012). *The new Jim Crow: Mass incarceration in the age of colorblindness.* New York: The New Press.

Becker, G. (1968). "Crime and punishment: An economic approach". *Journal of Political Economy,* 76(2), 169–217

Bilton, M. (2003). *Wicked beyond belief: The hunt for the Yorkshire Ripper.* London: HarperCollins.

Bittner, E. (1967). The police on skid-row: A study of peace keeping. *American Sociological Review,* 32(5), 699–715.

Corston, J. (Chair) (2007). *A report by Baroness Jean Corston of a review of women with particular vulnerabilities in the Criminal Justice System.* Retrieved from www.justice, gov.uk

Cross, S. (2010). *Mediating madness: Mental distress and cultural representation.* New York: Springer.

Cummins, I. (2016a). *Mental health and the criminal justice system: A social work perspective.* Northwich: Critical Publishing.

Cummins, I. (2016b). Putting diagnosis into brackets: Franco Basaglia, radical psychiatry, and contemporary mental health services. *Illness, Crisis & Loss,* 1054137316659206. doi: 10.1177/1054137316659206

Cummins, I. (2018). The impact of austerity on mental health service provision: A UK perspective. *International Journal of Environmental Research and Public Health,* 15(6), 1145. doi: 10.3390/ijerph15061145

Cummins, I. D. (2013). Policing and mental illness in the era of deinstutionalisation and mass incarceration: A UK Perspective. *International Journal of Criminology and Sociological Theory,* 6(4), 92–104.

Drucker, E. (2013). *A plague of prisons: The epidemiology of mass incarceration in America.* New York: The New Press.

Eastman, N., & Starling, B. (2006). Mental disorder ethics: Theory and empirical investigation. *Journal of Medical Ethics,* 32(2), 94–99. doi: 10.1136/jme.2005.013276

Fazel, S., & Seewald, K. (2012). Severe mental illness in 33 588 prisoners worldwide: Systematic review and meta-regression analysis. *The British Journal of Psychiatry,* 200(5), 364–373. doi: 10.1192/bjp.bp.111.096370

Foot, J. (2015). *The man who closed the asylums: Franco Basaglia and the revolution in mental health care.* London: Verso Books.

Foucault, M., 2012. Discipline and punish: The birth of the prison. New York: Vintage.

Foucault, M. (2003). *Madness and civilization.* doi: 10.4324/9780203164693

Garland, D. (2001). *The culture of control: Crime and social order in contemporary society.* Oxford: OUP.

Gunn, J. (2000). Future directions for treatment in forensic psychiatry. *The British Journal of Psychiatry,* 176(4), 332–338. doi: 10.1192/bjp.176.4.332

Her Majesty's Chief Inspector of Prisons Annual Report 2014–2015 (2015). Retrieved from https://www.justiceinspectorates.gov.uk/hmiprisons/wp-content/uploads/sites/4/2015/07/HMIP-AR_2014-15_TSO_Final1.pdf

HM Inspectorate of Prisoners for England and Wales (HMIP). (2015). HM Chief Inspector of Prisons for England and Wales Annual Report 2014–15. Inspectorate of Prisons.

Karban, K. (2017). Developing a health inequalities approach for mental health social work. *The British Journal of Social Work,* 47(3), 885–992. doi: 10.1093/bjsw/bcw098

Kelly, B. D. (2007). Penrose's Law in Ireland: An ecological analysis of psychiatric inpatients and prisoners. *Irish Medical Journal*, *100*(2), 373–374.

Large, M. M., & Nielssen, O. (2009). The Penrose hypothesis in 2004: Patient and prisoner numbers are positively correlated in low-and-middle income countries but are unrelated in high-income countries. *Psychology and Psychotherapy: Theory, Research and Practice*, *82*(1), 113–119. doi: 10.1348/147608308X320099

Lipkin, R. J. (1990). Free will, responsibility and the promise of forensic psychiatry. *International journal of law and psychiatry*, *13*(4), 331–359.

Marmot, M., Allen, J., Goldblatt, P., Boyce, T., McNeish, D., Grady, M., & Geddes, I. (2010). *The Marmot review: Fair society, healthy lives*. London: UCL.

Moon, G. (2000). Risk and protection: The discourse of confinement in contemporary mental health policy. *Health & Place*, *6*(3), 239–250. doi: 10.1016/S1353-8292(00)00026-5

Morse, S. J. (2003). Diminished rationality, diminished responsibility. *Ohio State Journal of Criminal Law*, *1*, 289.

Nagel, T. (1978). *The possibility of altruism*. Princeton: Princeton University Press.

Penrose, L. S. (1939). Mental disease and crime: Outline of a comparative study of European statistics. *British Journal of Medical Psychology*, *18*(1), 1–15. doi: 10.1111/j.2044-8341.1939.tb00704.x

Penrose, L. S. (1943). A note on the statistical relationship between mental deficiency and crime in the United States. *American Journal of Mental Deficiency*, *47*, 462.

Sainsbury Centre for Mental Health (2008) *Briefing Paper 39 Mental Health Care and the Criminal Justice System*.

Seddon, T. (2007). *Punishment and madness: Governing prisoners with mental health problems*. doi: 10.4324/9780203945377

Simon, J. (2007). *Governing through crime: How the war on crime transformed American democracy and created a culture of fear*. New York: Oxford University Press.

Simon, J. (2014). *Mass incarceration on trial: A remarkable court decision and the future of prisons in America*. New York: The New Press.

Singleton, N., Farrell, M., & Meltzer, H. (2003). Substance misuse among prisoners in England and Wales. *International Review of Psychiatry*, *15*(1–2), 150–152. doi: 10.1080/0954026021000046092

World Health Organization (2008). Trencin statement on prisons and mental health. *Copenhagen: World Health Organization Europe*. Retrieved from https://apps.who.int/iris/bitstream/handle/10665/108575/E91402.pdf

Wacquant, L. (2009). *Punishing the poor: The neoliberal government of social insecurity*. Durham: Duke University Press.

Walmsley, R. (2013) *World prison population listed*. London: International Centre for Prison Studies.

Wolff, N. (2005). Community reintegration of prisoners with mental illness: A social investment perspective. *International Journal of Law and Psychiatry*, *28*(1), 43–58. doi: 10.1016/j.ijlp.2004.12.003

4

CONTAINING THEM, LIBERATING US

The *shadow* side of criminal psychopathy

Leon McRae

Robert Hare, the famous advocate of psychopathic diagnoses,[1] has suggested that "[t]he public is becoming increasingly more fascinated with psychopaths, both as villains and antiheroes" (2003, p. viii). Whether they be the beguiling, homicidal caricatures caught on screen, those in board rooms, propagating the narcissistic push and shove of Capitalism[2] or the sociopaths "next door" whose traits are "conveniently invisible to the world" (Stout, 2005, p. 2),[3] the psychopath is now firmly with and without us. So intolerable is the notion that there is a "spectrum of psychopathy along which each of us has our place" (Dutton, 2012, p. 10) that in the U.S. an offender diagnosed as psychopathic is more likely to face capital punishment in cases of first-degree murder (Hare, 1996; DeMatteo & Edens, 2006).[4] Counterintuitively, the medical evidence in such cases tends to suggest that the psychopath poses "a continuing threat of violence [to society], *even while confined in maximum security prisons*" (Bersoff, 2002, p. 571, emphasis added). In England and Wales, where capital punishment is antithetical to the best interests ethic upon which medicine is based (Gunn, 2007), psychiatrists instead ask: "how do we deal with [these] strange creatures ... in a manner that does not make monsters of the rest of us?" (Thomas, 2013, p. 46).

The answer has been to instrumentalise the unfounded, actuarial link between psychopathic diagnoses and the *risk* of serious violence (Rogers, 2000; Freedman, 2001) in order to operate an "exclusionary principle" within psychiatric hospitals and prisons (Seddon, 2008, p. 309). Within these technologies of power, the psychopathic offender is given to a rhetoric of rehabilitation, which serves to both justify (scientifically and fiscally) the labelling of 'psychopathic' personalities and, by extracting the criminal subject's cooperation in treatment, legitimise the mechanisms of power that orientate his exclusion from society.

Among the technologies of the past 20 years to have, in Mullen's words, benefitted from the belief "in [such] a ghost in the machine of crime" (2007a, s 8) are: the (now replaced) Dangerous and Severe Personality Disorder (DSPD) programme[5]; the (now abolished) Indeterminate Sentence for Public Protection (IPP); and the transfer of psychopathic prisoners to hospital late in their determinate sentences, on both sides of the Atlantic (see, for example, Sexual Violent Predator (SVP) legislation in the United States[6]). In this chapter, I frame these constructed technologies of power, and the subjectivities to which they give rise, from a postmodern application of psychoanalytic theory to critical criminology. My principal argument is that the obstensibly redeemable psychopath reflects our affinity for *archetypes*, or the "universal images that have existed since the remotest times" (Jung, 1954a/2000b, para. 2). It is suggested that, within the *collective unconscious*,[7] the motifs of two particular archetypes, the *trickster* (*qua* psychopath) and the *hero* (*qua* psychiatrist) (Jung, 1954b/2000c), facilitate the unconscious projection of "all those unpleasant qualities we like to hide" about ourselves (Jung 1953/2000g, para. 103n) onto this specific psychiatrised, criminal subject. In so doing, I argue, the personal unconscious, which always threatens to see itself in the psychopath, can remain orientated to the solidary demands for productivity in capitalist societies, free from *ego*-conflict.[8] To make this point, I begin by sketching the empirical landscape from which my ideas have necessarily surfaced.

Criminal psychopathy and the rehabilitation myth

Early in my career, I was fortunate to receive a handsome research grant (ESRC award: PTA-031-2006-00269) to undertake a three-year empirical study looking at the legal, medical and interrelational consequences of admitting offenders diagnosed with psychopathy under s 47 (Removal to hospital of persons serving sentences of imprisonment, etc.) of the Mental Health Act 1983 (as amended: MHA) for up to two years' treatment. My interest in this area, at least initially, had been piqued by previous empirical research conducted by the Mental Health Act Commission (as it was; MHAC) in 2008. The MHAC evidenced that, once admitted to hospital, the vast majority of psychopathic patients were engaging cooperatively with treatments, such as cognitive behavioural therapy and group psychotherapy. In light of this unexpected finding,[9] it was argued:

> Patients with experience of serving prison sentences, especially if they have experience or knowledge of the parole system, may equate treatment compliance with the 'good behaviour' that leads to quicker release from custodial sentences or step-down from the higher security levels of the prison system, and (in most cases quite correctly) therefore view treatment compliance as likely to hasten their transfer to lower security hospitals and/or release into the community.
>
> *(p. 233)*

I was fascinated by the possibility that psychopaths were engaging with treatment for ulterior gain. Peay (1989) had previously shown that patients detained in a secure hospital were aware of the potential correlative effect of positive treatment engagement with the potential for expedited release. As one put it, "medication is my ticket out of here" (p. 52). My working hypothesis was that a particular criminal law sentence in vogue at the time, the Indeterminate Sentence for Public Protection (IPP), accounted for the empirical findings of the MHAC.

Introduced in April, 2005 by Part 12, Chapter 5 of the Criminal Justice Act 2003, a 'dangerous' adult-offender (s 225(1)(b))[10] convicted of a 'specified offence' (originally 153 offences under Schedule 15), not sufficient to warrant life imprisonment (s 225(2)) but attracting a maximum sentence of at least ten years, was handed a tariff equating to half of the equivalent determinate sentence for the same crime (based on the projected release of such prisoners at the halfway point in their determinate sentence: Powers of Criminal Court (Sentencing) Act 2000, s 82A). After serving their tariffs, prisoners deemed to no longer pose a "risk to life or limb" were eligible for release by the Parole Board (Parole Board, 2013, p. 3). In reality, evidence of risk reduction required engagement with 'relevant offending behaviour programmes' (*Walker and James v Secretary of State* [2008] EWCA Civ 30 (Court of Appeal), per Lord Phillips of Worth Matravers CJ, para. 69). The problem was that the prison system could not cope with the requirement to give all IPP-prisoners access to rehabilitative and resettlement programmes. Three years after its introduction, there were 4,619 IPP-prisoners,[11] and only 31 out of the 880 considered by the Parole Board had been granted release (Sainsbury Centre for Mental Health, 2008, p. 7). Absent proper resourcing, post-tariff IPP-prisoners challenged the sentence, *inter alia*, on the grounds of Articles 5(1)(a) and (4) (concerning the lawfulness of detention of post-conviction and its timely review) of the European Convention on Human Rights (ECHR). The Court of Appeal in *Walker* stated that the current system of seeking parole was an 'empty exercise' (*per* Lord Phillips of Worth Matravers CJ, para. 67), and that 'if so long elapses without a meaningful review [of the continued necessity for public protection] detention becomes disproportionate or arbitrary' under Article 5(1)(a) (ibid., para. 69). The House of Lords ruled, however, that a breach of ECHR rights necessitated a 'prolonged failure' (conceivably, "a period of years rather than months" (Annison, 2015, p. 12)), and otherwise appeared reassured that 'deficiencies [were], at last, being made good' (*R (James v Secretary of State for Justice; R (Lee) v Same; R (Wells) v Same* [2009] UKHL 22, *per* Lord Judge CJ, para. 121). But with no possible quick fix to the "erosion of hope caused by indeterminacy" (Sainsbury Centre for Mental Health, 2008: 42),[12] I was to uncover that patient-prisoners were seeking hospital admission in order to secure treatment that might satisfy the Parole Board of their suitability for release. Consider, for example:

> "I was kind of excited [by my pre-admission assessment], but I weren't [*sic*] really as honest, well, I think I was perhaps too honest in the assessment … I probably exaggerated some of my answers … I knew what kind of stuff [the practitioners] were looking for."
>
> *(Mr. D; McRae, 2015, p. 331)*

> "As soon as you get into groups and start talking with the nurses, it's like everyone puts a front on. You know, I have seen that when the [psychiatrists] come into certain meetings, as soon as, the [psychiatrist] comes in, certain patients will start talking differently. I think to myself: if I can see this, surely they can. I do think they get sucked in. I can predict what they're gonna say. They'll say they've put this skill into practice, when I know they haven't."
>
> *(Mr. C; McRae, 2013, p. 57)*

On account of these findings, I remained attentive to the possibility that patient-prisoners had no honest compunction to change their criminogenic outlook. The advice to researchers and practitioners that assertions of honest engagement be triangulated with other records and other informants (Harris & Rice, 2006) proved well-founded. For instance:

> ... elsewhere in [Mr. E's] medical records, a ward round note describes an incident in which he was one of the two patients who took an 'active dislike' to one another, each retaliating by 'saying the other was not committed to treatment; was putting a front on'.
>
> *(McRae, 2013, p. 58)*

> "[The psychiatrist commissioned during Mr. E's trial] concluded that [he] did not appear to be psychologically minded; his motivation to deal with problems appeared to be related to the fact he was facing [an IPP] sentence and that he had not taken part in previous offender related work."
>
> *(Unpublished data: prison records)*

Particularly motivating to the patient-prisoners was the two-year timeframe of hospital treatment on the ward. The perception of a potential pathway back into the community following treatment was in stark opposition to aspects of the admission criteria to the DSPD programme, which privileged the presumption of enduring risk.[13] Furthermore, attendant policy stipulated that one function of the programme was to accommodate those "near the end of their [determinate] sentence [at the behest of the Secretary of State]" *and* short-tariff IPP-prisoners in wait (as was typical) of "other placement options for the continuation of treatment" following three years' detention (Ministry of Justice & Department of Health, 2005, pp. 10, 17). By 2010, it was found that "few individuals [had] completed their treatment" (Hawes, 2010, p. 226). Whether through experience or intuition, patient-prisoners were unambiguous in their distrust of the DSPD's wide potential net:

> "My recommendation for sentencing was DSPD ... I was waiting for a referral from [a DSPD prison unit] ... They told me to expect to do 13 years, 13, 14 years. My tariff's 3 years ... I was told if I don't do a DSPD, it's

highly unlikely I'm being paroled. So, that's why I've come to this [hospital]. Hopefully, I can do enough [treatment] here to cancel out the DSPD. And I think I have."

(Mr. C; McRae, 2015, p. 331)

MR. M: 'What's your actual job?'
ME: 'I'm a university researcher and teacher.'
MR. M: 'Nothing to do with Rampton [DSPD unit]?'
ME: 'No, nothing to do with hospitals.'
MR. M: 'Right, let's go.'

(Unpublished data)

When the government subsequently announced it would "significantly increase treatment capacity" to 520 places in high secure prisons by disinvesting in the DSPD programme (Department of Health & Ministry of Justice, 2011, para. 26),[14] it was revealed that, on average, only two hours of psychological treatment had been made available each week to those detained (Burns et al., 2011). Forced to draw a parallel with the situation facing incapacitated sexually violent offenders (with personality disorder) in America, Mullen (2007a) defended the DSPD, pointing out that the SVP legislation lacks "even a semblance of an attempt to provide meaningful therapy and rehabilitation for those caught up in the system" (section 6).

In 2012, the semblances of rehabilitative intent were dealt a further blow. Following a combined application by IPP-prisoners James, Wells and Lee to the European Court of Human Rights, it was ruled that the sentence was contrary to Article 5(1)(a), for want of 'a real opportunity for rehabilitation' by reference to the need for public protection (*James, Wells & Lee v The United Kingdom*, App. Nos. 25119/09, 57715/09, and 57877/09 [2012] ECHR 1706, para. 209). The ruling swiftly led to the abolition of the IPP (meaning no new sentences could be imposed) and its replacement with the extended determinate sentence (EDS). Its logic, much like the IPP before it, was to "help [offenders] lead less destructive lives" through provision of treatment (Department of Health & Ministry of Justice, 2011, p. 5).

Elsewhere, I have noted that the 'new' sentencing approach is impractical on the account of with two contextual limitations never addressed in government policy or medical literature (see, McRae, 2015). First, those serving sentences of less than ten years are automatically released at the two-thirds point of the EDS, followed by a period of probation. Only for sentences beyond this does the Parole Board have jurisdiction to prevent release on the basis of risk. This suggests that the overall take-up of treatment, compared to the IPP, is likely to be low. Second, as of 30 June 2018, 2,745 IPP-prisoners were yet to be paroled (down only by 18% in the last 12 months), with the total number of EDS-prisoners at 4,718 (up 23%) (Ministry of Justice, 2019, p. 4). As such, any treatment-seeking EDS-prisoners with longer sentences will face stiff competition for resources from incapacitated IPP-prisoners.

Drawing on past experiences (see MHAC, above), one result of treatment disengagement among EDS-prisoners may be increased use of late hospital transfers to coincide with offenders' release dates. Should the patient-prisoner maintain his refusal to engage with treatment, it could be cited as a breach of his probation licence (see, for example, Morris et al., 2007). The result would be his return to prison for the remainder of his licence.[15] If he does engage, his liberty may be further restricted on account of the introduction of Psychologically Informed Planned Environments (PIPEs) in prisons, *and* "in a number of community-based hostel settings" for both "personal development" and to ensure, rather incongruously, that "ongoing risks are appropriately managed and monitored" (National Health Service & National Offender Management Service, 2015, p. 10).[16] By comparison, those remaining IPP-prisoners who complete a period of treatment in hospital are likely to find that it is deemed by the Parole Board to be inequivalent to treatment received in prison. Patient-prisoners observed:

> [B]ecause [treatment is] not recognised, some people do see it as a waste of time [...] You have to start somewhere and work your way through.
> *(Mr. E; McRae, 2013, p. 64)*

> [They] lose motivation some people, because they get towards the end [of treatment] and they don't see that parole's gonna happen, so they think I'm just gonna go back to where I started from…'.
> *(Mr. C; ibid., p. 63)*

Amid the plurality of strategies and resistances characterising these technologies of power,[17] two theoretical observations are possible. First, the diagnosis of psychopathy pertains only to how the offender may be "subjected, [re-] used, transformed and improved" (Foucault, 1977, p. 136). Second, medical professionals, trained in the art of psychopathic resocialisation,[18] curiously depart from the traditions of medicine by administering preventative strategies. In the service of incapacitation, they typically end by becoming executants in a "subordinate role, while managerial policy formation is allowed to develop into a completely autonomous force" (Castel, 1991, p. 281). This has led to many dissenting clinical voices, particularly during the DSPD-era (see, for example, Chiswick, 1999; Haddock et al., 2001; Coid & Maden, 2003; Grounds, 2004; reports in Duggan and Kane, 2010). Nevertheless, medical practitioners continue to "gratefully accept government money and a captive 'treatment' audience, only to bemoan their connivances later on" (McRae, 2015, p. 347). On the eve of his retirement from forensic psychiatry, Duggan (2011) reflected:

> [A]re we *sufficiently conscious* of the very wide margin of error when we detain someone against their will on the basis of risk that they might pose to themselves or to others? Although the DSPD initiative has been criticised

(rightly) in riding roughshod over many aspects that professionals regard as important, is there not a nagging suspicion that in many respects it was doing explicitly what many psychiatrists practise implicitly?

(pp. 432–434, emphasis added)

If, as Duggan implies, the maladministration of psychopathy is linked to the effects of *un*-conscious decisions by medical practitioners, what is the individual gain? Referring to meritocratic neoliberalism, Ingleby (1985) acknowledges the scope for increased professional power through patient interest in a highly structured social order, but rightly acknowledges that this schema appears "unmediated by any cognitive processes" and as a "case of professionals unconsciously acting out a latent social tendency in favour of [social] stability" (p. 174). In effect, he is posing the questions: Must we confuse individuality with the performance of a socially mandated role? What is the gain to the *collective* (rather than conflicted personal) *unconscious* by deploying the psychiatric gaze within incapacitating technologies of power? It is my contention that answers to these questions reveal there to be a forced distinction between us and the psychopathic other.

The bio-politics of psychopathic correction

The 'psychopath' has always been with us, for the longest time free from the psychiatric gaze. Writing, for instance, in 1699, la Bruyère, on translating the writings of Theophrastus (c. 371-287 B.C.) on moral turpitude in Athens, observed: "Sciences daily improve, yet Vice and Folly get footing in the World" (preface).[19] Much later, Foucault (1961/2009) designated the "strange takeover" of normal behaviour (including indigence, idleness, marginalised sexuality and madness) by medical reason to an economic and moral invention of capitalist systems (p. 44).[20] With power given to ensuring, sustaining and instrumentalising life, breaches of law punishable by death ("the macrophysics of sovereignty": Foucault, 2006, p. 27) were increasingly replaced by "an entire series of interventions and *regulatory controls: a bio-politics of the population*" (Foucault, 1978a, p. 139).[21] In this new realm of *bio-power*, confinement (whether in prisons, asylums or workhouses) became milieu for corrective justice ("the microphysics of discipline" (Foucault, 2006, p. 27)), organised through micro-punishments[22] within 'panoptic' architecture,[23] allowing the few to watch the many (possibly) self-govern in accordance with the norm.

In this ideal-type "automatic functioning of [scientistic] power" (ibid., p. 203), the reality is, of course, that technologies of power consistently fail to "reduce [subjects] to giving up the struggle" for individuality (Foucault, 1982, p. 225). The object of governance refuses, for instance, psychiatric medication unless compelled (e.g. Chamberlin, 1998[24]) and prison remains a revolving door (for 37% of all offenders[25]). The typical counter is that the "devious and supple" system of *bio-power* (Foucault, 1978a, p. 86) needs time to have its way. As one Occupational Therapist put it in the study:

> "I suppose, ultimately, gaining parole is one of the main motivating factors for a lot of the guys on the ward. And you can often find once you get somebody into more of a therapeutic environment, their gaining parole is the end point, but they actually perhaps see there's a process in between, which they can benefit from."
>
> *(McRae, 2013, p. 58)*

When time inevitably bears witness to empirical failures of corrective justice (for example the DSPD programme), [26] this is taken not as a failure of bio-politics but as a need to "*reshape* services to provide more effective treatment for those offenders with severe forms of personality disorder?" (Ministry of Justice, 2010, p. 4, emphasis added). The diverting of spending from DSPD services to high secure prisons to increase treatment capacity (OPDP, above, Department of Health & Ministry of Justice, 2011) is a recent, notable simile.[27] The development of progression units, or PIPEs (see above, National Health Service & National Offender Management Service, 2015[28]), for treatment-completers is its extension.

How then, is this proliferation in the face of failure justified? Through "concern that some offenders who complete high intensity programmes may not [*yet*] have applied this learning to practice" (Turley et al., 2013, p. 4), and thus may merely require a "long period of time over which progress is made and *evidenced*" (National Health Service & National Offender Management Service, 2015, p. 3, emphasis added). In others jurisdictions, like the United States, the fact that future dangerousness has been evidenced to predicate on criminal history and impulsivity, *not* personality traits (Yang et al., 2010), has been replaced with the construction that "psychopathy has *come to connote* a static, life-long condition that is not amenable to treatment or intervention" (Vitacco & Salekin, 2013, p. 82, emphasis added). Through the spurious conclusion that the psychopath must be offered up to incapacitation (or death, depending on the jurisdiction), it is as if the collective unconscious knows what is at stake by uncoupling him from the bind of medical power.

A further ornament of the bio-politics of psychopathy is the insistence on the confessional. For as long as there has been a problematization of health, the confession has been "a communication at the very least imagined between doctor and patient" acting to orientate moral and therapeutic attitudes in society (Foucault, 1961/2009, p. 307). In the courtroom, psychiatrists are routinely called upon to show "who one is" (Foucault, 1982, p. 212), so that methods of punishment-correction can be evaluated. When the defendant, diagnosed as psychopathic, evidences difficulty in moral knowledge,[29] we nonetheless deny him, for instance, the defence of legal insanity on the basis that he knows he did legally wrong.[30] When, instead, a defendant comes with a motiveless crime (for example, 'I felt like killing him'[31]), and does not otherwise appear insane, the psychiatrist must furnish an account of the differences within and between mad and bad individuals in order to retain the "preposterous stance" (Foucault, 1978b, p. 6) that crimes of moral unreason are pathological.

Containing them, liberating us   53

While, today, it is tacitly accepted that "[p]sychopaths are infamous for their immoral behaviour" (Borg & Sinnot-Armstrong, 2013, p. 107), historically, such a visible sign of madness was initially "so foreign and so unacceptable" that its subsequent acceptance by the courts needed to be explained through a conflation of psychopathy with "living conditions (overpopulation, overcrowding, urban life, alcoholism, debauchery)" (Foucault, 1978b, p. 6, emphasis added). In so doing, the psychopath became collectively, and conveniently, "*perceived* as a source of danger for oneself, for others, for one's contemporaries" (ibid., p. 7). Research into responses to community reintegration of psychopathic sex offenders in the United States, for instance, is telling of this strategic manoeuvre:

> Many protesters expressed anger and frustration at the fact that their fate was to be decided by faceless bureaucrats who rarely lived in such areas themselves ... Council tenants who were expected to put up with living next to an incinerator, playgrounds built on polluted sites, damp housing or a failing local school, now were also expected to tolerate the country's most dangerous predators.
>
> *(Kitzinger, 2004, p. 152)*

Through protest, the psychopath ("a [false] source of danger") forcibly meets with collective fears of crime, which have long become "an inseparable part of society [and] thus perpetually inscribed in each individual consciousness" (Foucault, 1978a, p. 12). It is not by accident that the protester's placard is held aloft, where the author cannot see it, such is the fragile fictive relationship that Western societies have created between the constructed self and indespensible psychopath. In this way, the drama of dramatic discourse reveals the constant tension, if not societal *raison d'être*, of an unrealised (psychopathic) self. Foucault seems to foreground this general problematic of *bio-power* in his early work on prisons, before returning to it in a seminar convened before his death:

> The [psychopathic] criminal designated as the enemy of all, *whom it is in the interest of all to track down* ..., disqualifies himself as a citizen [through incarceration] and emerges [through diagnosis], bearing within him as it were, *a wild fragment of nature*.
>
> *(1977, p. 101, emphasis added)*

> [T]echnologies of the self, which permit individuals to effect by their own means or *with the help of others* a certain number of operations on their own bodies and souls, thoughts, conduct, and a way of being, so as to transform themselves in order to attain a certain state of happiness, purity, wisdom, perfection, *or immorality*.
>
> *(1982/1988, p. 16, emphasis added)*

In Foucauldian discourse, technologies of self, or *subjection*, presuppose that the *bio-politique* has "mask[ed] a substantial part of itself" (Foucault, 1978a, p. 86). It is on account of this strategic poise that resistance of the criminal psychopath within technologies of power, as a form of coming *within* power-knowledge, is supposed to foreshadow his rehabilitation. As one consultant psychiatrist put it: 'I don't care if [they're] manipulative, as long as they engage' (unpublished data; see also the account of the Occupational Therapist, above: McRae, 2013, p. 58). The inherent contradiction of these empirical accounts and Foucault's analytic is that it continues to be in "the interest of all to track down" psychopaths even though psychiatrisation habitually fails to effectively tackle crime. It points towards a singularity that has, thus far, been missed: the instrumentality of the psychopath relates to an *unconscious* subjection of *our*-selves. Writ more optimistically, the almost mythical psychopath, primed for incapacitation because of his relationship to us, denotes the potential for a transformative experience of our own immorality, our own instinctual "wild fragment of nature", which we take great care to conceal from ourselves, and others.

Confessing the *shadow* self

Much of Foucault's work on *bio-power* can now be read as an attempt to show that "we have indirectly constituted ourselves through the exclusion of some others" (Foucault, 1988, p. 146). By giving criminality and madness to exclusion, we have enlivened the possibilities for conscious self-examination of our more problematic instincts. Since there is "no illness intrinsic to instinct" to enable this process (Foucault, 2003, p. 299), one must be created through psychiatric nosology.[32] The resultant technologies of psy-power, however, are both liberating and constraining. They are liberating because the fashioning of (legal) psychiatric norms invites mundane transgressions that tell us more about ourselves, about what it means to be human. They are potentially constraining because technologies of self, like the criminal confession linked to them, require "the drives to seek within the self any *hidden feeling*, ... any desire disguised under *illusory forms*" (Foucault, 1988, p. 16, emphasis added).

The psychoanalytic movement, which matured alongside *bio-power*,[33] lays claim to the view that an analysand can be "led back to the nature law of his own [instinctual] being" by reconnecting with the mythological *archetypes* of the collective unconscious (the so-called "illusory forms") (Jung, 1934/2000j, para. 351).[34] Foucault (1961/2009), by comparison, posits that the fruits of self-examination of the instincts are inevitably rooted in prescriptive, scientific vocabularies of historical regression.[35] With the view that science precedes, there can be no place in ethnology for a collective unconscious, animated by archetypes to understand the psychopathic posture, except within the terms set by the human sciences. Thus,

> a system of *cultural unconscious* [is] the totality of formal structures which render *mythical discourse significant*, give their coherence as necessity to the rules that regulate needs, and provide the norms of life ....
> *(Foucault, 1970/2002, p. 414, emphasis added)*

Having forced a bio-political articulation on archetypes ("mythical discourse" related to instinct) Foucault makes the abstract claim that we—the administrators of *bio-power* (i) and (i) the subjects of it—are invested "in the [same] panoptic machine ..., which *we bring to ourselves*" (Foucault, 1978a, p. 217, emphasis added). But, without an archetypal frame of reference; to justify self-governance according to *bio-power*, Foucault must concede that resistance, that is, the "unbalanced, heterogeneous, unstable, and tense [hegemonic] relations" (ibid., p. 93) characterising *bio-power* comes first. Rather, the 'visibility' of archetypes is evidenced by the several practical realignments that psychiatry would face if the collective unconscious were not guided, in Foucault's words, by 'mythical discourse' to accent its intrusions and limitations.[36]

First, in a highly visible, delocalised, mass-mediated age, where heinous acts rarely escape our attention, psychiatrists would lose their authority (some would say "mandate": Ingleby, 1985) to characterise irredeemable "psychopathic" crime. Second, we would recognise that by containing the psychopath we, paradoxically, contain ourselves. As Reid (1985) once put it:

> [W]e frustratedly give up the ability to move about as we please after dark, to take that romantic walk through the woods, to send the children to play on their own ... in order to contain the antisocial element. In doing so we may, by our own hand, become victims before we have even been victimized.
>
> *(p. 79)*

Third, we would more widely acknowledge that 'playing' the coercive criminal justice system to expedite parole is not evidence of psychopathology; rather, in the words of one clinical psychologist: "You don't need to have psychopathy to have [that] motivation. You can understand it" (McRae, 2015, p. 331). Strategy, including lying and manipulation, would thus be read into the "whole field of responses, reactions, results, and possible inventions" that characterise *bio-power* for us *all* (Foucault, 1982, p. 220). Fourth, and related, the panoptic viewing of *many* (psychopaths) by the *few* (experts) in technologies of power would be seen to correspond to a *synoptic* viewing of the *few* (archetypal psychopaths) by the *many* (society, including experts) for collective gain.[37] Orientated in this way, the many might be compelled to ask: What archetype did *bio-power* forget to keep the psychopathic diagnosis free of us?

The answer, I argue, is the *trickster* (Jung, 1954b/2000c): an archetype of "primitive or barbarous consciousness" (paras. 465–466) and "evil qualities" (para. 475), representing the polaristic struggle between a psyche that has "hardly left the animal level" (ibid., para. 465) and the search for higher levels of civilisation connected to the desire for capitalist production. The *trickster* is, for instance, the obscene clown in carnivalesque festivals using wit and deception to mock the restrained social order[38]; the Chief of "licenced anarchy" and breaker of taboos in Winnebago (*Wakdjunkaga*) culture (Velie, 1991, p. 45), seemingly in want of "values, moral or social" (Radin, 1953, p. xxiii); the shapeshifting animal and human embodiment of our potential to feel "shame and identity" in films like *Thor* (2011), *The Avengers* (2012), *Thor: The Dark World* (2013) (Bassil-Morozow, 2017, p. 90) and *Avengers: Endgame* (2019); the wily animal in childhood fairy tales, who acts on "unconscious fantasies relating to primitive impulses" that we must not visit in our own lives, except vicariously (Crowther et al., 1998, p. 208); and the myriad other culture-specific creations that arise in a "doubtful or critical [social] situation" (Jung, 1954b/2000c, para. 469).

The development of *bio-power* in industrial societies onwards of the 1700s – a time when "appetite in its natural state" (*libido*) (Jung, 1948/2000e, para. 194) began to react to moral and legal directionality – was an especially "critical" and "doubtful" period in the *trickster* life cycle. The, possibly reductionist, use of the term *libido* to denote a sexual function that "cannot be eliminated from psychic life by any device" (Freud, 1917/2001c, p. 357) nevertheless comments on the affinity of a *trickster* motif for the failure of familial and societal conditioning to direct our instinctual energy to "higher, asexual [capitalist] aims" (Freud, 1901/2001a, p. 50). Foucault, indeed, suspects that the policing of sexual perversions in the nineteenth century, for capitalist demands, merely effected a "valorization and intensification of indecent speech" (1978a, p. 18). More recently, the contemporary rise of sadistic sex crimes like rape porn, revenge porn, date rape, stealthing, sexsomnia (McRae, 2019) and child offences show that to "refuse the dark side of one's nature is to store up or accumulate the darkness" (Johnson, 1991, p. 26). Thus, in "synoptic" art and media, the sexual motif is given metaphorical force through modulated *trickster* figures to assault the "decency and propriety" of forbidding structural forces (Bassil-Morozow, 2017, p. 91). Elsewhere, the "vast amount of sadism in which no sexual behaviour is [apparently] involved" (Fromm, 1973, p. 378) is made knowable in the cold, unfeeling eyes of *masked* killers in horror franchises, who permit us to be repelled and yet "imagine [if subconsciously] something as evil or demonic" in our own lives, within the collective *shadow* (Abrams & Zweig, 1991, p. xx).[39] Periodically, as in the transmuted case of the psychopath, the 'psychopathic' killer in these dramas is entrapped, only to escape shortly thereafter, often by fault of human hand,[40] because a system's attempt at "authoritativeness and *exactitude*" of the instincts through science is never permitted to accumulate beyond a counterweight (Bassil-Morozow, 2017, p. 86, emphasis added). We want both to have control and to be defenceless without it.

In this artistic cycle of ego-defence and necessary self-renewal, the conflict of opposites sees Eros, our potential for "psychic relatedness" and a "connective quality" (Jung, 1928/2000i: para. 255),[41] posture for "what Logos sundered" (para. 275). Logos, that "realm of the scientifically applied intellect [that] finds expression on the battlefield and in the state of [a] bank balance" (para. 237), corresponds to the archetypal "ways that the past shows [us] … are insufficient for the [collective, capitalist] needs of the present" (para. 240). Jung (1954b/2000c) is right to caution:

> [We think] the meaning of existence would be discovered if food and clothing were delivered to him gratis on his own doorstep, or if everybody possessed an automobile. *Such as the puerilities that rise up in place of an unconscious shadow and keep it unconscious.* As a result of these prejudices, the individual feels totally dependent on his environment and *loses all capacity for introspection.* In this way his code of ethics is replaced by a knowledge of what is permitted or forbidden or *ordered* [through law] … From this point of view *we can see why the myth of the trickster was preserved and developed:* like many other myths, it is supposed to have a *therapeutic effect.*
>
> *(paras. 479–480, emphasis added)*

The psychopath-*trickster*, then, has become the supra-scientific part of imperfect personalities that "cannot be argued out of existence or rationalized [by logos] into harmlessness" (Jung, 1954a/2000b: para. 43). He (not she[42]) is the projective identification of transgressions that socialisation will not permit us to perform "behind Mother's back" (Redfearn, 1979, p. 190)[43]; the successive iterations of collective anxiety brought by trespasses against petty laws ("whether from stupidity, temptation, or mere viciousness" (1928/2000i: para. 265)), which inspire psychiatrisation of criminals[44]; the affinity of the confession for the psychopathic, criminal subject; an elucidation of why no definitive author of (subversive) *biopower* will ever be found[45]; and, finally, proof that Logos is male.[46] How else could Capitalism, another historical, male prerogative (Jung, 1928/2000i), forget our "subhuman" past (Jung, 1954b/2000c: para. 475) except by referring psychopathic maleness to the same principles of calculation, objectivity, categorisation and generalisability that underpin Logos' sphere?

This collective fix ends by producing a paradoxical situation, however. On the one hand, following the Global Financial Crisis, psychopaths were blamed for creating the Machiavelli of the new corporate realm (see, for example, Boddy, 2011). The term "business psychopathy" was used to denote a neglected population (Furnham, 2015), more numerous than "household psychopathy" by a factor of three (Babiak & Hare, 2006). Practices of "[a]ccounting fraud, tax evasion, toxic dumping, product safety violations, bid rigging [and] overbilling" were cited as evidence that morality in the market is a category error endorsed by the wealthy minority (Deresiewicz, 2012: SR5). On the other hand, it was argued that the (non-psychopathic) majority players of meritocratic neoliberalism had, especially over the past 30 years, fallen victim to the problem of responsibility for self-identity in an economy favouring competition, superficial alliances and displaced aggression, typically arising through fear of failure and a "broader social fear of the threatening other" (Verhaeghe, 2014). General 'inhuman' narratives of "disregard for or even delight in the suffering of others, the casual use of violence to dominate and inflict pain" (Pillsbury, 2013, p. 311) were simply written out of history by a convenient monolith.

In the ever-narrowing, social margins of psychopathic-*trickster*, the psychiatrist has become indispensable. Functioning as the *hero* archetype[47], our *shadow* is cast by professional performance over certain forms of criminal: the sorts who never get to grips with the personas that society accepts[48]; those who are without the opportunities or connections to see a boardroom[49]; those who find solace in being a criminal[50]; and those who will freely, if foolishly, declare a wish to sadistically "[strike] someone's fingers with a hammer one at a time until they bend to his will" (Prison report of Mr. C; unpublished data). In so doing, that "the monster of darkness" (psychopathy) and "the *long-hoped-for* and expected triumph of consciousness over [our] unconscious" (Jung, 1950/2000a: para. 284, emphasis added) is kept from fulfilling its promise. In extended metaphor, the psychopath's journeying between different 'therapeutic' technologies of power (what Jung would describe as *archetypes of transformation*[51]) may now be understood as the blocking of escape routes for our disinclination to lose our animal beginnings, in a world now projected as evil, wicked and unsafe.

The criminal psychopath will, therefore, remain "the great monster" (Foucault, 1978b, p. 5) for as long as we willingly "confuse one's clothing for one's skin" (Whitmont, 1991, p. 161). In refusing nakedness sometimes, we only fasten more tightly the wears of our social roles. The psychiatric practitioner, among others, will express cynicism about the merits of psychopathic rehabilitation,[52] forgetting that psychopathy and crime are no different at the outset. S/he may, in time, experience "feelings of [professional and personal] inadequacy" due to a lack of belief in what they [have to] do (Ministry of Justice, 2011, p. 113). Those experiencing this inner state of division often complain of feeling "flat and listless" (Stevens, 1994, p. 67) or depressed, because the truth is that reason and unreason has always traded places under *bio-power*; psychic liberties have been 'forgotten' for over 200 years to a particular mode of repression. More recently, psychopaths have had their lives cut short, in order that the beneficiaries of this unconscious delirium of vice might be kept virtuous.

Does this mean unconsciousness will always cast a collective *shadow* over the psychopath (because there will always be crime and vice)? According to Page (1999), a psychoanalyst in non-forensic settings, typologies can change if a practitioner "form[s] a relationship with the *actual person* who is the client" (ibid., 1999, p. 76, emphasis added). Ostensible examples of this from the study include:

> 'We're all personality disordered here. [The nurse turns and laughs with her colleague] Where do you go if you're a tree but the forest'.
> *(Unpublished data)*

> 'Everyone's a PD'.
> *(Health support worker; unpublished data)*

A key difference between these accounts and Page's optimism is that he is envisioning a differentiated unconscious, where the personal and collective posed as equal ("individuation": see, e.g., Jung, 1950/2000a). By comparison, the second quote is a confession. It has a "directly productive role" both on the viability of discourse and "the divisions, inequalities, and disequilibrium" to which it gives rise (Foucault, 1978a, p. 94). A psychiatrist (the *hero*) receiving the psychopathic confession will necessarily speak of wishing to "constitute, positively, a new self" out of crime (Foucault, 1982/1988, p. 48); the nurse who confesses her-*self*, however, is already in a position of exteriority to the discourse now affirmed. As such, she evidences the move *towards* the polaristic struggle between the self and the psychopath. What she later says in interview speaks directly to the persistence of a *trickster* motif in technologies of power:

> [Mr D], for example, he's been here for quite some time, excellent paper work, problem solving, done [*sic*] all the groups, getting along quite well in the meetings and stuff like that… You know, and you just think to yourself: Is he taking it all on board this time? He appears to be. *But does he just behave in the way that, you know, he thinks we want him to behave? Does he say the things that we want him to say?*
>
> (McRae, 2013, p. 60, emphasis added)

We know quite well that he does. It is merely that the "tangled web of fate" (Jung, 1954b/2000c: para. 487) between the *trickster*-figure and *shadow* creates such an unconscious, harrowing situation for the rest of us that his confession, dramatic or verbalised, must be imagined capable of being different from our own.

Conclusion

Over the last 20 years, offenders diagnosed with psychopathy have become the subject of numerous criminal justice and mental health interventions, often at huge financial cost. Despite successive policies framing those technologies of power in terms of rehabilitate intent, they have become better known as expensive sites of exclusion from, and for, the public. In seeming contradiction, the mass-media has numerously depicted the psychopath as the archetypal *trickster* of myth, fairy tale and folklore: "a faithful reflection of an absolutely undifferentiated human consciousness" (Jung, 1954b/2000c: para. 465), freed for our amusement from the shackles of over 200 years of morality-making under *bio-power* (Foucault, 1978a). Guggenbühl-Craig (1980) suggests that:

> [Psychopathy] forces us to consider why we are not amoral in spite of the fact that we have tendencies to amorality within us. We consider our feelings, asking ourselves about the nature of ethics and love. Psychopathy is a tool with which we can better understand ourselves.
>
> *(p. 43)*

Away from such contrivances, daily, psychopathic residues accumulate through war, strikes, racial intolerance (Johnson, 1991, p. 26); the relentless seeking of "sex, possession, money, and fame" in capitalist economies (Fromm, 1973, p. 282); and in the repressed sadism that finds a channel, despite the fact "[w]e *know* that it is very bad taste to delight in another's pain or misfortune" (Abrams & Zweig, 1991, p. 42). At the micro-level, these psychopathic motifs enter the collective *shadow* (Jung, 1954b/2000c), owing to societal and familial repressions. At the macro-level, these repressions are actively sustained through the deployment of psychiatric discourse within the forensic criminal justice and mental health institution. Within these technologies of power, the psychiatrist, as a function of the *hero* archetype (see Jung, 1928/2000i), enters into symbolic battle with the shadow-in-the-psychopath to ensure that the disavowed elements of the collective unconscious are hidden from individual consciousness. Any empirical failings must be written into "the multiplicity of points of resistance" (Foucault, 1978a, p. 95) that economics, design and space have failed to address – this time. Such a perpetual *"living and lived myth"* that psychiatry will triumph over 'monsters' (Jung, 1954b/2000c: para. 180) goes to the very heart of our search for light after *shadow*.

Notes

1 Before Hare, no standard diagnostic criteria for psychopathy existed. In 1980, he developed the Psychopathy Checklist (PCL), now the PCL-R (Hare, 2003). The PCL-R is a 20-item measuring the presence of interpersonal (e.g. pathological lying, manipulativeness), affective (e.g. lack of remorse, callousness), lifestyle (e.g. impulsivity, irresponsibility) and antisocial (e.g. early behavioural problems, criminal versatility) based on semi-structured interviews, and collateral evidence. Scores of between 0 and 2 are given for each trait. A score of 30 would lead to a diagnosis of psychopathy. Fifteen per cent of male, and 7% of female, offenders are typically diagnosed with psychopathy (Hare, 2003). Related to psychopathy is the DSM-V (APA, 2013) diagnosis of antisocial personality disorder (ASPD) and the ICD (WHO, 1993) diagnosis of dissocial personality disorder. These emphasise antisocial and criminogenic behaviours rather than personality traits. Approximately 40–70% of UK and US prisoners have ASPD (Fazel & Danesh, 2002).
2 High levels of psychopathy correlate with the holding of high-ranking executive positions (Babiak & Hare, 2006).
3 Cf. Coid & Yang (2008): the prevalence of household psychopathy using a categorical rather than dimension model is 3.6% (95% confidence level).
4 'Murder is the unlawful killing of a human being with malice aforethought. Every murder perpetrated by poison, lying in wait, or any other kind of willful, deliberate, malicious, and premeditated killing; or committed in the perpetration of, or attempt to perpetrate, any arson, escape, murder, kidnapping, treason, espionage, sabotage, aggravated sexual abuse or sexual abuse, child abuse, burglary, or robbery; or perpetrated as part of a pattern or practice of assault or torture against a child or children; or perpetrated from a premeditated design unlawfully and maliciously to effect the death of any human being other than him who is killed, is murder in the first degree. Any other murder [with intent] is second degree murder': 18 U.S. Code, Section 1111. In a survey of 360 undergraduate university students in the U.S. (Edens, Guy and Fernandez (2003)), 36% the supported death penalty for *juveniles* with prototypical psychopathic traits (versus 22% without).

5 In 2011, a total of 350 places were developed at HMP Whitemoor and HMP Frankland, and the secure hospitals Broadmoor and Rampton. Additional services were also developed at HMP Low Newton (for women) and three medium secure hospitals.

6 In 21 U.S. states since 1990, SVP legislation allows for the preventative detention of sex offenders in hospital following the expiry of their fixed-term (determinate) sentence, if s/he is "likely to engage in predatory acts of sexual violence" [as a result of] "mental abnormality or personality disorder" (Washington State Legislation, RCW 71.09.030 (1990), subsection 18).

7 Jung (1969), a one-time contemporary of Freud, describes the collective unconscious as "the whole spiritual heritage of mankind's evolution, born anew in the brain structure of every individual" (para. 342). Freud (1905/2001b), by comparison, saw the unconscious as a personal affair linked to heredity and the "influences of actual life" (p. 171).

8 Freud coined the term *ego* to describe the weaving of character out of desires, impulses and defences aimed at controlling and, where possible, discharging uncomfortable internal stimuli (e.g. forbidden fantasies, wishes and experiences) so as to produce an *ego-ideal*. With the help of the *superego* (self-governance attuned to moral values), the aim of the *ego* is to keep the 'cauldron full of seething excitations' (instinctual drives (id)) under control (1933, p. 73). An element of self-deception, or repression, is necessary to achieve this.

9 Since the prototypical psychopath feels no remorse or empathy for victims, he is not expected to make use of treatment that aims for resocialisation. Reid and Gacono (2000) suggest: "The fact that antisocial symptoms are not painful or ego-dystonic in themselves makes it even less logical for the antisocial person to seek or tolerate treatment" (pp. 648–649).

10 In this context, 'dangerous' meant that there was a significant risk to members of the public of serious harm caused by the offender committing further specified offences (s 229(1)(b)).

11 Contextual reasons for the high numbers were that the judge was originally *compelled* to impose an IPP in the presence of a 'specified offence' and the absence of a minimum tariff (related to the maximum sentence than could be imposed for the particular crime). It was not until 14 July, 2008 that a notional minimum term was introduced (two years) and Schedule 15 was replaced with a reduced number of 'specified offences' under Schedule 15A (see the Criminal Justice and Immigration Act 2008). Nevertheless, approximately 70 new IPP-sentences were subsequently imposed each month (Jacobson and Hough, 2010: 19).

12 For instance, in most cases, IPP-prisoners who were transferred to alternative prisons for treatment were placed at the bottom of long waiting lists (Sainsbury Centre for Mental Health, 2008: 30). Prime Minister, David Cameron, subsequently acknowledged that there was a complete lack of 'any certainty about the sentence that [would] be served or when their assailants [would] be let out' (Cameron, 2011).

13 Even a cursory reading of the admission criteria evidenced the privileging of perceived risks posed by the patient-prisoners: "the victim would find it difficult or impossible to recover; and, [he] has a severe disorder of personality; and, [t]here is a link between the disorder and the risk of offending" (Ministry of Justice and Department of Health, 2005, p. 8).

14 Each place in a DSPD unit was £300,000 per annum, compared to £85,000 in prison (Department of Health & Ministry of Justice, 2011, para. 24).

15 EDS-prisoners remain on licence for the final third of their sentence, up to a maximum of five years for a violent offence and eight years for a sexual offence (and never less than one year) (s 226A(8), LASPO 2012). Whilst this is lower than the minimum of ten years that applied to IPPs (Criminal Justice Act 2003, s 25(4)), the more important figure is the rate of community recall: 22% (to 928) over the past year (Ministry of Justice, 2019, p. 4).

16 The government is unequivocal in its plan of "provid[ing], for some [psychopathic] offenders, arrangements for lifelong management" (Department of Health & Ministry of Justice, 2011: para. 39).

17 I mean to say "the manner in which a partner in a certain game acts with regard to what he thinks should be the actions of the others and what he considers the others think to be his own" (Foucault, 1984, p. 225).

18 For instance, various educational programmes, from diploma to PhD level, exist as part of the Knowledge and Understanding Framework. These are jointly commissioned by National Health Service England and Her Majesty's Prison and Probation Service, and delivered by the Institute of Mental Health: see https://www.institutemh.org.uk/education/knowledge-and-understanding-framework/143-overview

19 Referring to the impudent and covetous man, Theophrastus (successor to Aristotle in the Peripatetic School) writes:

> [This] vice may be defined a neglect of reputation, upon the account of sordid gain. A person influenced by this principle, will ask to borrow money off one whom he has already openly cheated ... [W]hen his meat is weighed, standing by the Scales, he will (if it be possible) put more in than is his due weight, if he be hindered from that, he will throw a Bone into the Scale, which if he can but carry off he is mightily pleased, but if he cannot he'll snatch some of the off all off the Stall, and go away laughing, When he has Strangers with him, that desire to see a Play, and give him money to pay for their places, he always contracts for himself to come in on freecost ...
>
> (p. 16)

20 Here, Foucault makes a more general point that the poor insane could no longer be seen as a form of mental alienation. Referring to England, Macdonald (1981) notes that they were now "terrifying and disgusting, impossible to control" and as "imperilling the fundamental principles of social life, household and hierarchy" (p. 147). By analogy, one reason to consider the diagnosis of ASPD will be evidence of "[c]onsistent irresponsibility, as indicated by repeated failure to *sustain consistent work behavior or honor financial obligations*" (American Psychiatric Association, 2013, p. 659, emphasis added).

21 Where it was maintained, it was to announce "the monstrosity of the criminal, his incorrigibility" and safeguard society from "a kind of biological danger" (Foucault, 1978b, p. 138).

22 These comprise

> a whole micro-penalty of time (lateness, absences, interruptions of tasks), of activity (inattention, negligence, lack of zeal), of behavior (impoliteness, disobedience), of speech (idle chatter, insolence), of the body (incorrect attitudes, irregular gestures, lack of cleanliness), of sexuality (impurity, indecency).
>
> (Foucault, 1977, p. 178)

An impressive form of micro-punishment which I witnessed on the secure ward hosting my research was peer-pressure:

> [O]n this ward, if someone is upset, and is distressed, is angry, hostile, aggressive, and refuses to go through to the dining room ... if someone refuses to do that, then no–one goes ... That would be happening quite a lot if we didn't have an effective way of dealing with that ... (Nurse)
>
> (McRae, 2013, p. 56)

One might describe this particular designation of the power relationship as "the manner in which a partner in a certain game acts with regard to what he thinks should be the actions of the others and what he considers the others think to be his own" (1984, p. 225). It presupposes the availability of resistance to patient-prisoners.

23 In a panopticon, buildings are divided into cells each containing two windows, which fit together like "small theatres in which each actor is alone, perfectly individualized and constantly visible" to the demands of disciplinary power (Foucault, 1977, p. 200). The windowed security office on the secure ward was a constant reminder of the conceptual importance of the medical gaze to surveying its subjects.
24 The MHA, s 63 permits the administration of medication without consent for the first three months of hospitalisation.
25 This is up 10% since 2011. The statistics relates to offenders with 15 or more previous cautions or convictions (Ministry of Justice, 2019, p. 7).
26 In 2010, it was reported that 58% of DSPD patients were reconvicted within two years after discharge (Yang et al., p. 7).
27 Note, however, that entry for the OPDP now only requires a "likely diagnosis" (National Health Service & National Offender Management Service, 2015, p. 5).
28 So far, PIPEs have been piloted on 820 prisoners in prison and probation settings.
29 Duff (2010) argues:

> [He] cannot understand how the interests or the suffering of others could have a claim on him, a claim that might outweigh his own inclination; or how honesty could matter in any terms other than those of immediate self-interest ... [Such a person] is not a morally ... responsible agent.
>
> (pp. 209–210)

See also, Duff (1977).
30 See the M'Naghten Rules (1843) and *R v Windle* [1952] 2 QB 826. *Contra*, in respect of offenders not diagnosed as psychopathic, courts are generally willing to accept testimony from psychiatrists on the defendant's immoral compass as evidence of his insanity (see Mackay & Kearns, 1999; acknowledged in *R v Johnson (Dean)* [2007] EWCA Crim 1978).
31 In the nineteenth century, those committing crimes of unreason were labelled as *monomaniacs* (Foucault, 1978b); today, we would understand shallow effect and lack of remorse as evidence of psychopathy.
32 Foucault (2003) cites the case of Charles Jouy of 1867, who dragged Sophie Adams, a young girl, to a ditch alongside a road to Nancy. Her family find evidence of sex on Sophie's clothes. Unusually, Jouy is charged with paedophilia and confined in an asylum for life. Foucault cites this as evidence that the family were "plugged into another system of control and [psychiatric] power" (pp. 295–296).
33 The earliest contributions of psychoanalytic theory were French (see, e.g., Charcot and Magnan, 1882; Binet, 1887).
34 Jung (1954a/2000b) defines archetypes as the universal, "primordial types [of model image or role] ... that have existed since the remotest times [of unconsciousness]" to pre-define the instincts in personified form (para. 5). We typically see them in myth, art, literature, religion and fairy tales, owing to "[e]ndless repetition [that] has engraved [the] experiences into our psychic constitution" (Jung, 1936/2000f: para. 99). Examples include the mother, father, child, maiden, hero, wise old man, persona, shadow and trickster.
35 Foucault suggests that discourse is not "the majestically unfolding manifestation of a thinking, knowing subject" but "a totality, in which the dispersion of the subject and his discontinuity with himself may be determined" (1972, p. 55).
36 Foucault (1961/2009) may have (unconsciously) acknowledged this point when he wrote that psychoanalysis provided "an experience of [madness] that psychology, in the modern [panoptic] world, was meant to disguise" (p. 339).
37 The term 'synopticism' was coined by Mathiesen (1997); however, his use of the words presumes subjection of the masses by institutional elites, who organise media to foster consciousness in accordance with economic and industrial aims by promoting

"the deviant, the shuddering, the titillating ..., the concrete misery of the world" (p. 230). I use it in a much broader sense of the contested meaning of 'truth'.

38 More recently, he is the child-killing clown adapted for big screen from the Stephen King novel. In 2017, the film grossed more than any other horror film in history in its first weekend ($117.2 m). The first public comment on *The Guardian* website refers to "inherent untrustworthiness of adulthood" depicted in the film (Guardian Film and Agencies, 2017).

39 Jung (1937/2000d) elaborates:

> Unfortunately there can be no doubt that man is, on the whole, less good than he imagines himself or wants to be. Everyone carries a shadow, and the less it is embodied in the individual's conscious life, the blacker and denser it is.
>
> (para. 131)

40 In the original Friday the 13th series (1980–1989), mostly set in Camp Crystal Lake, the heroine is attacked by Jason Vorhees in child form and pulled into the lake (Pt 1); another fails to properly restrain Jason in the shack where he is maimed, following multiple murders of camp counsellors (Pt 2); an orderly fails to fasten the door to a hospital morgue where he lay undead (Pt 4); the wish of a survivor from the last two instalments to ensure that Jason is dead in his grave leads to his being struck by a reviving lightning strike (Pt 6); he escapes the lake after his restraint is damaged by the careless use of telekinetic powers (Pt 7); and, finally, he returns to mayhem after a power cable is damaged by an ill-driven yacht, while its marked owners have sex in the cabin (Pt 8). "The lake in the valley is the unconscious", Jung states (1954a/2000b), "usually with the pejorative connotation of an inferior consciousness" (para. 40).

41 Freud (1905/2001) had earlier used the term to denote our gravitation towards reproductive unities, friendships, families, communities, corporations and nations, following a break with our primary attachment.

42 Just as the vast majority of dramatic versions of the *trickster* are rooted in the male persona, 97% of the IPP-population was once shown to be male (Jacobson & Hough, 2010, p. 42), with over two-thirds being estimated to meet the diagnostic criteria for psychopathy (Sainsbury Centre for Mental Health, 2008, p. 39).

43 We suffer cultural indoctrination and the familial repression of instincts due to our need for attachment. Bowlby (1988) writes: "During infancy and childhood bonds are with parents (or parent substitutes) who are looked to for protection, comfort, and support" (p. 136).

44 An earlier, more sanguine attempt to constitute psychopaths as, "abnormal personalities who either suffer personally because of their own abnormality or make the community suffer because of it (Schneider, 1958, p. 3) was ironically criticised as "usefully but dangerously indeterminate, a rubric that comfortably encompassed incarcerated criminals and dissipated high-livers, promiscuous girls and lazy men, deficiencies so vague, so numerous and, in the end, so elusive that some wondered whether it referred to anything at all." (Lunbeck, 1994, p. 65)

45 The 'tactics' of bio-power are 'intentional and nonsubjective', Foucault (1978a) argues: they "end by forming comprehensive systems: the logic is perfectly clear, the aims decipherable, and yet it is often the case that no one is there to have invented them, and few who can be said to have formulated them" (pp. 94–95).

46 Jung (1928/2000i) states: "Woman's psychology is founded on the principle of Eros, the great binder and loosener, whereas ... the ruling principle ascribed to man is Logos" (para. 255).

47 The psychiatrist has been the cornerstone of hospital admission since the mid-1800s (Unsworth, 1987). Today, hospital admission cannot occur without the recommendation of at least one psychiatrist (MHA, s 12(2)).

48 As one high-profile, psychopathic lawyer attests:

> It was in my preteen years that I realized how crucial it was to actively cultivate attractive personality traits … Not only could I wear any number of masks to suit any situation, I had learned how to wear them with consistency.
>
> (Thomas, 2013, p. 107)

49 They compare with those who are blamed for economic disaster, who begin "new roles advising governments how to prevent such economic disasters" (Boddy, 2011, p. 256).

50 Mr. D states: "[W]hen I was out in the community and things got tough, I thought I'll go back to jail; fuck it, I'll go out and do something stupid. That was my answer to everything" (unpublished data).

51 "They are not personalities, but are typical situations, places, ways and means, that symbolize the kind of transformation in question" with an "almost limitless wealth of reference" (Jung, 1954a/2000b, pp. 80–81).

52 For example,

> [W]hat you've got to watch here with PD patients, is they can be manipulative, and they can say that they're doing, they're getting better, and they can conform to all the treatments they're having and they're not, they're only doing it for their own benefit. To get out of this place. And when they've been discharged, they've reoffended.
>
> (nurse in Bowers, 2002, p. 40)

References

Abrams, J., & Zweig, C. (Ed.). (1991). *Meeting the shadow: The hidden power of the dark side of human Nature*. New York, NY: Penguin.

American Psychiatric Association. (2013). *Diagnostic and statistical manual of mental disorders* (5th ed.). Arlington, VA: American Psychiatric Publishing.

Annison, H. (2015). *Dangerous politics: Risk, political vulnerability, and penal policy*. Oxford, UK: Oxford University Press.

Babiak, P., & Hare, R. D. (2006). *Snakes in suits: When psychopaths go to work*. New York, NY: HarperCollins.

Bassil-Morozow, H. (2017). Loki then and now: The trickster against civilization. *International Journal of Jungian Studies*, *9*(2), 84–96. doi: 10.1080/19409052.2017.1309780

Bersoff, D. N. (2002). Some contrarian concerns about law, psychology, and public policy. *Law and Human Behavior*, *26*(5), 565–574. doi: 10.1023/A:1020260123477

Binet, A. (1887). Le fétichisme dans l'amour'. *Revue Philosophique*, *24*, 143–167.

Boddy, C. R. (2011). The corporate psychopaths theory of the global financial crisis. *Journal of Business Ethics*, *102*(2), 255–259. doi: 10.1007/s10551-011-0810-4

Borg, J. S., & Sinnot-Armstrong, W. P. (2013). Do psychopaths make moral judgments. In K. A. Kiehl & W. P. Sinnot-Armstrong (Eds.), *Handbook on psychopathy and law* (pp. 107–131). Oxford, UK: Oxford University Press.

Bowers, L. (2002). *Dangerous and severe personality disorder: Response and role of the psychiatric team*. London, UK: Routledge.

Bowlby, J. (1988). *A secure base: Clinical applications of attachment theory*. London, UK: Routledge.

Bruyère, J. de la (1699) *The characters of Theophrastus, or the manners of the age* (J. de la Bruyère, Trans.). London, UK: Henry E. Huntington Library.

Burns, T., Yiend, J., Fahy, T., Fitzpatrick, R., Rogers, R., Fazel, S., & Sinclair, J. (2011). Treatments for dangerous severe personality disorder (DSPD). *The Journal of Forensic Psychiatry & Psychology*, *22*(3), 411–426. doi: 10.1080/14789949.2011.577439

Cameron, D. (2011). *Press conference on sentencing reforms*. Retrieved from https://www.gov.uk/government/speeches/pms-press-conference-on-sentencing-reforms.
Castel, R. (1991). 'From dangerousness to risk. In G. Burchell, C. Gordon, & P. Miller (Eds.), *The Foucault effect: Studies in governmentality* (pp. 281–298). Chicago, IL: University of Chicago Press.
Chamberlin, J. (1998). Confessions of a noncompliant patient. *Journal of Psychosocial Nursing and Mental Health Services, 36*(4), 49–52. doi: 10.3928/0279-3695-19980401-17
Charcot, J., & Magnan, V. (1882). Inversion du sens sénital. *Archives de Neurologie, 3,* 53–60.
Chiswick, D. (1999). Preventive detention exhumed and enhanced. *Psychiatric Bulletin, 23,* 703–704.
Coid, J., & Maden, T. (2003). Should psychiatrists protect the public?: A new risk reduction strategy, supporting criminal justice, could be effective. *BMJ, 326*(7386), 406–407. doi: 10.1136/bmj.326.7386.406
Coid, J., & Yang, M. (2008). The distribution of psychopathy among a household population: Categorical or dimensional? *Social Psychiatry and Psychiatric Epidemiology, 43(10),* 773–781.
Crowther, C., Haynes, J., & Newton, K. (1998). The psychological uses of fairy tales. In I. Alister & C. Hauke (Eds.), *Post-Jungian perspectives from the Society of Analytical Psychology* (pp. 211–229). London, UK: Routledge.
DeMatteo, D., & Edens, J. F. (2006). The role and relevance of the psychopathy checklist-revised in court: A case law survey of U.S. courts (1991–2004). *Psychology, Public Policy, and Law, 12*(2), 214–241. doi: 10.1037/1076-8971.12.2.214
Department of Health & Ministry of Justice. (2011). *Consultation on the offender personality disorder pathway implementation plan*. London, UK: Department of Health.
Deresiewicz, W. (2012, May 13). Capitalists and other psychopaths. *New York Times*. Retrieved from www.nytimes.com.
Duff, A. (1977). Psychopathy and moral understanding. *American Philosophical Quarterly, 14*(3), 189–200. Retrieved from JSTOR.
Duff, A. (2010). Psychopathy and answerability. In L. Malatesti & J. McMillan (Eds.), *Responsibility and psychopathy: Interfacing law, psychiatry, and philosophy* (pp. 199–212). Oxford, UK: Oxford University Press.
Duggan, C. (2011). Dangerous and severe personality disorder. *The British Journal of Psychiatry, 198*(6), 431–433. doi: 10.1192/bjp.bp.110.083048
Duggan, C., & Kane, E. (2010). Developing a National Institute for Health and Clinical Excellence guidelines for antisocial personality disorder. *Personality and Mental Health, 4,* 3–8.
Dutton, K. (2012). *The wisdom of psychopaths: What saints, spies and serial killers can teach us about success*. New York: Farrar, Straus and Giroux.
Edens, J. F., Guy, L. S., & Fernandez, K. (2003). Psychopathic traits predict attitudes toward a juvenile capital murderer. *Behavioral Sciences and the Law, 21*(6), 807–828.
Fazel, S., & Danesh, J. (2002). Serious mental disorder in 23 000 prisoners: A systematic review of 62 surveys. *The Lancet, 359*(9306), 545–550. doi.org/10.1016/S0140-6736(02)07740-1
Foucault, M. (1961/2009). *History of madness*. London, UK: Routledge.
Foucault, M. (1970/2002). *The order of things: An archaeology of the human sciences*. London, UK: Routledge.
Foucault, M. (1972). *The archaeology of knowledge* (A. Sheridan, Trans.). London, UK: Tavistock.
Foucault, M. (1977). *Discipline and punish: The birth of the prison* (A. Sheridan, Trans.). London, UK: Allen Lane.
Foucault, M. (1978a). *The history of sexuality, vol. 1: The will to knowledge* (R. Hurley, Trans.). London, UK: Penguin.

Foucault, M. (1978b). About the concept of the 'dangerous individual' in 19th-century legal psychiatry. *International Journal of Law and Psychiatry, 1*(1), 1–18. doi: 10.1016/0160-2527(78)90020-1

Foucault, M. (1982). The subject and power. In H. L. Dreyfus & P. Rabinow (Eds.), *Michel Foucault: Beyond structuralism and hermeneutics*. Chicago, IL: University of Chicago Press.

Foucault, M. (1982/1988). Technologies of the self. In L. H. Martin, H. Gutman & P. H. Hutton (Eds.) *Technologies of the self: A seminar with Michel Foucault*. London, UK: Tavistock Publications.

Foucault, M. (1984). *The history of sexuality, vol. 2. The use of pleasure*. (R. Hurley, Trans.). London, UK: Penguin.

Foucault, M. (1988). The political technology of individuals. In L. H. Martin, H. Gutman & P. H. Hutton (Eds.), *Technologies of the self: A seminar with Michel Foucault* (pp. 145–163). London, UK: Tavistock Publications.

Foucault, M. (2003) *Abnormal: Lectures at the Collège de France, 1974–1975* (G. Burchell, Trans.). New York, NY: Picador.

Foucault, M. (2006) *Psychiatric power: Lectures at the Collège de France, 1973–1974* (G. Burchell, Trans.). London, UK: Palgrave Macmillan.

Freedman, D. (2001). False prediction of future dangerousness: Error rates and Psychopathy Checklist—Revised. *Journal of the American Academy of Psychiatry and the Law, 29*(1), 89–95.

Freud, S. (2001a). Fragment of an element of a case of hysteria. In J. Strachey (Ed.), *Complete psychological works of Sigmund Freud* (Vol. 7, pp. 3–125). London, UK: Hogarth Press. (Original work published in 1901).

Freud, S. (2001b). Infantile sexuality. In J. Strachey (Ed.), *Complete psychological works of Sigmund Freud* (Vol. 7, pp. 173–207). London, UK: Hogarth Press. (Original work published in 1905).

Freud, S. (2001c). The libido and narcissism. In J. Strachey (Ed.), *Complete psychological works of Sigmund Freud* (Vol. 16, pp. 412–431). London, UK: Hogarth Press. (Original work published in 1917).

Freud, S. (2001d). New introductory lectures on psycho-analysis. In J. Strachey (Ed.), *Complete psychological works of Sigmund Freud* (Vol. 22, pp. 3–185). London, UK: Hogarth Press. (Original work published in 1933).

Fromm, E. (1973). *The anatomy of human destructiveness*. London, UK: Penguin.

Furnham, A. (2015). *Backstabbers and bullies: How to cope with the dark side of people at work*. London, UK: Bloomsbury Publishing.

Grounds, A., Gelsthorpe, L., Howes, M., Melzer, D., Tom, B. D. M., Brugha, T., … Meltzer, H. (2004). Access to medium secure psychiatric care in England and Wales. 2: A qualitative study of admission decision-making. *The Journal of Forensic Psychiatry & Psychology, 15*(1), 32–49. doi: 10.1080/14789940310001648212

Guardian Film and Agencies. (2017, September 11) 'Stephen King's It breaks highest-grossing horror record. *The Guardian*.

Guggenbühl-Craig, A. (1980). *The emptied soul: On the nature of the psychopath*. Putnam, CT: Spring Publications.

Gunn, J. (2007). The death penalty: A psychiatrist's view from Europe. In: A. R. Felthous & H. Saß (Eds). *International handbook on psychopathic disorders and the law* (Vol 2). Chichester: John Wiley & Sons, Ltd

Haddock, A., Snowden, P., Dolan, M., Parker, J., & Rees, H. (2001). Managing dangerous people with severe personality disorder: A survey of forensic psychiatrists' opinions. *Psychiatric Bulletin, 25*(8), 293–296. doi: 10.1192/pb.25.8.293

Hare, R. D. (1980). A research scale for the assessment of psychopathy in criminal populations. *Personality and Individual Differences, 1*(2), 111–119. doi: 10.1016/0191-8869(80)90028-8

Hare,, R. D. (1996). Psychopathy and antisocial personality disorder: A case of diagnostic confusion. *Psychiatric Times, 13(2)*: https://www.psychiatrictimes.com.

Hare, R. D. (2003). *The hare psychopathy checklist – Revised* (2nd ed). Toronto, Canada: Multi-Health Systems.

Harris, G., & Rice, M. (2006). Treatment of psychopathy: A review of empirical findings. In C. Patrick (Ed.), *Handbook of psychopathy* (pp. 555–572). New York, NY: Guildford.

Hawes, V. (2010). Treating high-risk mentally disordered offenders: The dangerous and severe personality disorder initiative. In A. Bartlett & G. McGauley (Eds.), *Forensic mental health: Concepts, systems, and practice* (pp. 215–235). Oxford, UK: Oxford University Press.

Ingleby, A. (1985). Mental health and social control. In S. Cohen & A. Scull (Eds.), *Social control and the state: Historical and comparative essays* (pp. 141–188). Oxford, UK: Blackwell.

Jacobson, J., & Hough, M. (2010). *Unjust deserts: Imprisonment for public protection*. London, UK: Prison Reform Trust.

Johnson, R. A. (1991). *Owning your own shadow: Understanding the dark side of the psyche*. New York, NY: HarperCollins.

Jung, C. J. (2000a). A study in process of individuation. In G. Alder & R. F. C. Hall (Eds & Trans.). *The collected works of C. J. Jung* (Vol. 9, Pt 1). Princeton, NJ: Princeton University Press. (Original work published in 1950).

Jung, C. J. (2000b). Archetypes and the collective unconscious. In G. Alder & R. F. C. Hall (Eds & Trans.). *The collected works of C. J. Jung* (Vol. 9, Pt 1). Princeton, NJ: Princeton University Press. (Original work published in 1954a).

Jung, C. J. (2000c). On the psychology of the trickster-figure. In G. Alder & R. F. C. Hall (Eds & Trans.). *The collected works of C. J. Jung* (Vol. 9, Pt 1). Princeton, NJ: Princeton University Press. (Original work published in 1954b).

Jung, C. J. (2000d). Psychology and religion. In G. Alder & R. F. C. Hall (Eds & Trans.). *The collected works of C. J. Jung* (Vol. 11). Princeton, NJ: Princeton University Press. (Original work published in 1937).

Jung, C. J. (2000e). The concept of libido. In G. Alder & R. F. C. Hall (Eds & Trans.). *The collected works of C. J. Jung* (Vol. 5). Princeton, NJ: Princeton University Press. (Original work published in 1948).

Jung, C. J. (2000f). The conception of the collective unconscious. In G. Alder & R. F. C. Hall (Eds & Trans.). *The collected works of C. J. Jung* (Vol. 9, Pt 1). Princeton, NJ: Princeton University Press. (Original work published in 1936).

Jung, C. J. (2000g). The personal and collective (or transpersonal unconscious). In G. Alder & R. F. C. Hall (Eds & Trans.). *The collected works of C. J. Jung* (Vol. 7). Princeton, NJ: Princeton University Press. (Original work published in 1953).

Jung, C. J. (2000h). The structure of the psyche. In G. Alder & R. F. C. Hall (Eds & Trans.). *The collected works of C. J. Jung* (Vol. 8). Princeton, NJ: Princeton University Press. (Original work published in 1969).

Jung, C. J. (2000i). Women in Europe. In G. Alder & R. F. C. Hall (Eds & Trans.). *The collected works of C. J. Jung* (Vol 10). Princeton, NJ: Princeton University Press. (Original work published in 1928).

Jung, C. J. (2000j). The practical use of dream-analysis. In G. Alder & R. F. C. Hall (Eds & Trans.). *The collected works of C. J. Jung* (Vol. 16). Princeton, NJ: Princeton University Press. (Original work published in 1934).

Kiehl, K. A., & Sinnott-Armstrong, W. P. (2013). *Handbook on psychopathy and law*. Oxford, UK: Oxford University Press.

Kitzinger, J. (2004). *Framing abuse: Media influence and public understandings of sexual violence against children*. London, UK: Pluto Press.

Lunbeck, E. (1994). *The psychiatric persuasion: Knowledge, gender and power in modern America*. Princeton, NJ: Princeton University Press.

Macdonald, M. (1981). *Mystical bedlam: Madness, anxiety, and healing in seventeenth century England*. Cambridge, UK: Cambridge University Press.

MacKay, R. D., & Kearns, G. (1999). More fact(s) about the insanity defence. *Criminal Law Review* 725.

Mathiesen, T. (1997). The viewer society: Michael Foucault's 'panopticon' revisited. *Theoretical Criminology*, 1(2), 215–234.

McRae, L. (2013). Rehabilitating antisocial personalities: Treatment through self-governance strategies. *The Journal of Forensic Psychiatry & Psychology*, 24(1), 48–70. doi: 10.1080/14789949.2012.752517

McRae, L. (2015). The offender personality disorder pathway: Risking rehabilitation? *Medical Law Review*, 23(3), 321–347. doi: 10.1093/medlaw/fwv021

McRae, L. (2019). Blaming rape on sleep: A psychoanalytic intervention. *International Journal of Law and Psychiatry*, 62, 135–147. doi: 10.1016/j.ijlp.2018.12.004

Mental Health Act Commission (2008). *Risk, rights, recovery. Twelfth biennial report 2005–2007*. London, UK: The Stationary Office.

Ministry of Justice. (2010). *Breaking the cycle: Effective punishment, rehabilitation and sentencing of offenders*. Green paper evidence report. London, UK: The Stationary Office.

Ministry of Justice (2011). *Working with personality disordered offenders: A practitioners Guide*. London, UK: Ministry of Justice.

Ministry of Justice (2019). *Criminal justice statistics quarterly, England and Wales, October 2017 to September 2018*. London, UK: Ministry of Justice.

Ministry of Justice & Department of Health. (2005). *Dangerous and severe personality disorder (DSPD) high secure services for men: Planning and delivery guide*. London, UK: Ministry of Justice.

Morris, A., Gibbon, S., & Duggan, C. (2007). 'Sentenced to hospital'—A cause for concern? *Personality and Mental Health*, 1(1), 74–79. doi: 10.1002/pmh.10

Mullen, P. E. (2007a). Dangerous and severe personality disorder and in need of treatment. *The British Journal of Psychiatry*, 190(S49), s3–s7. doi: 10.1192/bjp.190.5.s3

Mullen, P. E. (2007b). Dangerous severe personality disorder. *Advances in Psychiatric Treatment*, 13, 325–332.

National Health Service & National Offender Management Service. (2015). *The offender personality disorder pathway strategy 2015*. London, UK: National Health Service.

Page, S. (1999). *The shadow and the counsellor: Working with the darker aspects of the person, role and the profession*. London, UK: Routledge.

Parole Board for England and Wales. (2013). *Guidance to members on LASPO Act 2012 – Test for release*. London, UK: Parole Board.

Peay, J. (1989). *Tribunals on trial: A study of decision–making under the MHA 1983*. Oxford, UK: Clarendon Press.

Pillsbury, S. H. (2013). Why psychopaths are responsible. In K. A. Kiehl & W. P. Sinnot-Armstrong (Eds.), *Handbook on psychopathy and law* (pp. 297–321). Oxford, UK: Oxford University Press.

Radin, P. (1953). *The world of the primitive man*. New York, NY: N. Schuman.

Redfearn, J. W. T. (1979). The captive, the treasure, the hero and the "anal" stage of development. *Journal of Analytical Psychology*, 24(3), 185–206.

Reid, W. H. (1985). Psychopathy and dangerousness. In M. Roth & R. Bluglass (Eds). *Psychiatry, human rights and the law* (pp. 72–810). Cambridge: Cambridge University Press.

Reid, W. H., & Gacono, C. (2000). Treatment of antisocial personality, psychopathy, and other characterologic antisocial syndromes. *Behavioral Sciences & the Law, 18*(5), 647–662. doi: 10.1002/1099-0798(200010)18:5<647::AID-BSL407>3.0.CO;2-O

Rogers, R. (2000). The uncritical acceptance of risk assessment in forensic practice. *Law and Human Behavior, 24*(5), 595–605. doi: 10.1023/A:1005575113507

Sainsbury Centre for Mental Health. (2008). *In the dark. The mental health implications of imprisonment for public protection*, London, UK: Sainsbury Centre for Mental Health.

Schneider, K. (1923/1958). *Psychopathic personalities* (9th ed.) (M. N. Hamilton, Trans.). London, UK: Cassell.

Seddon, T. (2008). Dangerous liaisons: Personality disorder and the politics of risk. *Punishment & Society, 10*(3), 301–317. doi: 10.1177/1462474508090230

Stevens, A. (1994). *Jung*. Oxford, UK: Oxford University Press.

Stout, M. (2005). *The sociopath next door*. New York, NY: Broadway Books.

Thomas, M. E., (2013). *Confession of a sociopath: A high life spent in plain sight*. Croydon, UK: Pan Macmillan.

Turley, C, Payne, C., & Webster, S. (2013). *Enabling features of Psychological Informed Planned Environments*. Ministry of Justice Analytical Series. London, UK: Ministry of Justice.

Unsworth, C. R. (1987). *The politics of mental health legislation*. Oxford, UK: Oxford University Press.

Velie, A. R. (1991). *American Indian literature: An anthology*. Oklahoma: University of Oklahoma Press.

Verhaeghe, P. (2014, May 29). Neoliberalism has brought out the worst in us. *The Guardian*.

Vitacco, M. J., & Salekin, R. T. (2013). Adolescent psychopathy and the law. In K. A. Kiehl & W. P. Sinnot-Armstrong (Eds.), *Handbook on psychopathy and law* (pp. 78–93). Oxford, UK: Oxford University Press.

Whitmont, E. C. (1991). *The symbolic quest: Basic concepts of analytical psychology*. Princeton, NJ: Princeton University Press.

World Health Organization (1993). *The ICD-10 classification of mental and behavioral disorders: Diagnostic criteria for research*. Geneva: World Health Organization.

Yang, M., Wong, S. C. P., & Coid, J. (2010). The efficacy of violence prediction: A meta-analytic comparison of nine risk assessment tools. *Psychological Bulletin, 136*(5), 740–767. doi: 10.1037/a0020473

5

COMMUNITY PUNISHMENT AND MENTAL ILLNESS AND DISORDER

Lol Burke

Given that only a small proportion of mentally disordered offenders will receive disposals under the Mental Health Act 1983 (Bourne et al., 2015) it is highly likely that a significant proportion of individuals with mental health problems will come into contact with probation services. This can either be through the imposition of a community order or following their release from custody on licence if they have served a determinate, extended or life sentence. Probation officers, therefore, have a significant role in the supervision of offenders with mental health problems in terms of helping them access services and alleviate personal and practical difficulties that might increase their vulnerability. Moreover, as Robinson (2011) contends, exposure to the criminal justice system in itself can induce feelings of social isolation and stigma that might lead to a deterioration in an individual's mental state. In the absence of other mental health professionals, it often falls on probation staff to recognise mental health issues and to make appropriate recommendations to the court through the provision of a Pre-Sentence Report. For this reason, the Bradley Report (2009) recommended that all probation staff should receive mental health awareness training, having found that existing provision was often non-existent or wholly inappropriate (Scott & Moffatt, 2012, p. 13).

A study by Brooker et al. (2012) into the prevalence of mental health disorders among a cohort of those under supervision in one probation trust in England and Wales found that around 39% of offenders experienced a mental illness whilst on probation, with half of that population having a past or lifetime disorder. In common with previous studies of prison populations, the researchers also found a strong correlation evident in terms of the co-occurrence of co-morbidity (the presence of a mental illness and a personality disorder) and of dual diagnosis (a mental illness and substance misuse). Such findings would appear to replicate and reinforce those found in studies undertaken in other jurisdictions (Lurigio et al.,

2003). Worryingly, Brooker et al. (2012) also found that the prevalence of psychosis was ten times higher than in the general population and suicide levels were rising among those being supervised in the community (accounting for one in eight deaths amongst offenders on probation). Whilst at the same time as suicide levels were declining among prisoners, who traditionally have been unacceptably high, suggesting that ultimately these trends will converge.

Offending lifestyles often involve significant levels of stress and anxiety that can exacerbate mental health problems. A combination of mental health problems and/or personality disorder and substance use can have a detrimental impact on treatment outcomes (DiClemente et al., 2008) and is often characterised by a lack of engagement with therapeutic services, poor motivation and relapse (Long et al., 2018). A study over three years of 613 probationers in the USA found that those with a mental illness were significantly more likely to have their orders revoked than those without (Skeem & Louden, 2006). This is often compounded by the complex personal backgrounds and chaotic lifestyles that are characteristic of many of those on probation. This, in turn, can lead to difficulties in forming positive relationships and a disenchantment with both mental health and criminal justice services. However, Skeem and Louden (2006) also note that these individuals are often failed by services that are not geared towards the needs of this population. This is because many mainstream community health services sometimes deem their needs too complex and struggle to meet their clinical needs (Vaughan & Stevenson, 2002) whilst criminal justice organisations, such as the probation service, are not always designed to meet the unique challenges that individuals with mental illness can at times pose.

McArt (2013, p. 191) warns that an increasing focus on the punitive aspect of community sentences could limit sentencers' options by making the punitive aspects mandatory in many cases. For those with a range of mental health-related needs, making sentences more onerous could create demands that they cannot meet in the community, thus resulting in a further period of imprisonment and thereby continuing the cycle of a lack of treatment in place of punishment. However, recently a more nuanced understanding of offending among people with mental illness has emerged (Louden et al., 2018) based on a strong evidence base that suggests that serious mental illness is not a strong predictor of re-offending symptoms and their symptoms are not directly related to the offences they commit. Instead, those with a mental illness tended to display more general risk factors for offending (such as criminogenic personality patterns) compared with non-disordered offenders. In this respect, 'mental illness appears to be an indicator of risk—because it is correlated with factors related to offending—rather than a causal mechanism itself' (Louden et al., 2018, p. 573).

The picture is further complicated by the conflation of mental disorder, risk and dangerousness in contemporary probation policies and practices. Castel (1991) suggests that up until the 1970s, dangerousness was viewed as an internal characteristic of certain pathological individuals and tended to be governed through institutional confinement. More recently, this approach has gradually been replaced by "interventions targeted at combinations of abstract factors identified as increasing the probability of undesirable behaviour" (Seddon, 2008, p. 307). Feeley and Simon (1992, 1994) see the emergence of risk-based strategies in correctional services as representing a new form of penology that places *actuarial justice* at its centre. According to the authors, this has marked a paradigm shift away from diagnosing, treating and punishing individual offenders towards one of regulating groups within the population as 'part of a strategy of managing danger' (Feeley & Simon, 1994, p. 173). Fitzgibbon and Green (2006) have conversely argued that there has been a corresponding dilution of the concept of serious mental illness, which has allowed a broader definition of mental health that could see those from socially excluded backgrounds being assimilated into this category of dangerousness. The current actuarial-based tools for risk assessment and prediction utilised within the probation service has according to the authors, simultaneously spread the net of dangerousness whilst at the same time failed to address the criminogenic needs of offenders effectively. The new generic 'dangerousness' provisions introduced by the Criminal Justice Act 2003 have become highly significant in this respect. Under this legislation, in addition to life sentences, the courts can now impose extended or indeterminate sentences (IPP) for sexual and violent offenders who pose a significant risk of serious harm to the public. Those subject to such sanctions must prove that their 'dangerousness' is reduced before they may be considered for release. However, as O'Loughlin (2014, p. 174) argues:

> If personality disorder continues to be tied to 'dangerousness', but no effective treatments or long-term management techniques for the disorder become available, such prisoners may continue to languish in prison for years to come and be punished far beyond what would be proportionate to the gravity of their crimes.

In short, the past two decades have brought about both a substantial amount of attention to offenders with mental illness. In the following sections, attention is turned to two of these developments – the Mental Health Treatment Requirement (MHTR) and the Offender Personality Disorder Pathway (OPDP) which have resulted in a noticeable shift in perceptions of best practices for managing this group in the criminal justice system.

The mental health treatment requirement

The Community Order was implemented as part of provisions of the 2003 Criminal Justice Act and brought together a range of community orders and requirements into what has been termed a 'smorgasbord' approach to sentencing (Von Hirsch & Roberts, 2004). Originally made up of ten different requirements, the intention behind the Community Order was to provide judges and magistrates with the flexibility to choose from a range of options when determining a sentence in the adult courts. In 2005 the Alcohol Treatment Requirement and the Mental Health Treatment Requirement were subsequently introduced in response to those particular issues. The Legal Aid, Sentencing and Punishment of Offenders (LASPO) Act 2012 made changes to the administration of the MHTR by amending provisions linked to the Criminal Justice Act 2003 and the Mental health Act 1983. The LASPO Act sought to make it easier for courts to use the MHTR as part of a Community Order or suspended sentence order by simplifying the assessment process and removed the requirement in the Criminal Justice Act 2003 that evidence of an offender's need for mental health treatment is given to a court by a Section 12 registered medical practitioner. Sentencers can now seek the views and assessments from a broader range of suitably trained mental health professionals (NOMS, 2014).

The primary purpose of the MHTR is to ensure that those individuals appearing before the courts with mental health issues are able to access appropriate treatment in the community (Scott & Moffatt, 2012). It is intended to target those individuals committing middle-range offences rather than the least severe end of the continuum where fines or conditional discharges might be more appropriate or those whose levels of seriousness mean that imprisonment or detainment under the Mental Health Act is inevitable. The MHTR is a 'bespoke' sentence and as such the nature of the treatment is not specified but in order to include an MHTR in a Community Order, the sentencer must be satisfied that three criteria have been met. Notably, that:

- they require treatment for mental health-related needs;
- there are concerns regarding future engagement; and
- the court is of the view that it is not appropriate to divert them from the criminal justice system altogether (Scott & Moffatt, 2012).

An MHTR requires offenders to engage in specific treatment for a specified period of time, the nature of which will depend on the nature of their condition. As such, it provides sentencers with the option to impose a criminal justice sanction on those individuals with mental health problems who have committed relatively minor offences. In this respect, it is "a form of diversion within rather than away from the criminal justice system, but outside custody" (Scott & Moffatt, 2012, p. 6).

The MHTR can be used in relation to any mental health issue, including personality disorders. This includes any mental health condition which is susceptible to treatment such as low-level depression or anxiety. The type of treatment is not defined and can cover a wide range of interventions. Treatment should be based on the offender being assessed as able to be treated for their mental health problem either in a community setting or as an outpatient in a non-secure setting (NOMS, 2014). MHTRs are rarely made as stand-alone sanctions and are usually combined with a supervision requirement to support the rehabilitative endeavour and provide additional assistance. There must be a named registered medical practitioner or registered psychologist overseeing the treatment who will work collaboratively with probation staff. The focus of the latter will be on addressing other matters in relation to offending and monitor compliance with the order. In imposing a MHTR the recipient's consent is required reflecting "the treatment ethos of voluntary and motivated participation" (Pakes & Winstone, 2012, p. 109).

According to Pakes and Winstone (2012, p. 109) the MHTR makes 'intuitive sense' in that it potentially positively addresses the offender's needs and avoids the damaging impact of imprisonment which may only serve to exacerbate any lingering or manifest mental health problems. However, the implementation of the requirement has not been without problems. Perhaps the most telling of these has been the low-take up rate, an issue which also befell previous attempts to address the mental health issues of offenders through community sentences such as the Probation Order with Psychiatric Treatment (1948) and the Community Rehabilitation Order with a requirement for psychiatric treatment (2001) (Scott & Moffatt, 2012). Khanom et al. (2009) found that no more than 686 MHTRs were imposed, out of 221,700 requirements, in 2008. Recent statistical data suggests that not much has changed within this profile. The Offender Management Statistics for July–September 2010 show that there were 584 MHTRs for Community Orders and another 253 attached to Suspended Sentence Orders. As Pakes and Winstone (2012, p. 110) note, although these figures would appear to suggest an increase in the use of MHTRs since 2008, the trend is actually downward, 13% and 26%, respectively, from the same period the year before (Ministry of Justice, 2011).

Research has uncovered a range of reasons for the underuse of MHTR. There appeared to be a lack of knowledge and understanding about MHTRs among criminal justice and health professionals and uncertainty as to what their purpose was and which offenders would benefit from the imposition of a MHTR. As Pakes and Winstone note, the issue of identifying suitable individuals who might benefit from an MHTR is complex, partly due to the specifics of the legislation and the fact that the offence with which the individual is charged needs to be in the right sentencing bracket. There is some evidence that professionals have different views as to who should receive an MHTR and who should be excluded. In practice, professionals have tended to exclude certain groups, including those with personality disorders or those with depression or anxiety (Khanom et al., 2009). As Bourne et al. (2015, p. 277) note, "Often an offender has many complex problems and there can be differing views among professionals regarding who should receive an MHTR, with some arguing that mental health problems should not be dealt with via the criminal justice system". Scott and Moffatt (2012) for example, found that some psychiatrists were unlikely to recommend an MHTR for those individuals who may only require counselling or psychological treatment.

The use of the MHTR is likely to be limited by the requirement that there must be available treatment and the generally high thresholds set by mental health services for access to treatment. Local variations in the extent to which the MHTR is included are to be expected as the requirement depends on local arrangements (Pakes & Winstone, 2012). Local sentencing practices will no doubt also play a part. In their study into the use of requirements in community orders, Mair and Mills (2009) found that sentencers tended to be somewhat risk-averse in their use of requirements in community orders. They tended to consistently use those requirements they were familiar with and had confidence in the local probation service to deliver. Sentencers felt that their understanding of MHTRs was sparse and their knowledge of local mental health services was insufficient (Mair & Mills, 2009). As a result, mental health problems at court often go unidentified because many offenders with mental health problems also suffer from a multitude of other issues, including drug and alcohol abuse. Where this is the case, Drug Rehabilitation Requirements (DRR) and Alcohol Treatment Requirements (ATR) were far more likely to be imposed (Pakes & Winston, 2012). This was compounded by the fact that many offenders who could potentially be eligible for the requirement may have multiple problems and complex needs, which may preclude them from accessing certain services. As Scott and Moffatt (2012, p. 12) note:

> Unless services are available in the community to support clients with a dual diagnosis, it is likely that there will be cases where a person's mental health needs continue to go unaddressed and where it would be difficult to identify available treatment in order to make an MHTR.

Difficulties were encountered due to a lack of access to services and difficulties in obtaining mental health assessments by an appropriate mental health professional. Khanom et al. (2009) found that one of the biggest barriers to the use of MHTRs was there is a need for formal psychiatric reports. Obtaining these reports can be a lengthy process and requires additional funding through legal aid. A report by the National Audit Office (NAO, 2008) found that work with offenders with mental health needs cost an average of £3,700 in probation staff costs compared to about £650 for standalone supervision. From a probation perspective, that makes the MHTR the most expensive order (Pakes & Winstone, 2012). Current restraints on public spending could mean that services may not have the resources to provide the treatment required if the number of MHTRs increases (Scott and Moffatt, 2012).

A further issue that can also be a cause of tension between sentencers and mental health providers is the pressure that the former are under to produce 'swift justice' (Ministry of Justice, 2012). For example, courts want to avoid adjournments as much as possible and so cannot always wait for more accurate assessments of individuals (particularly when formal psychiatric reports can be challenging to obtain). This often runs contrary to the goals and attitudes of health professionals. There is the potential this tension will be exacerbated by the Government's current emphasis on speeding up the criminal justice process. It is therefore essential that sufficient safeguards are put in place to ensure that the needs of vulnerable defendants are identified and addressed (Scott & Moffatt, 2012, p. 14).

A previous study by Brooker et al. (2011) also found that a large proportion of those with a current mental illness were not receiving treatment: for example, 60% of those with a mood or anxiety disorder were not receiving any treatment, and only half of those with a current psychosis were receiving any support from mental health services. Moreover, the research suggests that mental health problems are under-identified by probation staff with only 33% of individuals identified as having a psychotic disorder subsequently recorded in probation files as having such a disorder. This under-identification could be partly explained by the limited opportunities available to probation staff to receive any form of mental health awareness training, with many grades of probation staff receiving no formal training in this area. In their report, Brooker et al. (2011) concluded that probation staff require at least a 'basic' level of mental health awareness in order to effectively perform tasks such as writing pre-sentence reports to advise on the disposal of offenders within the criminal justice or health systems, assessing risk, and liaising with health services in both community and prison settings on behalf of offenders (Scott & Moffatt, 2012, pp. 4–5).

A potentially contentious issue is that of enforcement in those cases when the individual does not comply with the court order. Enforcement can be viewed as a mechanism for ensuring compliance but can also blur the boundaries between therapy and coercion (Scott & Moffatt, 2012). Breach rates for community orders have traditionally been high (Mair & Mills, 2009) with an almost 500%increase in imprisonment for breach of non-custodial sentences between 1995 and 2009 (Ministry of Justice, 2009). Problems in engagement in those offenders identified as having mental health problems are well known with a 22% rate of failure to attend in previous surveys (Cohen et al., 1999). Probation relies on health professionals to report non-compliance but there is no specific guidance on how an offender can breach an MHTR and professionals may vary in how they interpret non-compliance with the requirement (Khanom et al., 2009). As those professionals involved in the MHTR process come from different professional cultures they may hold differing views and practices (Taylor, 2012). This is especially the case when it concerns the offender not taking medication or failing to attend medical appointments. Pakes and Winstone (2012) argue that "it is desperately unfair to invoke the threat of custody if individuals fail to comply with treatment due to the very nature of their illness and the lack of insight into their condition that mental health patients can have" (p. 115). However, on the positive side, Khanom et al. (2009) found that where there was such non-engagement that led to a breach, courts mostly allowed the order to continue or revoked the requirement without imposing a penalty.

Finally, it was found that communication between the health and justice systems was often poor and frequently ineffective. As Pakes and Winstone (2012) note, effective information sharing between agencies can obviously improve such processes dramatically, even though it is not without its pitfalls. Concerns about sharing information and breaching confidentiality can be a barrier to joint working.

Ensuring, therefore, that an individual's Community Order is appropriate to their needs and circumstances is crucial. If used appropriately, the support and treatment provided through the MHTR may also help offenders to comply with their Community Order and therefore, could help reduce the rate of breach of Community Orders. As Scott and Moffatt (2012) note, the MHTR will not be the appropriate solution for every individual with a mental health need who comes into contact with the criminal justice system. However, it has unfulfilled potential to offer offenders with mental health problems the option of a sentence in the community, which will enable them to engage with appropriate treatment and support. In doing so, any wider use of the MHTR could result in improved health outcomes and reduced reoffending, cutting the costs of crime for the wider community (Scott & Moffatt, 2012, p. 10).

The offender personality disorder pathway

It has been estimated that almost two-thirds of the offender population experience some form of personality disorder (Singleton et al., 1998) and probation staff play a pivotal role in managing this group. The term 'personality disorder' is a contentious one but is generally used to describe a set of behaviours that are considered to deviate significantly from 'normal' behaviour. Someone who behaves in a way consistent with a personality disorder diagnosis often adopts behaviour that is inflexible and hard to change, despite changing contexts and situations. Often these traits are present since adolescence and result in significant distress or impaired functioning in a number of different areas such as relationships and employment (Ramsden & Lowton, 2014). As mentioned, the notion of what constitutes a personality disorder has not been without its critics and has been seen as "pejorative and largely unhelpful" (Skett et al., 2017, p. 215). Pilgrim (2001), for example, argues that the concept of personality disorder is fundamentally flawed and acts as a dustbin category of problematic "behaviour".

Nevertheless, for service providers, these behaviours are highly problematic because they can obstruct a meaningful working alliance and/or therapeutic relationship. Personality difficulties also provide challenges to offender management, particularly in regard to risk and diagnosis and so it is vital that probation workers are attuned to the relationship between serious harm, offending and personality disturbance. Identifying personality problems in high-risk offenders is therefore crucial because as Minoudis et al. (2011, p. 34) note:

> This helps to isolate cases who are more likely to reoffend, more likely to commit a high harm offence and more likely to fail in the community and on treatment programmes. In terms of caseload management, identifying offenders with personality disturbance helps probation officers to prioritize higher risk cases which require more time and resources. It facilitates the anticipation of future difficulties, which in the long run is likely to be more efficient than reacting to the time-consuming management of crises.

Minoudis et al. (2011) identified two separate subgroups of offenders within the categorisation of personality disorder. The first are those individuals who are severely anti-social, prolific offenders who are likely to fail on orders, and drop out of treatment and re-offend (possibly with a serious further offence). These individuals tend to be identified on probation caseloads because they display a greater number of past offences, substance misuse, childhood behavioural disturbances and previous breaches/recalls. Second, there are those individuals with a more diverse personality profile (including borderline, paranoid and narcissistic features) who cause serious harm to others. These individuals may be less likely to be picked up by screening, as often the risk is less immediate although they present a longer-term management issue, associated with high harm.

For many years, services failed to respond to personality disorder, believing that it was untreatable. This situation changed following the brutal attacks against the Russell family by Michael Stone who, although a diagnosed psychopath, did not meet the criteria for treatment under the 1983 Mental Health Act and as such could not be detained indefinitely despite his obvious risk to the public. This led to the introduction of the first Dangerous and Severe Personality Disorder (DSPD) services in prisons and special hospitals. However, it became increasingly evident that there might be other personality disordered offenders who could benefit from the pro-social environments of the DSPD but did not meet the admission criteria (Lloyd & Bell, 2015). This, in turn, led to the development of a comprehensive strategy for the treatment and management of personality disordered offenders at all levels of security and resulted in the Offender Personality Disorder Pathway (OPDP) being introduced in 2011. Alongside this new approach in working with personality disordered offenders, Psychologically Informed Planned Environments (PIPEs) were rolled out across the prison estate and probation approved premises for those individuals who had completed a period of treatment in custody to ensure that this was followed up in the community.

The OPD pathway target population is those offenders who are aged 18 years and over and are managed by the National Probation Service (NPS). The specific risk criteria differ for men and women. Men are eligible for the pathway if they are assessed as presenting a high or very high risk of serious harm to others at any point during their sentence and are also likely to have a severe personality disorder for which there is a clinically justifiable link with that person's risk. The criteria for women are as the same as for men but without the necessity to be high risk (Skett et al., 2017). The four high-level outcomes that are the aims of the OPD pathway are reducing repeat serious offences, improving the psychological well-being of offenders, producing a competent and trained workforce, and using resources efficiently (Skett et al., 2017).

A key element of the pathway framework is a recognition that working with personality disordered offenders is the responsibility of both criminal justice and health services. Offenders with personality disorders who present a high-risk to the public will primarily be managed by the offender manager working in conjunction with psychologically trained staff. At the heart of the offender pathway is a request of offender managers to engage in a challenging process of change in the way they think about and carry out their work, particularly where difference may emerge between traditional risk management strategies and psychologically informed approaches to risk management (Harvey & Ramsden, 2017). Key to this is developing the skills and understanding of the offender manager to draw out key events and their significance and meaning in an individual's life history. This involves creating a safe containing space (Harvey & Ramsden, 2017). These formulations are then used to better manage interactions and work with the offender, forming in some cases the basis of a sequenced plan of intervention, or in others simply a guide to cope with difficult exchanges (Cluley & Marston, 2018).

Harvey and Ramsden (2017, p. 21) identifies a number of essential principles that should underpin psychologically informed practice. These include:

- the development of the practitioners' understanding of, and ability to have, psychologically informed conversations with offenders;
- the development of practitioners' reflective capacity to facilitate a thoughtful, self-aware and non-reactive approach to offenders and case management decisions;
- the use of the process consultation model (Schein, 1988) acknowledging previously unseen aspects of a process or problem, including the roles and reactions of individuals and organisations;
- the focus on the 'organisational mind' and the augmentation of the reflective capacity of the systems around the men and women involved with the criminal justice system who present with challenging personality traits;
- the need for organisations, and the individuals in the organisations, to act as containers for emotion, as per the Knowledge and Understanding Framework (KUF) awareness training.

Working with high-risk service users with personality disorders presents a range of complex challenges for probation practitioners and can induce feelings of being "helpless and de-skilled, confused and hopeless" (Murphy & McVey, 2010 in Ramsden & Lowton, 2014, p. 150). The lives of many individuals who are in contact with the criminal justice system are often a result of unresolved past trauma and so the work can involve:

> bearing witness to someone's distress and trauma by working with them to try and work out how to build a safe relationship, distinct from those in the past that may have been traumatizing.
>
> *(Cluley & Marston, 2018, p. 90)*

Probation staff are therefore faced with a range of contradictions that involve, "being caring whilst detaining; knowing about early life trauma whilst managing a 'perpetrator'; meeting high levels of need and deprivation whilst managing high levels of risk" (Fellowes, 2018, p. 154). Caught between the non-compliance of service users and the system's reliance on custodial sanctions, practitioners and the influence of adverse familial and statutory relationships practitioners need to persevere in the face of chronic mistrust and paranoia, sometimes for years (Fellowes, 2018). Therefore, as valuable as psychologically informed practice is, it is also a challenging relational and emotional endeavour. If staff are to offer supervision attuned to service users' particular needs, then the wider system needs to afford the opportunity for this work to be both safe and sustainable (Fellowes, 2014). Research suggests that for workers in this field, emotional resilience, more effective outcomes and improved service delivery are all more likely within a structured and supportive organisational climate where staff possess high levels of professional competency (Shaw et al., 2011). However, in her small-scale of probation officers who worked as personality disorder leads on the OPDP, Fellowes (2018) found that the complexity of the work was not always acknowledged in the policies and procedures that govern the organisation of probation. As a result, government and partnership agencies failed to fully appreciate the needs of these service users or provide the resources to meet their psychosocial needs. Nevertheless, the introduction of the pathway was welcomed by practitioners for the skills and the psychological support it offered (Fellowes, 2018, p. 164).

The benefits and challenges of working in partnership with a different organisation and organisational culture were also found by Ramsden et al. (2016). Utilising real-life case examples and qualitative data from focus groups, the authors highlighted some of the innovative practice developments that have emerged from this formulation-led psychologically informed way of working. Similarly, with regard to the PIPEs, early evidence suggests that this is an effective model for achieving a high-quality relational environment where residents feel better equipped to deal with impulsive behaviours and challenging interactions (Turley et al., 2013). Whilst these findings are encouraging and appear to support the aims of the pathway, Ramsden et al. (2016) warn that there is still work to be undertaken to ensure that the psychologically informed theory and principles that underpin this approach are meaningfully applied to traditional probation procedures.

Concerns have also been raised that recent changes to the organisational structure of the probation service have undermined the operationalisation of the pathways. As part of the governments *Transforming Rehabilitation* reforms (Ministry of Justice, 2013), the probation service was split into two parts. The National Probation Service (NPS) works directly with the Courts and victims and manage high-risk offenders, and the 21 new privately owned Community Rehabilitation Companies (CRCs) manage and deliver rehabilitation interventions to all low and medium risk offenders, both on community sentences and on licence after release from prison. These new structures have been criticised for needlessly fragmenting service provision with inherent difficulties of co-ordination and communication and have negatively impacted upon staff morale in the probation service (Kirton & Guillaume, 2015; Robinson et al., 2016; Burke et al., 2017). There is a further challenge of co-ordination in that these new structures are also not coterminous with NHS commissioning teams in NHS Clinical Commissioning Groups (CCGs) (Brooker, 2015).

Nichols et al. (2016) claim that because there is no remit for involvement through the pathways with those individuals identified as medium- or low-risk and supervised by the Community Rehabilitation Companies, this has narrowed the focus of the pathways to those deemed to be high-risk and as such under the supervision of the National Probation Service. This could reduce the number of those screened for personality disorders and, as the authors warn, could be seen as another failing in the way that risk is conceptualised within Transforming Rehabilitation in that the division of organisational responsibilities fails to acknowledge the dynamic nature of the behaviours involved and that individuals assessed as low or medium risk can and do sometimes go on to commit serious violent and sexual offences. This could undermine the government's intention, embodied in the pathway framework, to provide a consistent and coherent series of health interventions across both custodial and community settings and in doing so negatively impact on the equity of service provision.

Conclusion

Both the MHTR and the OPDP can be viewed as positive developments in terms of addressing the needs of those offenders under the supervision of the probation service in the community even if the potential of either initiative has not yet been fully realised. Both are grounded in notions of effective multi-agency collaboration, which is essential to successful rehabilitation given the complex nature of the psychological, social and forensic problems presented by those subject to community supervision. However, at a more fundamental level, there is, and there has been for some time, a strong argument for diversion, that is, to take individuals with mental health issues, where appropriate, out of criminal justice contexts and link them up with other community facilities. Operating at the interface between criminal justice and mental health services, liaison and diversion services could play an essential part in ensuring that the mental health needs of those in contact with, or at risk of entering, the criminal justice system are identified or addressed. It is of course equally imperative that local commissioning bodies and authorities ensure that there are adequate and appropriate services available in local areas that offenders can be diverted to (Scott & Moffatt,

2012, p. 8). However, as Pakes and Winstone (2012) note, despite a steady stream of Home Office circulars and reports provision remains patchy and piecemeal. The government intends to extend NHS England liaison and diversion services from 50% population coverage to 75% by 2018 (GOV.UK, 2018). The concern is that these encouraging developments, working alongside the MHTR and OPDP will be undermined by the on-going organisational turbulence regarding the delivery of community sentences in the wake of the Transforming Rehabilitation reforms. Current plans to address them (Ministry of Justice, 2018) do not inspire confidence – persisting as they do with a model of private-sector outsourcing that has at best been problematic.

References

Bourne, R., Rajput, R., & Field, R. (2015). Working with probation services and mentally disordered offenders. *BJPsych Advances, 21*(4), 273–280. doi: 10.1192/apt.bp.114.013342

Brooker, C. (2015). Healthcare and probation: The impact of government reforms. *Probation Journal, 62*(3), 268–272. doi: 10.1177/0264550515587971

Brooker, C., Sirdifield, C., Blizard, R., Denney, D., & Pluck, G. (2012). Probation and mental illness. *The Journal of Forensic Psychiatry & Psychology, 23*(4), 522–537. doi: 10.1080/14789949.2012.704640

Brooker, C., Sirdifield, C., Blizard, R., Maxwell-Harrison, D., Tetley, D., Moran, P., ... Turner, M. (2011) *An investigation into the prevalence of mental health disorder and patterns of health service access in a probation population*. Lincoln: University of Lincoln.

Burke, L., Millings, M., & Robinson, G. (2017). Probation migration(s): Examining occupational culture in a turbulent field. *Criminology & Criminal Justice, 17*(2), 192–208. doi: 10.1177/1748895816656905

Castel, R. (1991). 'From dangerousness to risk', in C. Gordon & P. Miller (eds), *The Foucault effect: Studies in governmentality*, 281–298. Hemel Hempstead: Harvester Wheatsheaf.

Cluley, E., & Marston, P. (2018). The value of 'bearing witness' to desistance: Two practitioners' responses. *Probation Journal, 65*(1), 89–96.

Cohen, A., Bishop, N., & Hegarty, M. (1999). Working in partnership with probation: The first two years of a mental health worker scheme in a probation service in Wandsworth. *Psychiatric Bulletin, 23*(7), 405–408. doi: 10.1192/pb.23.7.405

DiClemente, C. C., Nidecker, M., & Bellack, A. S. (2008). Motivation and the stages of change among individuals with severe mental illness and substance abuse disorders. *Journal of Substance Abuse Treatment, 34*(1), 25–35. doi: 10.1016/j.jsat.2006.12.034

Feeley, M. M., & Simon, J. (1992). The new penology: Notes on the emerging strategy of corrections and its implications*. *Criminology, 30*(4), 449–474. doi: 10.1111/j.1745-9125.1992.tb01112.x

Feeley, M., & Simon, J. (1994) 'Actuarial justice: The emerging new criminal law', in D. Nelken (ed), *The futures of criminology*, 173–201. London: SAGE.

Fellowes, E. (2014). 'What's needed as part of probation practice when working with personality disordered offenders? The importance of avoiding errors of logic' – A practitioner response. *Probation Journal, 61*(2), 192–199. doi: 10.1177/0264550514532155

Fellowes, E. (2018). The ultimate shock absorber: Probation officers' experience of working with male service users on the Offender Personality Disorder Pathway. *Probation Journal, 65*(2), 152–169.

Fitzgibbon, W., & Green, R. (2006). Mentally disordered offenders: Challenges in using the OASys risk assessment tool. *British Journal of Community Justice, 4*(2), 35–46. Retrieved from https://uhra.herts.ac.uk/dspace/bitstream/2299/876/1/103449.pdf

GOV.UK (2018) *£12 million to fund major expansion of services so more people who are arrested get a mental health assessment.* Retrieved from https://www.gov.uk/government/news/increased-mental-health-services-for-those-arrested (accessed 8 August 2018).

Harvey, D., & Ramsden, J. (2017). Contracting between professionals who work with offenders with personality disorder. *Probation Journal, 64*(1), 20–32. doi: 10.1177/0264550516677769

Khanom, H., Samele, C., Rutherford, M., & Sainsbury Centre for Mental Health. (2009). *A missed opportunity?: Community sentences and the mental health treatment requirement.* London: Sainsbury Centre for Mental Health. Retrieved from https://www.bl.uk/britishlibrary/~/media/bl/global/social-welfare/pdfs/non-secure/m/i/s/missed-opportunity-community-sentences-and-the-mental-health-treatment-requirement.pdf

Kirton, G., & Guillaume, C. (2015) *Employment relations and working conditions in probation after transforming rehabilitation: With a special focus on gender and union effects.* Centre for Research in Equality and Diversity School of Business and Management Queen Mary University of London. Retrieved from https://www.napo.org.uk/sites/default/files/BR%20112-2015%20Appendix%20A%20-%20Gill%20Kirton%20Report_0-2.pdf

Lloyd, M., & Bell, R. (2015). Editorial comment: Personality disorder in offenders then and now. *Prison Service Journal, 218,* 2–3. London: Centre for Crime and Justice.

Long, C. G., Dolley, O., & Hollin, C. (2018). The use of the mental health treatment requiremnt (MHTR): Clinical outcomes at one year of collaboration. *Journal of Criminal Psychology, 8*(3), 215–233.

Louden, J. E, Manchak, S. M., Ricks, P. E. and Kennealy, P. J. (2018). The role of stigma towards mental illness in probation officers' perceptions of risk and case management decisions. *Criminal Justice Behavior, 62*(3), 629–654.

Lurigio, A. J., Cho, Y. I., Swartz, J. A., Johnson, T. P., Graf, I., & Pickup, L. (2003). Standardized assessment of substance-related, other psychiatric, and comorbid disorders among probationers. *International Journal of Offender Therapy and Comparative Criminology, 47*(6), 630–652. doi: 10.1177/0306624X03257710

Mair, G., Mills, H., & Centre for Crime and Justice Studies (Great Britain). (2009). *The community order and the suspended sentence order three years on: The views and experiences of probation officers and offenders.* Retrieved from https://nls.ldls.org.uk/welcome.html?ark:/81055/vdc_100061262978.0x000001

McArt, D. (2013). Mental health conditions of offenders supervised by probation services. *Probation Journal, 60*(2), 191–192.

Ministry of Justice (2009). *Story of the prison population 1995–2009.* London: Stationary Office

Ministry of Justice (2011). *Offender Management Statistics Bulletin,* England and Wales. London: Ministry of Justice.

Ministry of Justice (2012). *Swift and sure justice: The government's plans for reform of.*

Ministry of Justice (2013). *Transforming rehabilitation: A revolution in the way we manage offenders.* London: Stationary Office.

Ministry of Justice (2018). *Strengthening probation, building confidence*. London: Ministry of Justice.

Minoudis, P., Shaw, J., Bannerman, A., & Craissati, J. (2011). Identifying personality disturbance in a London probation sample. *Probation Journal*, 59(1), 23–38. doi: 10.1177/0264550511429842

National Audit Office (2008). *National Probation Service: The supervision of community orders in England and Wales*. London: The Stationary Office.

Nichols, F., Dunster, C., & Beckley, K. (2016). Identifying personality disturbance in the Lincolnshire Personality Disorder Pathway: How do offenders compare to the London pilot? *Probation Journal*, 63(1), 41–53. doi: 10.1177/0264550515620691

NOMS (2014) *Mental health treatment requirements guidance on supporting integrated delivery*. London: NOMS.

O'Loughlin, A. (2014). The offender personality disorder pathway: Expansion in the face of failure? *The Howard Journal of Criminal Justice*, 53(2), 173–192. doi: 10.1111/hojo.12058

Pakes, F., & Winstone, J. (2012). 'The mental health treatment requirement: The promise and the practice', In A. Pycroft & S. Clift (Eds), *Risk and rehabilitation: Management and treatment of substance misuse and mental health problems in the criminal justice system* (pp. 107–118). Bristol: Bristol University Press. Retrieved from www.jstor.org/stable/j.ctt9qgz5r.10

Pilgrim, D. (2001). Disordered personalities and disordered concepts. *Journal of Mental Health*, 10(3), 253–265. doi: 10.1080/09638230125289

Ramsden, J., Joyes, E., Gordon, N., & Lowton, M. (2016). How working with psychologists has influenced probation practice: Attempting to capture some of the impact and the learning from the offender personality disorder pathway project. *Probation Journal*, 63(1), 54–71. doi: 10.1177/0264550515620694

Ramsden, J., & Lowton, M. (2014). Probation practice with personality disordered offenders: The importance of avoiding errors of logic. *Probation Journal*. doi: 10.1177/0264550514523815

Robinson, A. (2011). *Foundations for offender management: Theory, law and policy for contemporary practice* (1st ed.). doi: 10.2307/j.ctt1t894t2

Robinson, G., Burke, L., & Millings, M. (2016). Criminal justice identities in transition: The case of devolved probation services in England and Wales. *The British Journal of Criminology*, 56(1), 161–178. doi: 10.1093/bjc/azv036

Schein, L. (1988) *Process consultation: Its role in organizational development, Vol 1*. London: Prentice Hall.

Scott, G., & Moffatt, S. (2012). *The mental health treatment requirement: Realising a better future*. London: Centre for Mental Health.

Seddon, T. (2008) Dangerous Liasions: Personality disorder and the politics of risk. *Punishment and Society*, 10(3), 301–317.

Shaw, J., Minoudis, P., Hamilton, V., & Craissati, J. (2012). An investigation into competency for working with personality disorder and team climate in the probation service. *Probation Journal*, 59(1), 39–48. doi: 10.1177/0264550511429843

Singleton, N., Meltzer, H., & Gatward, R. (1998). *Psychiatric morbidity among prisoners in England and Wales*. London: HMSO.

Skeem, J. L., & Louden, J. E. (2006). Toward evidence-based practice for probationers and parolees mandated to mental health treatment. *Psychiatric Services (Washington, D.C.)*, 57(3), 333–342. doi: 10.1176/appi.ps.57.3.333

Skett, S., Goode, I., & Barton, S. (2017). A joint NHS and NOMS offender personality disorder pathway strategy: A perspective from 5 years of operation. *Criminal Behaviour and Mental Health*, 27(3), 214–221. doi: 10.1002/cbm.2026

Taylor, P. (2012). Severe personality disorder in the secure estate: Continuity and change. *Medicine, Science and the Law*, *52*(3), 125–127. doi: 10.1258/msl.2011.011112

Turley, C., Payne, C., & Webster, S. (2013). *Enabling features of psychologically informed planned environments*. London: Ministry of Justice.

Vaughan, P., & Stevenson, S. (2002). An opinion survey of mentally disordered offender service users. *The British Journal of Forensic Practice*, *4*(3), 11–20. doi: 10.1108/14636646200200017

Von Hirsch, A., & Roberts, J. V. (2004). Legislating sentencing principles: The provisions of the Criminal Justice Act 2003 relating to sentencing purposes and the role of previous convictions. *Criminal Law Review*. August, 639–652

6

UNEASY BEDFELLOWS

Imprisonment, mental health and public service austerity

Jane Senior

Mental health issues have been at the forefront of political, practice and media debates around imprisonment since reformer John Howard's eighteenth-century examination of the state of prisons in the UK and Europe.

First, this chapter will provide a brief historical review of the prison-based treatment of mental health issues centred around England and Wales, the expansion and increased plurality of service provision achieved over the last two decades through partnership with the National Health Service (NHS), including prevalence of disorder, ways to meet the needs of discrete populations, for example, older prisoners and former military personnel, and the challenges of ensuring a continuum of care between prison and the community. Second, the chapter will critically consider the current state of mental healthcare in prisons in the context of the sustained public sector austerity agenda and other similar policy and societal influences, and the challenges faced by practitioners and managers to improve individual and public health outcomes for this disadvantaged and marginalised community.

The history of mental healthcare in prisons

Early days

The role that prisons have played in the detention and 'care' of the mentally ill first came properly to public attention in 1777 when social reformer John Howard published *The State of the Prisons in England and Wales*, highlighting neglect and disinterest by gaolers and a sense of moral decay and idleness pervading prison institutions. Howard blamed an unsuitable population mix within the prisons as contributing to the problem whereby children, petty thieves and the mentally disordered were housed with the most experienced offenders – the mentally disordered often unintentionally providing a source of amusement for other prisoners (Howard, 1777).

During the nineteenth-century efforts were made to remove some of the most obviously mentally disordered from prison, notably through the opening in 1861 of a separate wing for criminal lunatics at the Bethlem Hospital, London, followed in 1863 by the opening of Broadmoor criminal lunatic asylum. However, this initiative did not herald an end to the detention of the mentally disordered in prison as, contemporaneously, special provision was being created within the prison system for those who were not to be transferred to hospital. Thus, in 1864, the population of mentally disordered prisoners housed at Dartmoor prison was transferred to Millbank Penitentiary in London and, in 1897, Parkhurst prison was used to house prisoners assessed as "unfit for ordinary penal discipline because of some mental instability other than insanity" (cited in Gunn, 1985). In 1895, the Report of the Gladstone Committee recommended that all prison medical officers be experienced in the subject of lunacy, thus acknowledging the likelihood of the mentally disordered remaining a significant presence in prisons.

As the twentieth century unfolded, prison medical officers began publishing case studies of mentally disordered prisoners in their care, and judicial interest in the possibility of facilitating treatment for this group, instead of imposing punishment, began. In the 1920s and 1930s the medical officer of HMP Birmingham, Dr Hamblin-Smith, recommended the establishment of treatment units within prisons and, in 1939, the visiting psychotherapist to HMP Wormwood Scrubs, Dr W.H. Hubert, and a prison medical officer, Dr Norwood East, recommended the establishment of a special penal institution with a psychiatric emphasis to ascertain the value of psychological treatment in the 'prevention and cure' of crime. Delayed until 1962, Hubert and East's recommendations were fulfilled with the opening of HMP Grendon Underwood therapeutic community prison. Hamblin-Smith later concluded that, because of their punitive ethos, prisons were, in fact, unsuitable environments for proper therapeutic interventions (Gunn, *op cit.*).

During this period, belief in the need for medical intervention with mentally disordered prisoners took hold, and the Prison Medical Service expanded rapidly, employing full and part-time medical officers. The role of hospital officer was instigated in 1899. These men were drawn from the ranks of the discipline officers and provided with a brief general healthcare training (Bluglass, 1990). While there was concern about the physical health of prisoners, it was acknowledged that the vast majority of a prison medical officer's work concerned mental disorder, with the main emphasis being placed on diagnosis and the provision of reports to courts rather than on the provision of treatment (Grounds, 1994). When the NHS was established in 1948, it did not cover the care provided to prisoners; rather, the Prison Medical Service remained a discrete entity, located within the Home Office.

In the latter part of the twentieth century, the Prison Medical Service was the subject of much public criticism concerning the numbers of suicides in prisons, alleged inappropriate use of psychotropic medication as a disciplinary aid for refractory prisoners, and poor overall standards of care (Ralli, 1994). The service was also criticised for being "invisible" and lacking any external accountability (Smith, 1984).

The future organisation of prison healthcare and beyond

The separation of healthcare for prisoners from the wider population of England and Wales began to be robustly challenged in the closing decade of the twentieth century. The overarching recommendation of the discussion paper *Patient or Prisoner?* (HMCIP, 1996) was that the NHS should assume overall, national, responsibility for the delivery of healthcare in prisons, based on the concept of equivalence, whereby it was acknowledged that:

> prisoners are entitled to the same level of health care as that provided in society at large. Those who are sick, addicted, mentally ill or disabled should be treated... to the same standards demanded within the National Health Service.
> *(HMCIP, 1996)*

The report noted that current care provision was out-dated, lacked continuity with community services and delivered by a professionally isolated workforce. Despite this, care was more than twice as expensive, per person, than that provided by the NHS for the wider community.

In the following year, the Health Advisory Committee for the Prison Service published a report on the specific topic of the provision of mental healthcare in prisons (HAC, 1997) which noted that the prison population was, in fact, a subset of the population as a whole and, as such, health policies and priorities set for the wider community should apply equally in prisons. Although less weight was given to the earlier recommendation that healthcare be wholly transferred to the NHS, the emphasis was placed on the need for the Prison Service and NHS to develop a joint policy on mental healthcare, to ensure broad consistency in terms of access to services, and quality and variety of provision.

In response to the challenge to improve services, *The Future Organisation of Prison Healthcare* (HMPS & NHS Executive, 1999) set out a roadmap for progress. The document accepted that, historically, healthcare in prisons was:

> often reactive rather than proactive, over-medicalised and only exceptionally based on systematic health needs assessment... (with an) over reliance on healthcare beds within prisons and a medicalised model of care.
> *(HMPS & NHS Executive, 1999)*

The document set out a future partnership arrangement, comprising HM Prison Service, adopting "a more collaborative and coordinated approach with the

NHS, supported by a recognised and formal duty of partnership" (ibid). The recommendation of a formal partnership fell short of earlier calls which overwhelmingly supported a move of prison healthcare services to be wholly within the NHS. However, it was argued that a partnership arrangement was, in fact, a more pragmatic approach to effecting change, allowing the experience of each agency to be drawn upon in a complex work programme.

Of particular relevance in the current context, the developmental needs for mental healthcare were later specifically encompassed in a document outlining a joint Department of Health/HM Prison Service approach to mental health policy, *Changing the Outlook* (DH/HMPS, 2001). The document focussed on a number of strands of work, including the need to improve staff training, peer support schemes and an emphasis on developing *"healthy prisons"*; improving mental health provision at primary care level; the development of wing-based services, known as in-reach, utilising a community mental health team model; the development of daycare services as an alternative to in-patient care; improvements in systems to transfer prisoners to hospital to minimise delays; and improving through-care and discharge planning to ensure that prisoners are discharged with appropriate aftercare plans.

Broadly speaking, the partnership arrangement set out in 1999 is the model still operational across the prison estate. Certain changes have occurred over time, perhaps most notably that budgets for prison-based healthcare and the direct commissioning of services now sit within NHS England. Another important development, perhaps unanticipated in 1999, has been the degree to which commercial healthcare providers now provide prison-based healthcare services. The impact of these and related developments will be discussed in the latter part of this chapter.

Prevalence of mental disorder

Prison-based mental health services have always dealt with higher levels of prevalence, for all types of disorder, than are found in the communities from which prisoners are drawn. This is true worldwide.

The last comprehensive prevalence study of psychiatric morbidity in prisoners in England and Wales is now over two decades old (Singleton et al., 1998). Using the same methodology as a contemporaneous study of psychiatric morbidity in the general population, researchers interviewed 3,142 prisoners across the 131 prisons open in England and Wales at the time. The study reported that prevalence rates for any functional psychosis over the past year ranged from 7% in the male, sentenced population, to 14% in the female population. Using an algorithm devised to calculate 'probable psychosis' in the whole population, it was suggested that 21% of the female remand population would probably have a psychotic disorder, as would 10% of the sentenced female population, 9% of male remands and 4% of male sentenced prisoners. Seventy-eight per cent of the male remand population and 50% of the female population were diagnosed as having a personality disorder. The most prevalent was antisocial personality disorder, identified in 63% of male remand prisoners and 31% of female prisoners.

With regard to neuroses, all types of prisoners returned high rates of symptoms such as sleep problems and worry. In common with findings from general household studies, women were significantly more likely to be positive for neurotic disorder and rates in remand prisoners were higher than those for the sentenced population. Seventeen per cent of male remand prisoners and 21% of female remand prisoners were diagnosed as experiencing a current depressive episode. Eleven per cent of both male and female remand prisoners were experiencing Generalised Anxiety Disorder.

However, it would seem to be the case that, due to the breadth of the survey, a close examination of overall prevalence rates is required if they are to inform policy decisions regarding the provision of treatment services usefully. For example, only 5% of male and 4% of female remand prisoners were not diagnosed with any form of mental disorder at all, but many prisoners were diagnosed only with disorders where motivation for change and a desire for treatment are vital, for example, personality disorder and substance misuse, so not all such prisoners would make demands for treatment. Similarly, disorders such as depressive episodes were not detailed in terms of severity; thus no judgement could be made as to how many prisoners would require intervention from services provided within prison settings, and/or at what level, nor how many would require transfer to NHS facilities.

Placing the findings of Singleton and colleagues into an international context, Fazel and Danesh (2002) completed a systematic review of surveys published on the prevalence rates of serious mental disorders in the prison populations of western countries. Studies with randomly selected prisoner participants which included diagnoses, made by clinical examination or examiners using diagnostic instruments, of psychosis or major depression within the previous six months were selected for inclusion. Diagnoses of substance abuse were excluded. Sixty-two studies from 12 countries were included, together with surveying the mental health of 22,790 prisoners, 81% of whom were male.

The results showed that 3.7% of men had psychotic illnesses, 10% major depression and 65% a personality disorder, including 47% with an antisocial personality disorder. In the sample of women, 4% had psychotic illnesses, 12% major depression and 42% a personality disorder, including 21% with an antisocial personality disorder. Significantly higher rates of psychosis were found in studies completed in the United States of America than those completed elsewhere. Studies showed substantial heterogeneity, but only a small proportion of this difference was explicable in terms of whether the sample populations were convicted or unconvicted prisoners.

Overall, the writers concluded that about one in seven western prisoners had psychotic illnesses or major depression, and about half of male and a fifth of female prisoners had antisocial personality disorders. These rates were greater than those found in the general population, by between two and four times for psychosis or major depression, and around ten times in terms of antisocial personality disorder. The authors concluded that these prevalence rates meant that there was a substantial burden of treatable mental disorder in prisons which, due to current limited resources, was likely to be inadequately addressed.

Since the seminal Singleton et al. study, the prevalence of mental disorder in prisons in England and Wales has been touched upon in some other pieces of smaller-scale research. One of the largest was conducted by Senior et al. (2013) as part of an evaluation of prison mental health in-reach services. The study sample comprised 3,492 prisoners and the researchers concluded that 23% had a serious mental illness, defined as a current episode of major depressive disorder, bipolar disorder and/or any form of psychosis. However, more importantly, the study identified that in-reach teams, the service heralded in the 2001 *Changing the Outlook* policy document as the main vehicle for improvement in for those with serious mental illness, assessed only 25% of these unwell prisoners, and accepted just 13% onto their caseload. The reasons behind this failure are many and complex but highlight the difficulties inherent in service innovation in this area (Senior et al., 2013).

Since these studies were conducted, the National Liaison and Diversion programme, led by NHS England, has been rolled out across most of England. Liaison and diversion services briefly described consist of mental health professionals embedded in police stations and some court settings to assess suspects, defendants or offenders with the aim of initiating contact with mental health services, where indicated, as early as possible into a person's criminal justice journey. Referrals to mental, substance misuse and/or social care services may involve people being diverted away from the criminal justice system into a more appropriate setting or may result in a different justice outcome, for example, community sentencing with support rather than imprisonment (NHSE & NHS Improvement, 2019). To date, although the early days of the liaison and diversion service model have been evaluated (Disley et al., 2016) it is too early to conclude whether it will have any impact on reducing the number of people with mental illness in prison custody and thus, the logical presumption is that prevalence rates remain significantly high and will be so for the foreseeable future.

Suicide and self-harm in prison

In prisons in England and Wales, men are five times, and women twenty times more likely to die by suicide than their counterparts in the general population (Fazel, Benning, & Danesh, 2005; Fazel & Benning, 2009). Rates of self-harm are similarly high; in the 12 months to September 2018, there were 52,814 reported incidents of self-harm across all prisons in England and Wales, an increase of 23% from the previous year (MoJ, 2019a). Self-harm and eventual suicide are closely related; a systematic review found that around 50% of those who died by suicide in prison custody had a history of self-harm (Fazel et al., 2008). A more recent study reported that 5–6% of male prisoners, and 20–24% of female prisoners, self-harmed every year and that a history of self-harm was positively associated with subsequent suicide in the prison setting (Hawton et al., 2014). Correspondingly, the Prisons and Probation Ombudsman (PPO) reported that, between 2012 and 2014, 70% of prisoners who died by suicide had mental health needs (PPO, 2016).

Suicide and self-harm identification and management are core tasks for prison staff from all professions. In 2005, the current system of risk identification and management – Assessment, Care in Custody and Teamwork (ACCT) – was rolled out across the English and Welsh prison estate, and what followed was an almost decade-long reduction in self-inflicted deaths (Shaw et al., 2013). In contrast to earlier systems, ACCT is based on personalised risk assessment and care planning and encourages staff to work collaboratively with at-risk individuals to pro-actively address issues which are contributing to their risk. The ACCT system is widely used; in 2017, over 48,000 case documents were opened (MoJ, 2018). Despite this, the majority of people who die by suicide in prison custody are not being managed under ACCT procedures at the time of their death, highlighting problems with the accurate identification of those at highest risk (PPO, 2016).

The most recent research into self-inflicted deaths in prisons in England and Wales and the ACCT system (Wainwright et al., 2020) highlighted ongoing concerns around safety in prison. The study collected health, social and criminogenic data on 286 self-inflicted deaths which occurred between 2016 and 2018. The majority of deaths were men (94%), of white ethnicity (87%), and sentenced (67%). Hanging (86%) was the most common method of death. This remains little changed from previous research in this area (Shaw et al., 2013), indicating a continued need to address risks in the physical environment. In contrast to the earlier study, a greater proportion of deaths occurred within the first week (16% vs 11%) or first month (26% vs 22%), highlighting that this is an extremely stressful and risky period for vulnerable people (ibid). Echoing the findings of the PPO (2016), only just over a third (35%) of this sample were considered at risk of suicide, as indicated by being cared for under ACCT procedures, at the time of death.

As part of the Wainwright et al. study, a total of 337 closed ACCT documents were audited from across 37 prisons in England and Wales. The audit revealed issues with a number of the fundamental requirements of the ACCT process. Issues included CAREMAPs (the individual care plan) not having been completed in 27% of cases, missing physical observations in 30% of cases and no evidence of a mental health assessment in 61%. Limited involvement of a person's family and friends was evident, with contact only made in 16% of instances. In just under a quarter (24%) of cases no post-closure interview was documented, a procedure designed to check on a person's welfare and reassess risk soon after the extra care and support offered during ACCT ends.

There is a substantial body of evidence around suicide and self-harm risks in custodial settings and little of it is contradictory or counter-intuitive. Prisons import people with established vulnerabilities in terms of risk of harm to self and have repeatedly failed to identify those risks early enough or systematically enough. When ACCT was rolled out, its implementation was supported by a comprehensive training package for staff and its operation was closely monitored by specialist Safer Custody staff in all establishments. Such a task is obviously labour intensive and requires the goodwill of both frontline staff and managers. While conducting their research, Wainwright and colleagues witnessed staff under pressure attempting to operate the ACCT system effectively, hampered by limited resources in terms of staff numbers and time to engage with at-risk individuals, compounded by a lack of access to training and support. These themes will be picked up later in this chapter.

Discrete challenges – older people and former armed forces personnel

Older people

Until recently, the prison was routinely viewed as a young man's domain, with troubled and anti-social youths "graduating" into an adult life of crime. Conversely, there are theories around how and why older adults, for complex and inter-connected reasons, appear to 'grow out of' criminality (Maruna, 1999; Richards, 2011). However, older people are now the fastest-growing demographic in prison in England and Wales.

The growing issue of older people in prison was first formally recognised by HM Chief Inspector of Prisons in their thematic review *No Problems – Old and Quiet* (2004), the title reflecting an entry found in an elderly prisoner's discipline record exemplifying the then stereotype of a quiet, helpful, older prisoner whose needs could easily be overlooked as staff dealt with the more acute and visible needs of younger prisoners. However, since the proportion of older prisoners in the prison population continues to rise, this stereotype is now being challenged by a growing body of research showing that they can have serious health, social and custodial needs which often go unidentified and unmet in the prison setting.

As of March 2019, there were 82,634 people in prison in England and Wales; of these 16% were older prisoners, defined as over 50 years old. Those aged 60+ are the fastest-growing group, followed by those aged 50–60. Between 2011 and 2019, the number of older male prisoners has increased from 3,038 to 4,930 aged over 60 years and 8,899 to 13,061 over 50 years. At the same time, the number of women over 60 has increased from 79 to 128, while those over 50 has increased from 397 to 559 (MoJ, 2019b). This growth is attributable in part to an overall ageing population but also increases in sentence length and the rise in historical sexual convictions (Howse, 2011). This substantial, and increasing, demographic presents discrete challenges in terms of delivering safe, rehabilitative imprisonment, a meaningful regime of age-appropriate activity and the provision of an environment in which health and social care needs can be addressed.

In terms of healthcare provision, it is widely accepted that older people in prison have greater levels of physical and mental health morbidity than both younger prisoners and an age-matched general population sample. Fazel and colleagues (2001a) reported that at least 85% of male prisoners aged over 60 years old had one or more major illnesses reported in their medical records, and 83% reported at least one chronic illness on interview. The most common illnesses were psychiatric, cardiovascular, musculoskeletal and respiratory. A more recent Ministry of Justice study reported that 31% of older people newly received into prison reported needing help with a medical problem, compared to 14% of younger prisoners (Omelade, 2014).

Although mental health and physical needs are significant in this group, there is a body of evidence confirming that such needs routinely remain unrecognised, or unmet, in practice. Fazel et al. (2001b), in their sample of 203 men in prison over the age of 60, identified through psychiatric interview one or more psychiatric illness in 108 individuals (53%). Importantly, while 30% of the sample had a diagnosis of clinical depression, only 12% of those were being prescribed anti-depressant medication.

More recent research, based on clinical interviews using standardised diagnostic instruments, estimated the rate of dementia and mild cognitive impairment in prisons in England and Wales to be 7%, which would equate to around 953 individuals at current population levels. The prison prevalence rate was approximately 2.5 times higher for those aged 60–69 and six times higher for those 70+, compared to the general community. In terms of under-recognition, only two people (3%) identified by researchers as likely having dementia or mild cognitive impairment had a relevant diagnosis recorded in their healthcare notes. This finding was augmented by an accompanying survey of all adult prisons regarding current practice in this area in which healthcare managers ($n = 77$), representing 71% of all adult prisons in England and Wales ($n = 109$) reported a cumulative figure of 198 people either referred for assessment or with an established diagnosis of dementia or mild cognitive impairment; this represents a significant under-representation of the issue; logically under-identification leads to under-treatment with people leading unnecessarily impoverished lives (Forsyth et al., 2020).

The challenge faced by policymakers and operational management and staff to improve the identification and subsequent care pathways for older people in prison is huge. Many prisons in the United Kingdom operate in buildings which date from the Victorian era or before. Such establishments are often in city centres, offering little or no opportunity to extend or build more suitable accommodation. Other prisons run in repurposed buildings, for example, former army barracks – buildings again designed to house able young men. Capital investment is needed to improve the built environment in most prisons for this purpose, including wheelchair accessible rooms, modified shower rooms with safety features, wings and housing units with no stairs to negotiate and highly visible signage.

In terms of better identifying dementia, prison-based services need meaningful links with community-based NHS assessment and treatment services. Equally importantly, local authority social care agencies need to fulfil their obligations under the Care Act (2014) which introduced a statutory framework for the delivery of social care in prisons (HM Government, 2014). Health and social care services for prisoners need to be *equivalent* to those available in the community and innovation is required to meet that objective. For example, many prisons already employ peer carers to assist frail elderly prisoners with day-to-day living tasks which fall short of the delivery of intimate, personal care. Prison staff need to proactively ensure that peer carers are appropriately trained and supervised in the conduct of their duties, to prevent the potential for abuse of vulnerable people and to assure the quality of the care being delivered.

As the number of older prisoners grows and if, as it should, the recognition of conditions such as dementia and mild cognitive impairment improves leading to more people receiving individualised health and social care plans, there is an urgent task for politicians and policy-makers to support governors, prison discipline staff and health and social care workers to innovate around how older prisoners are managed. Logical first steps to improvement include the further development of wings/discrete housing units for older prisoners; increased use of Release on Temporary Licence (ROTL) to suitable family or care home settings; and/or the development of a network of secure nursing/care homes, based on a model akin to regional medium secure units for mentally disordered offenders. Any reconfiguration of existing prison places and/or the development of new units is likely to require significant capital and ongoing investment.

Former armed forces personnel in prison

Former armed forces personnel, although less likely to offend than the general population, are the largest single occupational group within the prison system, with estimates of them comprising between 3.5 and 16.75% of the population of English and Welsh prisons (Howard League, 2011). In the absence of central recording upon first reception into custody of whether a person has a military background, different study methodologies account for the wide estimate range; the highest estimate is based on the findings of a Ministry of Defence study but should be treated with caution due to the very small scale, highly localised nature of the data collection.

Military mental health outwith the prison system has been examined in detail by the King's Centre for Military Health Research at King's College, London, through their extensive programme of longitudinal research. For example, Iversen et al. (2005) found that the most common diagnoses for ex-armed forces personnel in the community were for depressive episodes and anxiety disorders. Later research established that deployment was significantly associated with alcohol misuse, and combat personnel were more likely to report probable PTSD (Fear et al., 2010). Relevant to the current discussion about ex-military personnel in prison, pre-enlistment vulnerabilities such as poor family relationships and fighting at school have been found to be important determinants of the mental health of serving personnel. Iversen et al. (2007) reported that pre-enlistment vulnerability was associated with several negative health outcomes including general psychological ill-health, PTSD and alcohol use. A pre-enlistment vulnerability was also associated with having served in the Army at a lower rank, being single and having low educational attainment. The vulnerabilities for poor mental health in military personnel are thus very similar to the risk factors for engagement in criminal activity and subsequent imprisonment more widely (Tanner-Smith, Wilson, & Lipsy, 2012).

With regards to former military personnel in prison, a study undertaken across six prisons in England and Wales by Wainwright and colleagues was the first UK research to specifically identify the mental health needs, pathways to offending and barriers to receiving treatment of this group. In total 105 individuals, whose military service had been verified, took part in the study, having their mental health status assessed using a range of validated assessment tools and their offending histories recorded as fully as possible. Forty-three (41%) participants self-reported having a common mental health problem; however, of these, only 20 (47%) said that they were currently receiving treatment in prison, and a further 8 (19%) stated they were on a waiting list. In the healthcare records of participants, 39 (37%) had a mental health diagnosis recorded; the most common primary diagnoses recorded were PTSD ($n = 17$, 16%), depression ($n = 12$, 11%) and personality disorder ($n = 5$, 5%). Using the study measures, 40 (38%) participants screened positively for a current common mental health problem. Having a current mental health problem was significantly associated with being single, having low social contact, having money problems before prison and the types of pre-service vulnerabilities noted earlier (Wainwright et al., 2017a).

Substance misuse pre-custody was also prevalent in this group. Over half (56%) scored positively on a scale to measure harmful alcohol use and 28% on the scale for drug misuse. Those who screened positive for alcohol misuse were significantly more likely to be younger, single, have served as a Private (or equivalent rank) and to have had a shorter length of service than those without a diagnosis. Similarly, drug abuse was significantly associated with those who were younger, had served as a Private (or equivalent), to have served shorter service lengths and to report unemployment and limited social contact prior to entering prison (ibid.).

Of the whole sample ($n = 105$), around a third (32%) had committed violent offences and 28% sexual offences. The remainder had committed a range of acquisitive, drug-related and other miscellaneous offences. Thirty-eight participants (36%) reported having offended during their time in the armed forces; 10 (10%) had spent time in military prison. Violent behaviour prior to service was reported by more than half the sample with a high proportion (57%) reporting fighting often at school. Those with violent index offences were more likely to have had their service terminated, or to have been discharged than those with sexual or any other type of offences. Violent offenders were also more likely to have screened positively for alcohol misuse in the year before entering prison and to have offended prior to service in the armed forces. In terms of their current offence, 31 (30%) and 15 (14%) participants reported that they considered alcohol or drugs respectively as a contributing factor. Sexual offenders were significantly older than others and more likely to have offended at an older age (Wainwright et al., 2017b). Thus, while less likely to offend overall than the general public, ex-armed service personnel when imprisoned are more likely to have been convicted of violent or sexual offences than the prison population overall; for the prison population as a whole, 26% and 18% are imprisoned for violent and sexual offences, respectively (Sturge, 2019). This increased risk of violent and sexual offending has implications for mental health treatment services in terms of ensuring adequate, dynamic risk assessment and management strategies form a core part of treatment plans and self-help strategies.

From prison to community

As noted earlier, the prevalence of serious mental illness among prisoners is significantly higher than in the general population, and initiatives to improve prison-based mental health services have met with limited success, with the majority of people with serious mental illness remaining unidentified and/or untreated (Senior et al., 2013).

It is equally, if not, even more, challenging to engage people with appropriate mental health services upon release from prison, as efforts are compounded by the fact that people with criminal justice system (CJS) involvement frequently live challenging and chaotic lives and, as a result, may be more familiar with only engaging with healthcare services at times of crisis. A study conducted in the USA examined rates of hospitalisation and emergency department use by non-incarcerated individuals with CJS involvement and found significantly higher rates of both types of healthcare usage, compared to the general population. The study concluded that while CJS involved individuals made up only 4.2% of the US adult population, they accounted for 7.2% and 8.5% of hospital and emergency department expenditure respectively. Such use of non-routine services is costly and has inferior individual and public health outcomes compared to sustained engagement with routine services (Frank et al., 2014).

In the UK context, Lennox et al. (2012) reported rates of engagement with community mental health teams (CMHT) for those who had been under the care of specialist mental health services in prison. Of 20 people released from prison, for whom a CMHT was contacted directly and a referral made by a prison-based clinician, only four (20%) had been in touch with the CMHT in the first-month post-release. Of these, three had future appointments planned and one had informed the team that he did not wish to engage. An associated qualitative study examined this failure of engagement in further detail, identifying a mismatch between the priorities of prisoners and mental health professionals. Upon release, prisoners' priorities included issues such as accommodation, family relationships and financial and vocational matters rather than mental health treatment. The study concluded that to be successful, discharge planning for people with serious mental illness needs to be holistic, focussing not just on clinical issues, but also the wider determinants of social stability and long-term community tenure, such as substance use management, housing and employment (Bowen, Rogers, & Shaw, 2009).

To test this theory, Shaw and colleagues identified a particular case management approach, Critical Time Intervention (CTI), originally developed in the USA to support formally homeless people upon their discharge from psychiatric in-patient care (https://www.criticaltime.org/). In the original trials, the intervention had been shown to reduce the number of nights a person spent homeless after discharge, compared to treatment as usual (Herman et al., 2011). CTI is a holistic, time-limited, model of intensive case management which focuses on linking patients with standard community mental health and social support services. When individuals are firmly linked with local services, CTI ends. There are clear similarities between the original intended recipients, homeless people with mental illness, and discharged prisoners with SMI in terms of difficulties engaging with services and the risks inherent with the transition from one setting to another, including risks for suicide, homelessness or clinical relapse.

Adaptations to the model were made to suit its delivery in the UK setting and, following an encouraging pilot study (Jarrett et al., 2012), a full randomised controlled trial was undertaken. Briefly, the intervention consists of a prison-based mental health clinician maintaining contact with the person for a limited number of weeks following release. During that time, the clinician accompanies the person to appointments with community-based mental health services; works proactively to secure appropriate accommodation, financial support, work, education or other meaningful activity; and supports the person to re-establish contact with family, where possible.

The trial was conducted across eight English prisons; in total, 150 people with serious mental illness were randomised to the intervention ($n = 72$) or treatment as usual ($n = 78$). The main outcome measure was continued engagement with mental health services. At six weeks post-release, the people who had received the intervention were significantly more likely to be in contact with community mental health services than those who had received treatment as usual (53% vs 27%). The difference was maintained at six months' follow-up, but not sustained one-year post-release. Also, at six weeks, those who were in the intervention group were significantly more likely to be registered with a general practitioner, further stenting their links with routine, rather than emergency health services. Because of the increased number of contacts with clinicians experienced by those in the intervention group, CTI was more expensive per patient than treatment as usual. A longer-term evaluation is required to examine whether the additional costs are offset elsewhere, for example by a reduction in offending, or through less use of expensive emergency healthcare including ambulances and accident and emergency departments (Shaw et al., 2017).

What was clear from the study was that both patients and staff were positive about the benefits of the intervention. Patients reported feeling supported by staff attending appointments with them, in contrast to previous negative experiences when they had felt judged, and that mental health workers had not believed them or did not want to engage with potentially unreliable patients. Staff felt that the holistic model was more effective than a more limited emphasis on just establishing a diagnosis and concentrating solely on achieving adherence to medication (Lennox et al., 2020). The research evidence for the model is encouraging and it should be considered by those commissioning and proving services to this vulnerable group although, as discussed later, reduced public sector funding for such innovation is likely to be a barrier to implementation.

Prison healthcare in an era of public austerity

In 2010, the newly elected coalition government of the Conservative and Liberal Democratic parties embarked upon a programme of financial austerity, reducing central government grants to local and regional councils and significantly reducing the budgets of central government departments, directly affecting a range of public services, including police, fire and prison and probation services. When the Conservatives were elected as the sole party of government in 2015, austerity measures persisted.

Central government funding to the police service fell by 25% between 2010/2011 and 2015/2016; by March 2015, the total police workforce had been reduced by approximately 34,400 (14%). The majority of these staff, around 22,000, were police officers (Mann, Devendran, & Lundrigan, 2018). A number of negative trends in crime and detection correlated with the cuts to police budgets, for example, the proportion of investigations resulting in a suspect being charged or summoned to court has reduced by 9% and detection rates for homicide fell to 83% in 2010–2011 to 67% by 2017–2018 (Guardian, 2019).

Amid the cost-saving drive, fundamental changes to probation services were implemented in 2014 by the then Justice Minister Chris Grayling. *Transforming rehabilitation: A strategy for reform* (MoJ, 2013) paved the way for the community supervision of offenders to be partly privatised, whereby the National Probation Service supervised only high-risk offenders and several private providers oversaw low- and medium-risk offenders. In 2019, following sustained criticism of the "reforms", citing issues such as significant increases in people being recalled to prison, a 22% overall increase in the number of proven reoffences per reoffender between 2011 and March 2017, and the failure of Through The Gate resettlement initiatives (National Audit Office, 2019), Justice Minister David Gauke announced that all community supervision would be brought back under the auspices of the National Probation Service by 2021, requiring the early termination of contracts with the private sector at increased cost to the public purse.

Prison services have fared no better. Between 2010 and 2014, the number of core staff in public sector prisons fell by 27% (Institute for Government, 2020). As of 2017, there were 7,000 fewer officers in post than in 2010 (Fullfact.org, 2020). As with police and probation services, austerity has correlated with a number of negative indicators. Completed suicides in prisons stood at 56 in 2010; by 2016 they peaked at a record high of 119. Rates of self-harm are currently at an all-time high. Similarly, rates of violence have reached record highs, with 34,425 assault incidents in the 12 months to March 2019, up 11% from the previous year. In the same period, there were 10,311 assaults on staff, up 15% from the previous year, again a record high figure (MoJ, 2019a).

In terms of healthcare services in prisons during the austerity era, Ismail (2019) collates several issues of concern. These include the facts that, on average, prisoners miss 15% of medical appointments, predominantly due to a lack of prison officers to escort them to hospital and that two-thirds of those awaiting transfer to secure hospital for acute mental health problems wait for more than the 14-day target, with delays of over a year not unknown. While Her Majesty's Inspectorate of Prisons expects that prisoners should be unlocked for ten hours a day, in 2018 this was achieved for only 17% of the population, a situation likely to be harmful to mental health (ibid.).

How then, in such a political and economic climate, do healthcare providers deliver services that are of high quality, meet the needs of the population served and offer equivalence with the outside world?

Since prison-based healthcare services began being commissioned through competitive tendering, there has developed a complex landscape of different providers from public and private sector organisations. It has become commonplace for single prison establishments to host a variety of providers, each delivering discrete elements of service, for example, mental health, substance misuse, primary care and dentistry. The "market" has become very attractive to the private sector; the company Care UK, in particular, has determinedly pursued contracts and, at the time of writing, their corporate website states that they deliver healthcare in over 40 establishments across England and Wales. It is also not unusual that, where an NHS Trust holds a prison contract, the establishment will not necessarily be within the same geographical area as the other Trust sites and community services. This increase in out of area contracting and the emergence of powerful, national private providers raises concerns around how well integrated into local, non-custodial healthcare services prison-based services can become. Because of the vulnerabilities and levels of morbidity inherent in the prison population, all prisons need effective working relationships with local secondary services and it is the responsibility of clinicians to work towards integrating care within and without the prison walls to the benefit of their patient, regardless of whom they are employed by (Forrester et al., 2015).

An inherent difficulty in prison healthcare services, as evidenced earlier, is the ability to undertake effective, early identification of health issues, whether that be a risk of suicide and self-harm, serious mental or physical illness and/or dementia. Current systems are failing to identify these at-risk groups and increasingly stretched consistently, and inexperienced, staffing resources will not be able to improve this situation; in the current climate the often quoted mantra of 'doing more with less' is unimaginable.

That said, prison walls need to be permeable to improvement, with closer replication of community ways of working and greater integration with local services. A greater emphasis needs to be placed on conducting detailed assessments of all prisoners in the early days of custody to reduce deaths by suicide or by preventable natural causes and to improve treatment of chronic illness. This shift should equip services to *proactively respond* to the health needs of the prison population, rather than merely being able to *react* when things have already gone wrong. The need to work in a wholly different way, emphasising health rather than illness, has promoted calls for 'political courage' regarding a fundamental review of the prison health agenda to create an atmosphere in which clinicians can justly work in the best interests of their patients (Piper, Forrester & Shaw, 2019).

Conclusion

Prisons remain an unknown world to vast swathes of the general public who are influenced largely by the media and blustering political rhetoric about being tough on crime. Those in prison have behaved in ways which society disapproves of, but the pursuit of a punishment agenda is only part of the solution. The vast majority of people will enter and leave prison within a relatively short period of time and that time should be used to reduce the risks of them reoffending and increase their chances of making a positive contribution to society. That can be done through the provision of high-quality healthcare services to a vulnerable and needy group and the provision of a decent environment where respect can be earned and given.

To do this requires the delivery of holistic, multi-disciplinary interventions designed to improve a person's health, education and social status while in prison but, equally importantly, upon release. Healthcare services need to ensure that illnesses are effectively identified and treated, as well as offering a range of proactive health promotion and prevention interventions.

To achieve this requires money to be spent on the provision of a suitably trained and engaged workforce whereby specialist clinicians work alongside dedicated and motivated prison staff and all staff are supported to work to the best of their abilities in a learning, rather than blaming environment.

Public services at present are beyond the point where it is feasible to expect or believe that more can be achieved with less. It is disingenuous to criticise failing services while keeping them starved of resources. Now is the time to speak truth to power on these matters.

References

Bluglass, R. (1990). Prisons and the prison medical service. In Bluglass, R. & Boewn, P. (eds.), *Principles and practice of forensic psychiatry* (pp. 1321–1328). London: Churchill Livingstone.

Bowen, R. A., Rogers, A., & Shaw, J. (2009). Medication management and practices in prison for people with mental health problems: A qualitative study. *International Journal of Mental Health Systems, 3*(1), 24. https://doi.org/10.1186/1752-4458-3-24

Department of Health & HM Prison Service. (2001). *Changing the outlook. A strategy for developing and modernising mental health services in prisons.* London: Department of Health.

Disley, E., Taylor, C., Kruithof, K., Winpenny, E., Liddle, M., Sutherland, A., Lilford, R., Wright, S., McAteer, L., & Francis, V. (2016). *Evaluation of the offender liaison and diversion trial schemes.* Available at: https://www.rand.org/pubs/research_reports/RR1283.html (accessed 13.01.2020)

Fazel, S., & Benning, R. (2009). Suicides in female prisoners in England and Wales, 1978–2004. *The British Journal of Psychiatry, 194*(2), 183–184. https://doi.org/10.1192/bjp.bp.107.046490

Fazel, S., Benning, R., & Danesh, J. (2005). Suicides in male prisoners in England and Wales, 1978–2003. *The Lancet, 366*(9493), 1301–1302. https://doi.org/10.1016/S0140-6736(05)67325-4

Fazel, S., Cartwright, J., Norman-Nott, A., & Hawton, K. (2008). Suicide in prisoners: A systematic review of risk factors. *Journal of Clinical Psychiatry, 69*(11), 1721–1731.

Fazel, S., & Danesh, J. (2002). Serious mental disorder in 23 000 prisoners: A systematic review of 62 surveys. *The Lancet, 359*(9306), 545–550. https://doi.org/10.1016/S0140-6736(02)07740-1

Fazel, S., Hope, T., O'Donnell, I., Piper, M., & Jacoby, R. (2001a). Health of elderly male prisoners: Worse than the general population, worse than younger prisoners. *Age and Ageing, 30*(5), 403–407. https://doi.org/10.1093/ageing/30.5.403

Fazel, S., Hope, T., O'Donnell, I., & Jacoby, R. (2001b). Hidden psychiatric morbidity in elderly prisoners. *The British Journal of Psychiatry, 179*(6), 535–539. https://doi.org/10.1192/bjp.179.6.535

Fear, N. T., Jones, M., Murphy, D., Hull, L., Iversen, A. C., Coker, B., Machell, L., Sundin, J., Woodhead, C., Jones, N., Greenberg, N., Landau, S., Dandeker, C., Rona, R. J., Hotopf, M., & Wessely, S. (2010). What are the consequences of deployment to Iraq and Afghanistan on the mental health of the UK armed forces? A cohort study. *The Lancet, 375*(9728), 1783–1797. https://doi.org/10.1016/S0140-6736(10)60672-1

Forrester, A., Till, A., Senior, J., & Shaw, J. (2015). Competitive tendering and offender health services. *The Lancet Psychiatry, 2*(10), 859–861. https://doi.org/10.1016/S2215-0366(15)00414-9

Forsyth, K., Heathcote, L., Senior, J., Malik, B., Meacock, R., Perryman, K., Tucker, S., Domone, R., Carr, M., Hayes, H., Webb, R., Archer-Power, L., Dawson, A., Leonard, S., Challis, D., Ware, S., Emsley, R., Sanders, C., Karim, S., Fazel, S., Hayes, A., Burns, A., Piper, M., & Shaw, J. (2020). *Dementia and mild cognitive impairment in the prison population of England and Wales: Identifying individual need and developing a skilled, multi-agency workforce to deliver targeted and responsive services: A National Institute for Health Services and Delivery Research Programme report.* [In press].

Frank, J. W., Linder, J. A., Becker, W. C., Fiellin, D. A., & Wang, E. A. (2014). Increased hospital and emergency department utilization by individuals with recent criminal justice involvement: Results of a national survey. *Journal of General Internal Medicine, 29*(9), 1226–1233. https://doi.org/10.1007/s11606-014-2877-y

Full Fact. (2020). *Fewer prison officers in England and Wales.* Available at: https://fullfact.org/crime/prison-officer-numbers-have-fallen/ (accessed 13.01.2020)

Grounds, A. (1994). Mentally disordered prisoners. In Player, E. & Jenkins, M. (eds.), *Prisons after Woolf: Reform through riot* (pp. 190–201). London: Routledge.

Guardian. (2019). *Fewer criminals being caught after 28% drop in detective numbers.* Available at: https://www.theguardian.com/uk-news/2019/jun/24/police-lose-28-of-serious-crime-detectives-under-austerity (accessed 13.01.2020)

Gunn, J. (1985). Psychiatry and the prison medical service. In Gostin, L. (ed.), *Secure provision* (pp. 126–152). London: Tavistock.

Hawton, K., Linsell, L., Adeniji, T., Sariaslan, A., & Fazel, S. (2014). Self-harm in prisons in England and Wales: An epidemiological study of prevalence, risk factors, clustering, and subsequent suicide. *The Lancet, 383*(9923), 1147–1154. https://doi.org/10.1016/S0140-6736(13)62118-2

Health Advisory Committee for the Prison Service. (1997). *The provision of mental health care in prisons*. London: HM Prison Service.

Her Majesty's Chief Inspector of Prisons for England and Wales. (1996). *Patient or prisoner? A new strategy for health care in prisons*. London: Home Office.

Her Majesty's Chief Inspector of Prisons for England and Wales. (2004). *'No problems – Old and quiet': Older prisoners in England and Wales: A thematic review by HM Chief Inspector of Prisons*. London: Home Office.

Her Majesty's Government. (2014). *Care Act 2014 c.23*. London: HM Government.

Her Majesty's Prison Service & NHS Executive. (1999). *The future organisation of prison health care*. London: Department of Health.

Herman, D. B., Conover, S., Gorroochurn, P., Hinterland, K., Hoepner, L., & Susser, E. S. (2011). Randomized trial of critical time intervention to prevent homelessness after hospital discharge. *Psychiatric Services, 62*(7), 713–719. https://doi.org/10.1176/ps.62.7.pss6207_0713

Howard, J. (1777). *The state of the prisons in England and Wales*. Warrington: London.

Howard League for Penal Reform. (2011). *Report of the inquiry into former armed service personnel in prison*. London: Howard League.

Howse, K. (2011). Growing old in prison: A scoping study on older prisoners. Centre for Policy on Ageing and Prison Reform Trust. Available at: http://www.prisonreformtrust.org.uk/uploads/documents/Growing.Old.Book_-_small.pdf (accessed 13.01.2020)

Institute for Government. (2020). Prisons. Available at: https://www.instituteforgovernment.org.uk/publication/performance-tracker-2019/prisons (accessed 13.01.2020)

Ismail, N. (2019). Rolling back the prison estate: The pervasive impact of macroeconomic austerity on prisoner health in England. *Journal of Public Health*. https://doi.org/10.1093/pubmed/fdz058

Iversen, A. C., Fear, N. T., Simonoff, E., Hull, L., Horn, O., Greenberg, N., Hotopf, M., Rona, R., & Wessely, S. (2007). Influence of childhood adversity on health among male UK military personnel. *The British Journal of Psychiatry, 191*(6), 506–511. https://doi.org/10.1192/bjp.bp.107.039818

Iversen, A., Dyson, C., Smith, N., Greenberg, N., Walwyn, R., Unwin, C., Hull, L., Hotopf, M., Dandeker, C., Ross, J., & Wessely, S. (2005). 'Goodbye and good luck': The mental health needs and treatment experiences of British ex-service personnel. *The British Journal of Psychiatry, 186*(6), 480–486. https://doi.org/10.1192/bjp.186.6.480

Jarrett, M., Thornicroft, G., Forrester, A., Harty, M., Senior, J., King, C., ... & Shaw, J. (2012). Continuity of care for recently released prisoners with mental illness: a pilot randomised controlled trial testing the feasibility of a critical time intervention. *Epidemiology and Psychiatric Sciences, 21*(2), 187–193.

Lennox, C., Senior, J., King, C., Hassan, L., Clayton, R., Thornicroft, G., & Shaw, J. (2012). The management of released prisoners with severe and enduring mental illness. *The Journal of Forensic Psychiatry & Psychology, 23*(1), 67–75. https://doi.org/10.1080/14789949.2011.634921

Lennox, C., Stevenson, C., Edge, D., Hopkins, G., Thornicroft, G., Susser, E., Conover, S., Herman, D., Senior, J., & Shaw, J. (2020). Critical time intervention: A qualitative study of the perspectives of prisoners and staff. *The Journal of Forensic Psychiatry & Psychology, 31*(1), 76–89. https://doi.org/10.1080/14789949.2019.1665699

Mann, N., Devendran, P., & Lundrigan, S. (2018). Policing in a time of austerity: Understanding the public protection paradox through qualitative interviews with police monitoring officers. *Policing: A Journal of Policy and Practice, 47*, 1–13. https://doi.org/10.1093/police/pay047

Maruna, S. (1999). Desistance and development: The psychosocial process of 'going straight'. *The British Criminology Conferences: Selected Proceedings. Volume 2*. London: British Society of Criminology.

Ministry of Justice. (2013). *Transforming rehabilitation: A strategy for reform*. London: Ministry of Justice.

Ministry of Justice. (2018). *Her Majesty's Prison and Probation Service offender equalities annual report 2017/18*. London: Ministry of Justice.

Ministry of Justice. (2019a). *Safety in custody statistics, England and Wales: Deaths in prison custody to December 2018, assaults and self-harm to September 2018*. London: Ministry of Justice.

Ministry of Justice. (2019b). *Offender management statistics quarterly: October to December 2018*. London: Ministry of Justice.

National Audit Office. (2019). *Transforming rehabilitation: Progress review*. London: National Audit Office.

NHS England and NHS Improvement. (2019). *Liaison and diversion standard service specification 2019*. Available at: https://www.england.nhs.uk/wp-content/uploads/2019/12/national-liaison-and-diversion-service-specification-2019.pdf (accessed 13.01.2020)

Omelade, S. (2014). *The needs and characteristics of older prisoners: Results from the Surveying Prisoner Crime Reduction (SPCR) survey*. London: Ministry of Justice.

Piper, M., Forrester, A., & Shaw, J. (2019). Prison healthcare services: The need for political courage. *The British Journal of Psychiatry, 215*(4), 579–581. https://doi.org/10.1192/bjp.2019.43

Prison and Probation Ombudsman. (2016). *Learning from PPO investigations: Prisoner mental health*. London: Prison and Probation Ombudsman.

Ralli, R. (1994). Health care in prisons. In Player, E. & Jenkins, M. (eds.), *Prisons after Woolf: Reform through riot*. London: Routledge.

Richards, K. (2011). What makes juvenile offenders different from adult offenders? *Trends & Issues in Crime and Criminal Justice* No 409. February 2011. Canberra: Australian Institute of Criminology.

Senior, J., Birmingham, L., Harty, M. A., Hassan, L., Hayes, A. J., Kendall, K., King, C., Lathlean, J., Lowthian, C., Mills, A., Webb, R., Thornicroft, G., & Shaw, J. (2013). Identification and management of prisoners with severe psychiatric illness by specialist mental health services. *Psychological Medicine, 43*(7), 1511–1520. https://doi.org/10.1017/S0033291712002073

Shaw, J., Conover, S., Herman, D., Jarrett, M., Leese, M., McCrone, P., Murphy, C., Senior, J., Susser, E., Thornicroft, G., Wright, N., Edge, D., Emsley, R., Lennox, C., Williams, A., Cust, H., Hopkin, G., & Stevenson, C. (2017). *Critical time Intervention for Severely mentally ill Prisoners (CrISP): A randomised controlled trial*. Southampton: NIHR Journals Library. Available at: http://www.ncbi.nlm.nih.gov/books/NBK424457/

Shaw, J., Wainwright, V., Webb, R., Appleby, L., Piper, M., Rees, J., & Elder, R. (2013). *National study of self-inflicted death by prisoners 2008–2010*. (Report to Offender Health, Department of Health) Manchester: The University of Manchester. Available at: http://research.bmh.manchester.ac.uk/cmhs/research/centreforsuicideprevention/suicideinprisons/report_2013.pdf (accessed 13.01.2020)

Singleton, N., Meltzer, H., Gatward, R., Coid, J., & Deasy, D. (1998). *Survey of psychiatric morbidity among prisoners in England and Wales*. London: Department of Health.

Smith, R. (1984). *Prison health care*. London: British Medical Association.

Sturge, G. (2019). *UK prison population statistics House of Commons*, Briefing Paper Number CBP-04334. London: House of Commons.

Tanner-Smith, E. E., Wilson, S. J., & Wilson, M. W. (2012). Risk factors and crime. In Cullen, F. T. & Wilcox, P. (eds.), *The Oxford handbook of criminological theory*. Oxford: Oxford University Press.

Wainwright, V., Dawson, A., Senior, J., Appleby, L., Fazel, S., Forrester, A., Marriott, C., Perry, A., Pratt, D., Walker, T., & Shaw, J. (2020). *Managing the risk of self-inflicted death to support a psychologically safe and rehabilitative criminal justice pathway: A National Institute for Health Research Policy Research Programme Project*. [In press].

Wainwright, V., Lennox, C., McDonnell, S., Shaw, J., & Senior, J. (2017a). The mental health and substance misuse needs of male ex-armed forces personnel in prison. *The Journal of Forensic Psychiatry & Psychology, 29*(1), 146–162. https://doi.org/10.1080/14789949.2017.1352012

Wainwright, V., Lennox, C., Mcdonnell, S., Shaw, J., & Senior, J. (2017b). Offending characteristics of male ex-armed forces personnel in prison. *The Howard Journal of Crime and Justice, 56*(1), 19–33. https://doi.org/10.1111/hojo.12189

7

CONTINUITY AND CHANGE IN PENAL POLICY TOWARDS PERSONALITY DISORDERED OFFENDERS

Ailbhe O'Loughlin

The Dangerous and Severe Personality Disorder (DSPD) programme was established by New Labour in 2001 to test treatment, management and risk assessment techniques for individuals thought to pose a high risk of serious harm to the public stemming from a severe form of personality disorder (Home Office and Department of Health, 1999; see further O'Loughlin, 2014, 2019). The programme ran for over a decade and appeared to achieve some successes in managing a difficult population and reducing the risk of violence in the short term (Burns et al., 2011; Ministry of Justice, 2011). Patients and prisoners spent surprisingly few hours in therapy, however, and definitive conclusions on the effectiveness of treatment could not be drawn without a control group (Burns et al., 2011). Furthermore, the units experienced significant staffing and operational difficulties, progress through the programme was slow and pathways out of the units were unclear (Trebilcock & Weaver, 2010a, 2010b).

Despite these mixed results, in 2011 the government announced plans to decommission the hospital DSPD units and expand provision in prisons and the community under the new title of the Offender Personality Disorder Pathway (OPDP) (Department of Health and NOMS, 2011a, 2011b). While the primary objective of the OPDP is to improve public protection, its secondary aims are "reducing reoffending, improving psychological health and well-being and tackling health inequalities" (Department of Health and NOMS, 2011a, para. 36).

This chapter will explore the origins of the DSPD programme in England and critically evaluate the policies surrounding the OPDP. The contested nature of the personality disorder diagnosis and the vagaries of risk assessment will first be examined, grounding an exploration of the controversy provoked by the government's efforts to reform mental health legislation in the 1990s and early 2000s to facilitate the detention of dangerous personality disordered individuals regardless of their treatability. The discussion will unearth the long history of attempts by expert groups, policymakers and practitioners to respond to the challenges posed by personality disordered offenders and examine the reasons behind the mixed results of evaluations of the pilot DSPD programme. This will form the basis for a critical analysis of the ability of the OPDP to meet the potentially conflicting aims of improving health outcomes for offenders, managing a difficult group in institutions and protecting the public.

Personality disorder: a contested diagnosis

The fifth edition of the Diagnostic and Statistical Manual of Mental Disorders, DSM-V, defines personality disorder (PD) as

> an enduring pattern of inner experience and behaviour that deviates markedly from the expectations of the individual's culture, is pervasive and inflexible, has an onset in adolescence or early adulthood, is stable over time, and leads to distress or impairment.
>
> *(American Psychiatric Association, 2013, p. 645)*

The DSM-V also contains an alternative experimental set of "general criteria", which defines the "essential features" of PD as "moderate or greater impairment in personality (self/interpersonal) functioning" and the presence of "one or more pathological personality traits" (American Psychiatric Association, 2013, p. 761). These features are "relatively inflexible and pervasive across a broad range of personal and social situations" and "relatively stable across time" (American Psychiatric Association, 2013, p. 761). The inclusion of "relatively" reflects research showing variation and remission in PD symptoms over the life-course, indicating that PD traits may not be as inflexible and enduring as previously thought (see Zanarini et al., 2003; Gutiérrez et al., 2012).

DSM-V identifies three clusters of PD. Cluster B, the "dramatic, emotional or erratic" types include histrionic, narcissistic, antisocial and borderline PDs, which are associated with criminality (Jones, 2008, p. 63). The prevalence of PD amongst prisoners is up to ten times higher than that found in the general population and antisocial (ASPD) and borderline (BPD) types are particularly common (Fazel & Danesh, 2002). A systematic review of 28 surveys on prisoner mental health from 12 countries found that 65% of male and 42% of female prisoners surveyed had been diagnosed with a PD (Fazel & Danesh, 2002). Of these, 47% of adult male prisoners had been diagnosed with ASPD and 21% and 25% of adult female prisoners had been diagnosed with ASPD and BPD respectively (Fazel & Danesh, 2002). A survey of prisoners in England and Wales conducted by the Office of National Statistics found that 78% of male remand, 64% of male sentenced and 50% of female prisoners fulfilled the criteria for at least one PD (Singleton, Gatward & Meltzer, 1998, p. 10). Among a subset of prisoners who were clinically interviewed, 63% of male remand, 49% of male sentenced and 31% of female prisoners met the criteria for ASPD.

These figures may come as no surprise, as behaviours associated with criminality are incorporated into the diagnostic criteria of both ASPD and BPD. ASPD is associated with a failure to conform to social norms, deceitfulness, impulsivity, irritability and aggression, reckless disregard for the safety of self or others, irresponsibility and a lack of remorse (American Psychiatric Association, 2013, p. 659). The distinguishing features of BPD include frantic efforts to avoid real or imagined abandonment, a pattern of unstable and intense interpersonal relationships, identity disturbance, impulsivity, recurrent suicidal or self-mutilating acts, gestures, or threats, affective instability, chronic feelings of emptiness, inappropriate and intense anger or difficulties in controlling anger demonstrated by recurrent physical fighting, and transient paranoid ideation or severe dissociative symptoms in times of stress (American Psychiatric Association, 2013, p. 663).

ASPD, to some extent, overlaps with the construct of psychopathy, which similarly incorporates traits associated with offending behaviour. Psychopathy is defined by Robert D. Hare's Psychopathy Checklist Revised (PCL-R) (Hare, 1991), a diagnostic tool divided into two factors: Factor 1 (interpersonal/affective) and Factor 2 (unstable and antisocial lifestyle). Factor 1 includes the traits of glibness/superficial charm, grandiose sense of self-worth, pathological lying, conning and manipulativeness, lack of remorse or guilt, shallow affect, callousness or lack of empathy, and failure to accept responsibility for one's own actions. Factor 2 includes a need for stimulation or proneness to boredom, a parasitic lifestyle, lack of realistic long-term goals, impulsivity, irresponsibility, poor behavioural controls, early behavioural problems, juvenile delinquency, revocation of conditional release and criminal versatility (Hare, 1991).

Unsurprisingly, both ASPD and psychopathy have been criticised for their circularity, as "the psychopath's mental disorder is inferred from his anti-social behaviour while the anti-social behaviour is explained by mental disorder" (Wootton, 1981, p. 90). Thus, a diagnosis of ASPD or psychopathy "often does little more than recycle the history of prior offending behaviours in a different form, producing a potentially spurious association between PD and offending" (Mullen, 1999, p. 1147). Given a diagnosis of ASPD is often based on socially undesirable conduct, the construct has been criticised for its "moral overtones" (Gunn, 2003) and has even been branded "a moral judgement masquerading as a clinical diagnosis" (Blackburn, 1988, p. 511). These criticisms raise the question of whether these disorders cause, explain or merely describe the socially undesirable acts and tendencies of those who are so diagnosed.

Mental disorder tends to be associated with dangerousness, violence and unpredictability in the mind of the public and the media (see generally Thornicroft, 2006; Peay, 2011). While there is some evidence of an association between personality disorder and offending, the nature of this relationship is unclear, and it is difficult therefore to justify preventively detaining or treating individuals on the grounds of a PD diagnosis. The risk of violent offending amongst those with PD is about three times that of the general population and the risk of violence amongst those with ASPD is particularly high, at around 12.8 times that of the general population (Yu, Geddes & Fazel, 2012, p. 784). Causality between ASPD and violence is difficult to establish, however, due to the multiplicity of confounding factors, including comorbid substance abuse, mental illnesses and post-traumatic stress disorder (PTSD) (Duggan & Howard, 2009). Furthermore, the circularity of the ASPD diagnosis may mean that the association with antisocial behaviour is merely "trivial" or descriptive (Howard, 2015).

These uncertainties are compounded by the low predictive accuracy of actuarial risk assessment instruments when applied to individuals. Despite having an elevated risk of reoffending, only 14% of individuals diagnosed with ASPD in one study went on to be violent. This means that seven individuals with ASPD would have to be detained to prevent one violent act. Drug and alcohol abusers demonstrate a similar level of risk (Yu et al., 2012, p. 784) but tend to receive less public and political attention than the mentally disordered.

The ethical problems surrounding preventive detention and compulsory treatment for those with ASPD are compounded by a paucity of robust evidence for effective psychological or pharmacological treatments (Warren et al., 2003; Gibbon et al., 2010; Khalifa et al., 2010). While studies show some support for psychological and pharmacological interventions with BPD, the evidence continues to be limited by small sample sizes, short follow-up periods, the wide range of outcome measures used and poor controlling for comorbid psychopathologies (Bateman, Gunderson & Mulder, 2015). Furthermore, the effectiveness of existing treatments may be impeded by the fact that PD patients tend to have low motivation for treatment (Howells & Day, 2007). In particular, it is common for individuals diagnosed with ASPD tend to actively resist accepting help for their disorders (NCCMH et al., 2010, para. 2.4).

Notwithstanding these challenges, there is a growing literature on treatments that have shown some potential in treating PDs in serious offenders and several treatment models have emerged from the DSPD programme itself (e.g. Saradjian, Murphy, & McVey, 2010; Tennant & Howells, 2010; Tew & Atkinson, 2013). Nevertheless, the difficulties associated with conducting studies that meet the "gold standard" of the randomised controlled trial in forensic settings means that the evidence base for treatment effectiveness remains weak. Nonetheless, a policy push has come from the Department of Health to counteract therapeutic pessimism and to encourage a more inclusive and optimistic approach towards PD patients (see Pickersgill, 2012). Guidelines from the National Institute for Health and Care Excellence (NICE) recommend challenging negative attitudes towards ASPD patients and encouraging staff to develop "a stronger belief in the effectiveness of their own personal skills" (NCCMH et al., 2010, para. 4.3.1). Similarly, NICE recommends exploring treatment options with BPD patients "in an atmosphere of hope and optimism, explaining that recovery is possible and attainable" (NCCMH et al., 2009, para. 4.6.2.1).

History of the DSPD programme

The first mention of the term "DSPD" appeared in a joint consultation paper entitled *Managing People with Severe Personality Disorder* published by the Home Office and Department of Health in 1999. Individuals in the DSPD category were presented by politicians and policymakers as having fallen through the cracks in the mental health and criminal justice systems due to gaps in the law and the refusal of psychiatrists to take responsibility for patients they labelled "untreatable". "DSPD" was not a recognised clinical diagnosis but an administrative category that described a group with multiple complex problems. "Severe PD" was defined in the 1999 consultation paper as an "inability to relate to others, poor control of impulses and difficulty in learning lessons from previous experience" (Home Office and Department of Health, 1999, p. 7). This definition did not appear in any existing diagnostic manuals but appeared to describe a subset of individuals diagnosed with antisocial PD.

The consultation paper asserted that a significant number of individuals in the DSPD group had been given determinate sentences by the courts and had to be released from prison at the end of their sentences despite the risks they posed to the public (Home Office and Department of Health, 1999, p. 12). At the time, the Mental Health Act (MHA) 1983 only permitted the detention of individuals suffering from "psychopathic disorder" in hospitals if treatment was "likely to alleviate or prevent a deterioration" in their condition (former s.3.(2)(b)). This "treatability" criterion, coupled with a lack of adequate service provision, was presented as a stumbling block to the detention of dangerous individuals to protect the public (Seddon, 2008, p. 304; Peay, 2011, p. 176).

It was estimated that around 1,400 men in the DSPD group were detained in prison while about 400 were detained in psychiatric hospitals. A small group of between 300 and 600 men who had not been convicted of a recent offence were estimated to be abroad in the community (Home Office and Department of Health, 1999, p. 12). The number of women was expected to be much lower, at around 50 (DSPD Programme et al., 2006, p. 8). In addition to posing a risk to the public, the DSPD group posed "significant management challenges in institutional settings" and a "constant threat" to staff and other inmates (Home Office and Department of Health, 1999, p. 12). The DSPD group was not only portrayed as dangerous, however, but also as distressed and affected by a myriad of health and social problems, including substance misuse, suicide, depression, anxiety and illiteracy. Many had a history of poor relationships, unemployment and homelessness, and most were not receiving adequate support for their needs (Home Office and Department of Health, 1999, pp. 48–49).

The government put forward proposals to establish new powers for the detention of individuals in the DSPD group in a dedicated institution, separate from prisons and secure hospitals, for as long as they posed a risk and regardless of their treatability. Detention would not depend on a criminal conviction but would instead fall within the state's power to detain individuals "of unsound mind" under Article 5.1(e) of the European Convention on Human Rights (ECHR). An alternative, more modest set of proposals suggested removing the much-maligned "treatability" criterion to facilitate the preventive detention of individuals in the DSPD category in psychiatric hospitals, encouraging judges to make greater use of discretionary life sentences with this group, improving joint working between the mental health and criminal justice systems (Home Office and Department of Health, 1999).

The DSPD group would not merely be detained, however, but would be "helped and encouraged to co-operate in therapeutic and other activity designed to help them return safely to the community" (Home Office and Department of Health, 1999, p. 9). By allocating significant funding to research into tailored treatments, the government aimed to strike a "balance" "between the human rights of individuals [in the DSPD group] and the right of the public to be protected from these very dangerous people" (Boateng & Sharland, 1999, p. 7). If the risks posed by those in the DSPD group were found not to be reduced through treatment, however, there would be "no alternative but to continue to detain them indefinitely" (Home Office and Department of Health, 1999, p. 9).

The plans were widely interpreted by the media as a response to the case of Michael Stone. Stone was convicted of the murders of Lin Russell and her six-year-old daughter Megan and the attempted murder of her older daughter, Josie, then aged nine, in Chillenden, Kent in July 1996 (Francis, Higgins & Cassam, 2006, p. 11). Following his arrest, reports described Stone as a "psychopath" left free to kill after psychiatrists had refused to admit him to hospital because he was "untreatable" or "too dangerous" (Francis, Higgins & Cassam, 2006, Table 1.14). Some reports stated that in the days before the violent attack, Stone had told doctors he had fantasies of killing children and begged to be admitted to hospital (Francis, Higgins & Cassam, Table 14.1).

A subsequent independent inquiry into Stone's care and treatment exposed these claims as glaringly inaccurate (Francis, Higgins & Cassam, 2006). While Stone posed problems of diagnosis and there were some failings in his care, the Inquiry concluded Stone was "emphatically not a case of a man with a dangerous PD being generally ignored by agencies or left at large without supervision" (Francis, Higgins & Cassam, 2006, p. 5). Furthermore, if Stone had perpetrated the horrific crimes, the Inquiry "found no evidence that they would have been prevented if failings in the provision of treatment, care, supervision or other services to Mr Stone had not occurred" (Francis, Higgins & Cassam, 2006, p. 4). Michael Stone continues to protest his innocence.

While the announcement of the DSPD proposals coincided with Stone's conviction, it would be "a mistake to attribute too much significance to this piece of political theatre" (Maden, 2007, s.8). For Tony Maden, the "true motivation" for the proposals "was not a single case but longstanding frustration within government at the refusal of psychiatrists to address the problem of high-risk offenders with personality disorder" (Maden, 2007, s.8). The origins of the proposals may be traced further back, to the formation of a small group of officials drawn from the Home Office and Department of Health shortly after the election of the New Labour government in May 1997 (Rutherford, 2006). Andrew Rutherford argues that while the Stone case was not the catalyst, it provided "a narrative into which embryonic proposals might be located alongside the rationale and justification to carry them forward into the political arena" (Rutherford, 2006, p. 80).

Interdepartmental working on the problem addressed by the proposals may be traced further back still, however, to the establishment of the Butler Committee on Mentally Abnormal Offenders in 1972. In their memorandum of evidence to the Butler Committee, the Home Office and Department of Health and Social Security (DHSS) drew attention to "the problem of the legal obligation to release, at the end of determinate prison sentences, a small number of men who are probably dangerous but who are not acceptable for treatment in hospital" (Butler, 1975, para. 4.34). Butler proposed the creation of a new renewable sentence for dangerous offenders, but these were not taken forward by the government and interdepartmental work continued.

In 1986, a joint Home Office and DHSS working group was established to consider changes to the MHA 1983 to address the related problem of restricted patients being discharged from special hospitals by Mental Health Tribunals where they no longer met the medical criteria for detention but nevertheless presented a risk to the public (Home Office and DHSS, 1986). Responses from professionals to proposals published in 1986 were largely negative and they were quietly dropped (Peay, 1988).

The subsequent Review of Health and Social Services for Mentally Disordered Offenders, chaired by Dr John Reed (1992), led to the establishment of a Department of Health and Home Office working group on psychopathic disorder, which reported in 1994 (Reed, 1994). Reed later commented that psychopathic disorder "was by far the most difficult topic he had taken on to review" (Fallon, 1999, para. 6.1.75). Given the uncertainties surrounding the causes of PD and effective treatment, the Working Party's principal recommendation was to instigate "a comprehensive programme of research" (Home Office and Department of Health, 1999, p. 38).

At the time the DSPD proposals were under development, two further expert committees were working on these longstanding and thorny issues. An enquiry chaired by Peter Fallon QC was appointed in February 1997 to investigate allegations made by a former patient of the PD unit at Ashworth Special Hospital. Fallon examined in detail the controversies surrounding the diagnosis and treatment of PD and made recommendations regarding what services should be provided for those at "the severe end of the spectrum" (Fallon, 1999, para. 1.2.3). In October 1998, an Expert Committee chaired by Professor Genevra Richardson was appointed to conduct a review of the MHA 1983.

Despite then Home Secretary Jack Straw's claim in the House of Commons in October 1998 that the psychiatric profession had said that would "take on only patients whom it regards as treatable" (HC Deb, 26 October 1998, col. 9W), the Fallon Inquiry found a range of views on treatability. About 10% of psychiatrists "were totally dismissive of psychopaths and their treatability" while another 10% "stated equally vehemently that psychiatrists had a duty to treat this group of patients who caused suffering to themselves and society" (Fallon, 1999, para. 6.6.4). The rest were "somewhere in between" (Fallon, 1999, para. 6.6.4). The Inquiry heard evidence from psychiatrists who "who deem[ed] it right never to give up, and never to stop trying" and others who believed that treatment might succeed with some individuals but not with the more severe cases (Fallon, 1999, para. 6.65). However, it seemed that, due to a lack of robust empirical evidence, scepticism appeared to hold sway.

The Fallon Inquiry was asked to consider the option of a separate service for PD offenders but ultimately did not support it due to potential problems. These included additional bureaucracy, the potential rivalry between the Department of Health and the Home Office and the risk that the service would become isolated from the therapeutic mainstream and have difficulties attracting good staff. Finally, it commented that "concentrating the most problematic people in the system could be a recipe for disaster" (Fallon, 1999, para. 7.12.12). Some of these comments appear prophetic in light of the problems encountered by the DSPD programme, discussed further below.

Nevertheless, the Fallon Inquiry believed that it would not be acceptable to do nothing about the problem of dangerous offenders. It recommended the introduction of a reviewable prison sentence similar to that proposed by the Butler Committee, commenting that the government could choose to expand its application to other "dangerous offenders" who did not suffer from PD but who nevertheless posed "a substantial risk of causing harm to others after release from prison" (Fallon, 1999, para. 7.5.7).

In the same year as the Fallon report was published, the Richardson Committee presented proposals for a new Mental Health Act based on principles of capacity and reciprocity. Under the proposals, those with PD could only be detained where there was "a *substantial* risk of *serious harm* to the health or safety of the patient or to the safety of other persons" and "positive clinical measures [were] included within the proposed care and treatment which [were] *likely* to prevent deterioration or to secure an improvement in the patient's mental condition" (Department of Health, 1999, para. 5.95. Emphasis added). The latter condition was akin to the "treatability" test but the "substantial risk" and "serious harm" requirements set a higher threshold than the civil sections of the MHA 1983.

Like the Fallon Inquiry's reviewable sentence, the Richardson Committee's proposals did not provide an immediate solution to the problem of dangerous offenders being released from determinate prison sentences. It may not come as a surprise, therefore, that the Committee's proposals were accepted only in part and separate plans were drawn up for the DSPD group.

Controversy and compromise

Both Fallon and Richardson disapproved of the direction taken by the government on DSPD. Fallon criticised the overly optimistic presentation of current "good practice" in the 1999 consultation paper and urged the government to consider his Inquiry's reviewable sentence proposal (Select Committee on Health, 2000, Appendix 28). A subsequent White Paper entitled *Reforming the Mental Health Act* cherry-picked from Richardson, adopting a broad definition of mental disorder but abandoning the central principles of capacity and non-discrimination and focusing on minimising the risk of harm to the patient and others (Department of Health, 2000a, 2000b). The result, according to the Richardson Committee, was "an unfortunate hybrid" that would "significantly extend the use of compulsory powers" (Select Committee on Health, 2000, Thursday 6 April 2000).

The government's proposals also faced strident opposition from psychiatrists, lawyers, patient groups and civil liberties charities. In particular, psychiatrists were concerned about the ethical implications of detaining individuals who were unlikely to benefit from treatment and feared they would be expected to act as "judges and jailers" (Mullen, 1999, p. 1146). Legal commentators expressed the suspicion that the government aimed to circumvent the provisions of the European Convention on Human Rights and detain suspected offenders without the need for a criminal trial and conviction (Eastman, 1999). The plans for a separate service and legal regime for the DSPD group were eventually shelved, but the government pushed forward its reforms to mental health legislation.

After extensive debate, the MHA 2007 was passed, replacing the "treatability" criterion with a requirement that "appropriate medical treatment" be "available" to the patient and that the "purpose" of this treatment be "to alleviate, or prevent a worsening of, the disorder or one or more of its symptoms or manifestations" (MHA 1983, s.145(4)). A parallel development was the introduction of the sentence of imprisonment for public protection (IPP) by the Criminal Justice Act (CJA) 2003. Like the DSPD proposals, the IPP targeted the problem of dangerous offenders released from determinate prison sentences but did not apply retrospectively (Annison, 2015). The draconian IPP sentence created significant problems for an under-resourced and overcrowded prison system and the sentence was eventually abolished by the Legal Aid, Sentencing and Punishment of Offenders Act (LASPO) 2012.

While awaiting legislative change, a pilot DSPD programme was established in two high secure prisons for men (HMP Whitemoor and HMP Frankland) and one closed prison for women (HMP Low Newton) and two secure hospitals for men (Broadmoor and Rampton). Its "underpinning philosophy" was 'that public protection will be best served by addressing the mental health needs of a previously neglected group' and its aims were "improved public protection; provision of new treatment services improving mental health outcomes and reducing risk, and; better understanding of what works in the treatment and management of those who meet the DSPD criteria" (DSPD Programme et al., 2008, p. 6).

The DSPD programme: learning lessons?

Perhaps surprisingly, many of the myths and misinformation that were rife at the time the 1999 DSPD proposals were published live on in the minds of those involved in the OPDP. The discredited claim that Stone was "a diagnosed psychopath who did not satisfy the treatability criteria of the 1983 Mental Health Act and who could not therefore be detained indefinitely" was cited as recently as 2015 as one of the reasons behind the establishment of the DSPD programme (Lloyd & Bell, 2015, p. 2).

The officials responsible for designing and commissioning the OPDP have claimed that, before the DSPD programme, "many offenders perpetrating serious violence and sexual crimes were said to be untreatable" and there was "no place for them in a hospital" and mental health services were "almost exclusively for those deemed mentally ill" (Benefield et al., 2015, p. 4). These claims disregard the range of opinions on treatability noted by the Fallon Inquiry (Fallon, 1999) and the long history of PD patients detained in the special hospitals. In the 1980s, patients detained on the grounds of psychopathic disorder made up about a quarter of Broadmoor hospital's residential male population (Dell & Robertson, 1988, p. 63). Individual and group psychotherapy, social skills training and behaviour modification programmes were available in the hospital for this group. Half of the PD patients who had engaged in individual psychotherapy found it "very helpful" and a majority found behaviour modification and social skills programmes useful (Dell & Robertson, 1988, p. 87). At the time of the study, however, only a small minority of patients were taking part in any therapy, and much of the care was "custodial" in nature (Dell & Robertson, 1988, p. 87). Highlighting differences in what constitutes "therapy", practitioners at Broadmoor viewed life in a secure hospital setting as "milieu therapy", as patients were encouraged to learn acceptable behaviours through their interactions with staff and other patients (Dell & Robertson, 1988, p. 91). Many patients disagreed with this, however, and were disappointed with what they perceived to be insufficient levels of therapeutic input.

A small number of "hostile, bitter and uncooperative" patients who had been transferred there from prison for detention rather than treatment posed particular problems for Broadmoor. If their offences were sufficiently serious, such patients were effectively "undischargeable" (Dell & Robertson, 1988, p. 78). Similarly, there was pressure on Ashworth to take patients who could no longer be detained in prison, which could result in the hospital acquiring "a ward full of [...] people for whom nothing positive could be done" (Fallon, 1999, para. 1.38.2). The Fallon Inquiry concluded that secure hospitals were "being used as surrogate prisons" because there were no other means of detaining this category of dangerous offenders indefinitely (Fallon, 1999, para. 1.43.7).

Personality disordered individuals also caused difficulties within prisons, and the most disruptive prisoners were 'transferred from segregation unit to segregation unit' with 'little or nothing in the way of constructive activity or opportunity to address their behaviour' (Fallon, 1999, para. 1.35.8). Before the DSPD programme was introduced, prisoners with high psychopathy scores were often excluded from interventions aimed at reducing the risks they posed due to evidence that treatment could enhance their risk of recidivism (Rice, Harris & Cormier, 1992; D'Silva, Duggan & McCarthy, 2004).

It was against this background that the DSPD programme opened in the early 2000s. Evaluations of the programme reveal that, while the DSPD programme had some success in managing prisoners at a lower cost, many of the problems experienced by the secure hospital and prison systems were perpetuated under the DSPD programme. This raises the question of whether the programme was developed with due regard to the lessons from past failures noted by the Fallon Inquiry (1999). Given the seemingly low awareness amongst the creators of the OPDP of the institutional history surrounding PD offenders, there is a risk that these problems will continue.

The DSPD programme began with the aim of developing 'care pathways to allow a continuum of care across all levels of security' (Department of Health et al., 2003). The bulk of the funding was concentrated on high secure services, and no DSPD-specific services were established in lower security category prisons. Consequently, the options for onward progression from DSPD services were limited and uncertainties regarding pathways out of the units had a detrimental effect on prisoner and patient motivation and engagement with therapy (Trebilcock & Weaver, 2010a, 2010b; Burns et al., 2011).

An early evaluation of the DSPD programme by the IMPALOX group was highly critical, reporting that the units were administering "substantially different treatments […] with no apparent consistency or methodology being applied" and less than 10% of the time patients and prisoners spent in assessment and treatment constituted "direct therapeutic activity" (Tyrer et al., 2010, p. 97). The authors expressed the concern that the government was "warehousing" offenders in a programme that would allow them to "be 'parked' for long periods thereby preventing them from being released from custody and re-offending" (Tyrer et al., 2010, p. 97).

In response, Kevin Howells and colleagues affiliated with the DSPD unit at Rampton hospital attributed the low levels of therapeutic input to the premature commissioning of the evaluation (Howells et al. 2011). Some units did not reach full capacity until 2009 while the IMPALOX study concluded in 2006 (Tyrer et al., 2007). Much of the work of the units in the early stages was with men who had difficulty relating to others and who were "largely 'unready' to undertake intensive therapeutic work" (Howells et al., 2011, p. 132). The authors contended that one of the neglected successes of the programme was the fact it had managed to deliver therapy to a "challenging population" of "individuals who have typically failed to engage meaningfully in treatment […] or been denied treatment due to their so-called untreatability" (Howells et al., 2011, p. 130).

Nevertheless, subsequent evaluation of the DSPD programme by the IDEA group found similarly low levels of therapeutic activity, reporting that, on average, therapy sessions took up less than two hours per week (Burns et al., 2011, p. 237). This compared to nine hours of structured activities, including work, education and leisure (Burns et al., 2011, p. xiv). As may be expected, the greatest sources of dissatisfaction for patients and prisoners on the DSPD programme were boredom and frustration with "waiting" for treatment (Burns et al., 2011, pp. 205–206). These findings were surprising given the emphasis on therapy in programme delivery guides (DSPD Programme et al., 2006, 2008a).

The IDEA study found little difference between the prison and hospital units in terms of treatment outcomes. There were weak but statistically significant reductions in Violence Risk Scale (VRS) scores in both prisons and hospitals, suggesting treatment may have been beneficial in the short-term (Ministry of Justice, 2011a, p. 7). Due to the lack of a control group, however, it was not possible to say for certain whether these reductions were a result of treatment or other factors (Ministry of Justice, 2011a, p. 7).

The management of inmates in prisons may have been more effective than in hospitals, with fewer violent incidents being reported (Burns et al., 2011, p. 73, 177). However, the hospital units had to deal with a significant minority of patients who were unmotivated for or actively resisting therapy, and this was perceived by other patients and prisoners as having a negative influence on their own motivation (Burns et al., 2011, pp. 217–219). This indicates that some of the difficulties experienced by the secure hospitals in the past were perpetuated under the DSPD programme, despite the new enthusiasm and increased funding for research on treatment.

Despite these findings, the decision to decommission the DSPD programme in secure hospitals but to expand provision in prisons and in the community under the OPDP may be understood on economic grounds. The DSPD units offered a means of managing difficult and disruptive prisoners at £60,000 less per prisoner than existing close supervision centres (Department of Health, 2011, p. 6). In addition, if the DSPD programme were to close, managing this group of prisoners without therapeutic intervention was expected to result in increased violent disruption, putting additional pressure on the capacity of segregation units and leading to transfers between prisons (Department of Health, 2011, p. 6). It would also potentially lead to greater use of secure hospitals, where a bed costs around £290,000 per annum (Department of Health, 2011, p. 6). Thus, while robust evidence for the effectiveness of treatment on the DSPD programme is still elusive, the initiative performed relatively well against one of its original objectives: managing a difficult and disruptive group of prisoners. This aim has received less attention in the literature than treatment or risk reduction, but the survival of the DSPD programme in the form of the OPDP reveals its importance.

The OPDP

At first glance, the OPDP appears to be a more concerted effort to follow through on the original aims and methods of the DSPD programme and there is evidence that some lessons have been learned. The OPDP emphasises prisoner progression and investment in staff support and training, which may go some way to counteracting the high levels of burn-out and staff turnover experienced by the DSPD units (see Trebilcock & Weaver, 2010b). Other developments may, however, be questioned. The most resource-intensive treatment units in high-security prisons will focus on those prisoners who pose the highest risks to the public and those who are least likely to be motivated for treatment, indicating that these units will be particularly difficult to manage. Perhaps the most surprising element of the plans is that a "formal" diagnosis of PD will no longer be required for admission (Department of Health and NOMS, 2011a, para.17). This raises the question of what distinguishes PD offenders from others who pose management difficulties in prisons.

A significant difference between the OPDP and its predecessor is its scale. In response to media claims that the plans for the DSPD group would "involve sweeping large numbers of inoffensive people [...] off the streets", the government was at pains to emphasise in 1999 that only about 2,000 very seriously disordered and high-risk people would fall within the DSPD category (Boateng & Sharland, 1999). At 20,000, the number of men expected to be eligible for the OPDP is ten times higher (Benefield et al., 2015, p. 4). The number of women eligible has seen the most significant increase, from around 50 to between 1,000 and 1,500 (DSPD Programme et al., 2006, p. 8; d'Cruz, 2015, p. 48).

Recently published brochures outline 54 services for men and 24 services for women that are now available in prisons, secure hospitals and in the community under the OPDP (NOMS and NHS England, 2016a, 2016b). Based on the figures given in both brochures, there are now approximately 2,138 places for men and 611 for women in treatment, progression and resettlement services on the OPDP (NOMS and NHS England, 2016a, 2016b). While the bulk of provision is located within the criminal justice system, health services nevertheless retain a place on the OPDP. The former DSPD units at Broadmoor and Rampton secure hospitals have been decommissioned and now form part of the general PD service at each hospital, funded by NHS England.

The pathway will also integrate outcomes from "related programmes for young people and families [...] to contribute to breaking the intergenerational crime cycle" (Department of Health and NOMS, 2011a, para. 38). In this sense, the OPDP is now closer to achieving the original vision of the DSPD proposals, which called for a comprehensive strategy to identify the causes of severe PD and implement preventive interventions for children and adults at risk of developing it (Home Office and Department of Health, 1999, Annexe E).

It is estimated that around half of offenders found to meet the OPDP criteria will be willing or able to access treatment interventions (NOMS and NHS England, 2012, p. 20). The largest component of the OPDP will, therefore, consist of case formulation and case management and will include 20,000 individuals of both genders. This approach involves screening the NOMS prison and probation caseload to identifying offenders who meet the OPDP criteria early in their sentences and providing supported offender management, sentence planning, treatment service referrals, progress reviews and specialist training for staff (NOMS and NHS England, 2016a). This indicates that the monitoring and management of large numbers of problematic offenders have become a much more significant goal under the OPDP than under the DSPD programme.

Entry onto the DSPD programme depended on the fulfilment of three criteria, broadly the same for men as for women. The first requirement was that the candidate was likely to commit an offence that might be expected to lead to serious physical or psychological harm from which the victim would find it difficult or impossible to recover. Second, he or she had to be diagnosed with a severe PD. Third, a link between the disorder and the risk of offending was required (DSPD Programme et al., 2006, 2008a, 2008b). New, separate criteria for men and women have been devised for the OPDP and there are also indicative criteria for entry into high secure prison units for men and onto the hospital pathway. While the OPDP criteria follow a similar formula, they are significantly broader than the DSPD criteria, and the vast increases in the numbers eligible for the OPDP indicate that the criteria may be applied more flexibly.

Criteria for men's services:

At any point during their sentence, assessed as presenting a high likelihood of violent or sexual offence repetition and as presenting a high or very high risk of serious harm to others; and

1 Likely to have a severe PD; and
2 A clinically justifiable link between the PD and the risk; and
3 The case is managed by [the National Probation Service] (Benefield et al., 2015, p. 6).

Criteria for women's services:

1 Current offence of violence against the person, criminal damage, sexual (not economically motivated) and/or against children; and
2 Assessed as presenting a high risk of committing an offence from the above categories OR managed by the NPS; and
3 Likely to have a severe form of PD; and
4 A clinically justifiable link between the above (d'Cruz, 2015, p. 49).

The risk of serious harm threshold appears to be higher than under the DSPD programme, as the likelihood of reoffending now must be 'high'. However, as the Pathway will include male offenders who have been assessed as presenting a high or very high risk of harm to others 'at any point during their sentence' (Benefield et al., 2015, p. 6), it may be expected to draw in many individuals who would not have been eligible for the DSPD programme. These individuals are likely to have already made some progress on their sentences down through security categories.

The harm threshold for women entering the OPDP is lower than that required for men. This is intended to reflect 'the much *lower* numbers of women who are a high risk of harm to the general public, and the proportionately *higher* numbers of women offenders with mental health problems and self-harming behaviours' (Benefield et al., 2015, p. 6. Original emphasis). The inclusion of the

Continuity and change in penal policy **121**

offence of criminal damage without any additional requirement of harm to others will widen the net considerably. No further rationale is given for the inclusion of this offence or for offences against children.

Nevertheless, the strategy continues to focus on women assessed as presenting a high risk of relatively serious reoffending. Combined with the OPDP criteria for men, those who present a lower risk to the public but who may need better care may be left out. This calls into question the extent to which the initiative will reduce inequalities in mental health provision between prisons and the community.

Perhaps the most striking difference with the DSPD criteria is that individuals now need only be 'likely' to suffer from a severe PD before they can be referred to the OPDP. Indeed, the 'focus of work, in most cases, will be in relation to offenders who do not have a formal PD diagnosis' (Department of Health and NOMS, 2011a, para. 17). These individuals will 'have complex needs consisting of emotional and interpersonal difficulties, and display challenging behaviour of a degree that causes concern in relation to their effective management' (Department of Health and NOMS, 2011a, para. 17). This gives an indication that the focus of the OPDP will be on individuals who cause disruption in institutional settings as well as on those who pose a high risk to the public. A formal diagnosis will, however, be required for some forms of treatment on the OPDP (Department of Health and NOMS, 2011a, para. 17).

The incorporation of individuals who have not been formally diagnosed into a 'PD pathway' is problematic. While those on the OPDP are no longer described as 'dangerous', the PD label itself is stigmatising (Tyrer et al., 2011) and can affect a patient's care pathway and subsequent sentencing and custody decisions (Witharana, Ho, & Larkin, 2011). The continuing uncertainty about the effectiveness of the treatment may mean that a stigmatising label will be attached to offenders without giving them any effective means of progressing past it. On the flip side, the OPDP's focus on serious offenders may result in under-diagnosis, with some individuals slipping through the net and being left out of services that could benefit them (Witharana, Ho, & Larkin, 2011). This again highlights that the OPDP will struggle to meet the aim of reducing health inequalities and enhancing well-being, as the overarching emphasis is on public protection and facilitating the management of difficult prisoners (O'Loughlin, 2019).

In view of the controversy surrounding the DSPD diagnosis, it is perhaps surprising that the generality of the criteria for the OPDP has received such little attention. The reason for this may be because the OPDP mainly targets individuals who are within the NOMS caseload and are therefore subject to a prison sentence or licence conditions. Detention in hospital units included on the OPDP will depend on meeting the criteria in the MHA 1983, which include the requirement that the patient suffers from a 'disorder or disability of the mind' (s.1 MHA 1983).

The 2011 consultation document specifies additional criteria for entry into PD units in Category A prisons (Department of Health and NOMS, 2011a, para. 49).

These include 'a history of serious violent and/or sexual offences', which may include 'excessively violent or sadistic aspects', and 'an imminent risk of serious harm to others if released' (Department of Health and NOMS, 2011a, para. 49). Other criteria include failing to acknowledge the harms they have caused, tending to minimise the impact of their offending on others, blaming others for their problems or circumstances, exploiting others and abusing trust or friendships, and having a history of breaching parole, bail conditions or community sentences (Department of Health and NOMS, 2011a, para. 49). These criteria may be expected to yield a much higher concentration of prisoners exhibiting antisocial or psychopathic personality traits and behaviours than was the case under the DSPD programme.

Psychopathy ratings were high amongst those on the DSPD programme, with an average score of 28 on the PCL-R scale and 40% of participants scoring 30 and above (Burns et al., 2011, p. xi). However, 17.2% of patients and prisoners were admitted under the third diagnostic category, which did not require a high PCL-R score (Burns et al., 2011, Table 3.8). The lowest recorded PCL-R scores were 13 in the prisoner group and 18.9 in the hospital patient group, well below the cut-off point for psychopathy of 26 (Burns et al., 2011, Table 3.14, p. 46). Prisons and hospitals were more likely to refer to the DSPD programme 'individuals who [stood] out in terms of their behaviour or who are difficult to manage' (Kirkpatrick et al., 2010, p. 278). This included individuals 'characterised by high levels of emotional instability or repeated incidents of self-harm indicative of BPD' (Kirkpatrick et al., 2010, p. 278). Those with a primary diagnosis of BPD may be more treatment-seeking and more amenable to treatment given the more encouraging evidence base for treating BPD (NCCMH et al., 2009). They may now be excluded from high secure units focusing on those with a more antisocial profile, presenting difficulties in terms of equivalence of services between prison and the community.

While individuals diagnosed with BPD tend to be demanding of services, those diagnosed with ASPD tend to resist treatment (NCCMH et al., 2009, 2010). Success in treating this population is often calculated in terms of reduced risks to others rather than a benefit to patients (NCCMH et al., 2010). Offenders who already have a low motivation for treatment may be even less likely to engage with treatments primarily aimed at reducing risk to the public. This is compounded by the fact that candidates for high secure services will be selected explicitly on the grounds that they are 'unlikely to be very motivated, but likely to benefit from work to increase [...] motivation and engagement' (Department of Health and NOMS, 2011a, para. 49). Given the implications for staff working primarily with a resistant group of prisoners, the extent to which the OPDP builds on learning from the DSPD programme may be questioned.

High staff turnover and burnout presented operational difficulties for the high secure DSPD units and limited the number of treatment hours available (Trebilcock & Weaver, 2010b). The medium secure hospital units also struggled to retain staff (Fortune et al., 2010). The development of staff training under the PD Knowledge and Understanding Framework (KUF) may go some way towards combatting these problems, but the concentration of treatment-resistant prisoners makes it likely that the high secure prison units will be particularly difficult to manage. The units may, therefore, continue to struggle to attract and retain competent staff. This was one of the disadvantages of the separate service option noted by Fallon, again indicating that insufficient regard may have been had to the potential problems associated with concentrating treatment-resistant individuals in one place.

It is notable that some services on the OPDP, including prison PIPEs and therapeutic communities, require candidates to be self-motivated and some explicitly exclude individuals for whom engagement with the programme is a mandatory part of their sentence plan (NOMS and NHS England, 2016a). This indicates that the approach of the OPDP to those individuals who present the highest risks is more coercive, while the approach to lower risk individuals is more cooperative. In order to have a chance at success, psychological treatments for PD require patient engagement and motivation to change, and motivational interventions became a large part of the work of the DSPD units (Burns et al., 2011). In light of this, Peter Tyrer and colleagues suggested that 'concentrating the resources on those who are clearly motivated and determined to overcome their propensity to re-offend may be one way forward' (Tyrer et al., 2010, p. 98). However, the OPDP continues to prioritise high-risk prisoners with low motivation for admission to services in costly high-security settings, raising the question of whether this is the best use of resources.

Hospital services will be expected to relieve the prison service of its most challenging and complex cases without the additional staffing and resources of the DSPD units. Broad criteria for entry onto the hospital pathway include uncertain, changing or disputed diagnosis or risk levels, a need for interventions not readily available in prison, deliberate self-harm, co-morbid mental illnesses requiring stabilisation in hospital, and complexity compounded by borderline intellectual functioning or neurological impairment (NOMS and NHS England, 2015, p. 17). Also mentioned are 'repeated failure in a prison setting', 'irretrievable breakdown of relationships in custody' and 'therapy-interfering behaviours' such as 'litigiousness, breaches of boundaries [and] pathological attachments' (NOMS and NHS England, 2015, p. 17).

The hospital pathway will also continue to be used for the preventive detention of individuals who have been transferred to hospital from prison under s.47 of the MHA 1983 but whose prison sentences have since expired (NOMS and NHS England, 2015, p. 17). However, one of the aims of case formulation is to identify prisoners early in their sentences so that they can be treated on the prison pathway or promptly transferred to hospital. This suggests that lessons have been learned from the experience of the hospital DSPD units in dealing with a disgruntled group of patients transferred from prison (Trebilcock & Weaver, 2010b; Burns et al., 2011).

The Court of Appeal took a dim view of late transfers from prison to hospital in the case of *R. (TF) v. SS for Justice* [2008] EWCA Civ 1457, stating that 'heightened scrutiny' should be applied by courts and the Secretary of State to the evidence supporting such decisions and that it hoped that transfers close to a prisoner's release date would only take place in 'very exceptional circumstances' (*TF*, para. 18). The Ministry of Justice now instructs that prisoners 'should not be transferred to hospital at the end of sentence unless there is clear evidence that hospital admission is necessary on clinical grounds' (National MAPPA Team et al., 2012, pp. 123–124). However, the MHA 1983 does not present a barrier to late transfer decisions motivated by public protection so long as 'appropriate medical treatment' is 'available' to the patient in hospital (*R (SP) v. Secretary of State for Justice* [2010] EWCA Civ 1590; O'Loughlin, 2019). Despite the change in policy, therefore, secure hospitals can legally continue to be used for preventive detention. The problems disgruntled patients posed for the DSPD units and secure hospitals in the past may therefore recur in future.

Conclusion

While the stated aims of the OPDP are similar to those of the DSPD programme, improving wellbeing seems to take second place to the goals of protecting the public and managing disruptive offenders. There are also indications of a movement away from treating the DSPD group as a case apart and towards assimilating them into the mainstream prison population. On the other hand, these trends could be construed as the beginning of a movement towards interpreting the behaviour of all high risk disruptive prisoners through the lens of PD and the medicalisation of offending. For individuals who do not have a formal diagnosis of PD, this may result in stigmatisation and impede their progress through the system.

The focus of the new pathway on high-risk offenders and on those who are least likely to be motivated to engage with treatment indicates that the goal of reducing health inequalities is pursued inconsistently by the OPDP. Overall, these trends indicate that the DSPD programme has been co-opted by a criminal justice system geared towards protecting the public from crime and monitoring and managing the risks posed by offenders within institutions rather than meeting their mental health needs. This casts doubt on the ability of the initiative to meet the stated aim of reducing health inequalities amongst prisoners in the spirit of the Bradley Report (2009).

References

American Psychiatric Association (2013) *Diagnostic and Statistical Manual of Mental Disorders: DSM-5*. Washington, D.C: American Psychiatric Association.

Annison, H. (2015) *Dangerous Politics: Risk, Political Vulnerability and Penal Policy*. Oxford: Oxford University Press

Bateman, A.W., Gunderson, J. and Mulder, R. (2015) "Treatment of Personality Disorder", *Lancet*, 385, 735–743.

Benefield, N., Joseph, N., Skett, S., Bridgland, S., d'Cruz, L., Goode, I. and Turner, K. (2015) "The Offender PD Strategy Jointly Delivered by NOMS and NHS England", *Prison Service Journal Special Edition: Working with People with PD. Prison Service Journal*, 218, 4–9.

Blackburn, R. (1988) "On Moral Judgments and Personality Disorders: The Myth of the Psychopathic Personality Revisited", *British Journal of Psychiatry*, 153, 505–512.

Boateng, P. and Sharland, A. (1999) "Managing Dangerous People with Severe PD", *Criminal Justice Matters*, 37(1), 4–9.

Bradley, K. J. C. (2009) *The Bradley Report: Lord Bradley's Review of People with Mental Health Problems or Learning Disabilities in the Criminal Justice System*. London: Department of Health.

Burns, T., Yiend, J., Fahy, T., Fazel, S., Fitzpatrick, R., Sinclair, J., Rogers, R., Vasquez Montes, M. and the IDEA Group (2011) *Inclusion for DSPD: Evaluating Assessment and Treatment (IDEA): Final Report to NHS National R&D Programme on Forensic Mental Health*. London: Ministry of Justice.

Butler, R.A. (1975) *Report of the Committee on Mentally Abnormal Offenders*. London: H.M.S.O.

d'Cruz, L. (2015) "Implementing an Offender PD Strategy for Women", *Prison Service Journal*, 218, 31–34.

D'Silva, K., Duggan, C. and McCarthy, L. (2004) "Does Treatment Really Make Psychopaths Worse? A Review of the Evidence", *Journal of Personality Disorders*, 18, 163–177.

Dell, S. and Robertson, G. (1988) *Sentenced to Hospital: Offenders in Broadmoor*. Oxford: Oxford University Press.

Department of Health (1999) *Report of the Expert Committee: Review of the Mental Health Act 1983*. London: Department of Health.

Department of Health (2000a) *Reforming the Mental Health Act: Part I: The New Legal Framework. Cm 5016-I*. London: Stationery Office.

Department of Health (2000b) *Reforming the Mental Health Act: Part II: High Risk Patients, Cm 5016-II*. London: Stationery Office.

Department of Health (2011) *PD Pathway Implementation Plan: Impact Assessment*. Available at: https://www.gov.uk/government/publications/personality-disorder-pathway-implementation-plan-impact-assessment. Accessed 6 April 2020.

Department of Health and NOMS (2011a) *Consultation on the Offender PD Pathway Implementation Plan*. Available at: http://data.parliament.uk/DepositedPapers/Files/DEP2011-0319/DEP2011-0319.pdf. Accessed 6 April 2020.

Department of Health and NOMS (2011b) *Response to the Offender PD Consultation*. Available at: https://webarchive.nationalarchives.gov.uk/20130104190523/http://www.dh.gov.uk/en/Consultations/Responsestoconsultations/DH_130566. Accessed 6 April 2020.

Department of Health, Home Office and HM Prison Service (2003) *DSPD in the Community: Factsheet*. Home Office Communication Directorate.

DSPD Programme, Department of Health and Ministry of Justice (2008) *Forensic PD Medium Secure and Community Pilot Services Planning and Delivery Guide*. London: Ministry of Justice and Department of Health.

DSPD Programme, Department of Health, Home Office and HM Prison Service (2006) *Dangerous and Severe/Complex PD High Secure Services Planning and Delivery Guide for Women's DSPD Services (Primrose Programme)*. London: Home Office.

DSPD Programme, Department of Health, Ministry of Justice and HM Prison Service (2008) *Dangerous and Severe PD (DSPD) High Secure Services for Men: Planning and Delivery Guide*. London: Home Office.

Duggan, C. and Howard, R. (2009) "The 'Functional Link' Between Personality Disorder and Violence: A Critical Appraisal". In: McMurran, M. and Howard, R. (eds) *Personality, Personality Disorder and Violence: An Evidence-Based Approach*. Chichester: John Wiley and Sons., 19–38.

Eastman, N. (1999) "Public Health Psychiatry or Crime Prevention?", *British Medical Journal*, 318, 549–550.

Fallon, P. (1999) *Report of the Committee of Inquiry into the Personality Disorder Unit, Ashworth Special Hospital*. London: Stationery Office.

Fazel, S. and Danesh, J. (2002), "Serious Mental Disorder in 23,000 Prisoners: A Systematic Review of 62 Surveys", *Lancet*, 359, 545–550.

Fortune, Z., Rose, D., Crawford, M., Slade, M., Spence, R., Mudd, D., Barrett, B., Coid, J. W., Tyrer, P. and Moran, P. (2010) "An Evaluation of New Services for Personality-Disordered Offenders: Staff and Service User Perspectives", *International Journal of Social Psychiatry*, 56(2), 186–195.

Francis, R., Higgins, J. and Cassam, E. (2006) *Report of the Independent Inquiry into the Care and Treatment of Michael Stone*. South East Coast Strategic Health Authority, Kent County Council and Kent Probation.

Gibbon, S., Duggan, C., Stoffers, J., Huband, N., Völlm, B. A., Ferriter, M. and Lieb, K. (2010) "Psychological Interventions for Antisocial PD", *Cochrane Database of Systematic Reviews*, Issue 6.

Gunn, J. (2003), "Psychopathy: An Elusive Concept with Moral Overtones"., in Millon, T., Simonsen, E., Birket-Smith, M. and Davis, R. D. (eds.), *Psychopathy: Antisocial, Criminal and Violent Behaviour*. London: Guildford Press, 32–39.

Gutiérrez, F., Vall, G., Peri, J. M., Baillés, E., Ferraz, L., Gárriz, M. and Caseras, X. (2012) "Personality Disorder Features through the Life Course", *Journal of Personality Disorders*, 26(5), 763–774.

Hare, R. D. (1991) *The Psychopathy Checklist-Revised (PCL-R)*. Toronto: Multi-Health Systems.

Home Office and Department of Health (1999) *Managing Dangerous People with Severe PD: Proposals for Policy Development*. London: Home Office.

Home Office and Department of Health and Social Security (1986) *Offenders Suffering from Psychopathic Disorder*. London: Department of Health and Social Security.

Howard, R. (2015) "PDs and Violence: What is the Link?", *Borderline PD and Emotion Dysregulation*, 2(12), 1–11.

Howells, K. and Day, A. (2007) "Readiness for Treatment in High Risk Offenders with Personality Disorders", *Psychology, Crime and Law*, 13(1), 47–56.

Howells, K., Jones, L., Harris, M., Wong, S., Daffern, M., Tombs, D., Kane, E., Gallagher, J., Ijomah, J., Krishnan, G., Milton, J. and Thornton, D. (2011) "The Baby, the Bathwater and the Bath Itself: A Response to Tyrer et al.'s Review of the Successes and Failures of Dangerous and Severe Personality Disorder", *Medicine, Science and the Law*, 51(3), 129–133.

Jones, D.W. (2008) *Understanding Criminal Behaviour: Psychosocial Approaches to Criminality*. Cullompton: Willan.

Khalifa, N., Duggan, C., Stoffers, J., Huband, N., Völlm, B. A., Ferriter, M. and Lieb, K. (2010) "Pharmacological Interventions for Antisocial PD", *Cochrane Database of Systematic Reviews*, Issue 8.

Kirkpatrick, T., Draycott, S., Freestone, M., Cooper, S., Twiselton, K., Watson, N., Evans, J., Hawes, V., Jones, L., Moore, C., Andrews, K. and Maden, T. (2010) "A Descriptive Evaluation of Patients and Prisoners Assessed for Dangerous and Severe PD", *Journal of Forensic Psychiatry and Psychology*, 21(2), 264–282.

Lloyd, M. and Bell, R. (2015) "Editorial Comment: Personality Disorder in Offenders then and now". *Prison Service Journal*, 218, 2–3.

Maden, A. (2007) "Dangerous and Severe PD: Antecedents and Origins", *British Journal of Psychiatry*, 190 (supp. 49), s8–s11.
Ministry of Justice (2011) *The Early Years of the DSPD (Dangerous and Severe PD) Programme: Results of Two Process Studies*. Research Summary 4/11. London: Ministry of Justice.
Ministry of Justice (2011a) The Early Years of the DSPD (Dangerous and Severe Personality Disorder) Programme: Results of Two Process Studies. Research Summary 4/11. London: Ministry of Justice.
Mullen, P. E. (1999) "Dangerous People with Severe Personality Disorder", *British Medical Journal*, 319, 1146–1147.
National Collaborating Centre for Mental Health, National Institute for Health and Clinical Excellence, British Psychological Society and Royal College of Psychiatrists (2009) *Borderline PD: The NICE Guideline on Treatment and Management*. National Clinical Practice Guideline Number 78. London: British Psychological Society and Royal College of Psychiatrists.
National Collaborating Centre for Mental Health, National Institute for Health and Clinical Excellence, British Psychological Society and Royal College of Psychiatrists, National Institute for Health and Care Excellence (NICE) (2010) *Antisocial PD: Treatment, Management and Prevention*. National Clinical Practice Guideline Number 77. London: British Psychological Society and Royal College of Psychiatrists.
National MAPPA Team, National Offender Management Service, Offender Management and Public Protection Group (2012) *MAPPA Guidance 2012. Version 4*. Available at: https://www.justice.gov.uk/downloads/offenders/mappa/mappa-guidance-2012-part1.pdf. Accessed 6 April 2020.
National Offender Management Service and NHS England (2015) *The Offender Personality Disorder Pathway Strategy 2015*. Available at: https://www.england.nhs.uk/commissioning/wp-content/uploads/sites/12/2016/02/opd-strategy-nov-15.pdf. Accessed 6 April 2020.
NOMS and NHS England (2012) *F5793 Community PD Service Specification – FINAL12.09.12*. Obtained from NOMS PD Team.
NOMS and NHS England (2015) *The Offender Personality Disorder Pathway Strategy*. London: NOMS and NHS England. Available at: https://www.england.nhs.uk/commissioning/wp-content/uploads/sites/12/2016/02/opd-strategy-nov-15.pdf. Accessed 1 May 2020.
NOMS and NHS England (2016a) *Brochure of Offender PD Services for Men*. May 2016. Obtained from NOMS PD Team.
NOMS and NHS England (2016b) *Brochure of Offender PD Services for Women*. June 2016. Obtained from NOMS PD Team.
O'Loughlin, A. (2014) "The Offender PD Pathway: Expansion in the Face of Failure?", *Howard Journal of Criminal Justice*, 53(2), 173–192.
O'Loughlin, A. (2019) "De-Constructing Risk, Therapeutic Needs and the Dangerous Personality Disordered Subject", *Punishment & Society*, 21(5), 616–638.
Peay, J. (1988) "Offenders Suffering from Psychopathic Disorder: The Rise and Demise of a Consultation Document", *British Journal of Criminology*, 28(1), 67–81.
Peay, J. (2011) *Mental Health and Crime*. Abingdon: Routledge.
Pickersgill, M. (2012) "How Personality Became Treatable: The Mutual Constitution of Clinical Knowledge and Mental Health Law", *Social Studies of Science*, 43(1), 30–53.
Reed, J. (1992) *Review of Health and Social Services for Mentally Disordered Offenders and Others Requiring Similar Services: Final Summary Report*. London: HMSO.
Reed, J. (1994) *Report of the Department of Health and Home Office Working Group on Psychopathic Disorder*. London: Department of Health.
Rice, M. E., Harris, G.T. and Cormier, C. A. (1992) "An Evaluation of a Maximum-Security Therapeutic Community for Psychopaths and other Mentally Disordered Offenders". *Law and Human Behavior*, 16, 399–412.

Rutherford, A. (2006) "Dangerous People: Beginnings of a New Labour Proposal". In: Newburn, T. and Rock, P. (eds.) *The Politics of Crime Control: Essays in Honour of David Downes*. Oxford: Oxford University Press.

Saradjian, J., Murphy, N. and McVey, D. (2010) "Delivering Integrated Treatment to People with PD". In: Murphy, N. and McVey, D. (eds) *Treating PD: Creating Robust Services for People with Complex Mental Health Needs*. London: Routledge, 99–157.

Seddon, T. (2008) "Dangerous Liaisons: PD and the Politics of Risk", *Punishment & Society*, 10, 301–317.

Select Committee on Health (2000) Fourth Report: Provision of NHS Mental Health Services. Volume II: Minutes of Evidence and Appendices to the Minutes of Evidence. Available_at:_http://www.publications.parliament.uk/pa/cm199900/cmselect/cmhealth/373/37302.htm. Accessed 6 April 2020.

Singleton, N., Gatward, R. and Meltzer, H. (1998) *Psychiatric Morbidity among Prisoners in England and Wales*. London: Stationery Office.

Tennant, A. and Howells, K. (2010) *Using Time, Not Doing Time: Practitioner Perspectives on PD and Risk*. Chichester: Wiley-Blackwell.

Tew, J. and Atkinson, R. (2013) "The Chromis Programme: From Conception to Evaluation", *Psychology, Crime and Law*, 19(5–6), 415–431.

Thornicroft, G. (2006) *Shunned: Discrimination against People with Mental Illness*. Oxford: Oxford University Press.

Trebilcock, J. and Weaver, T. (2010a) *Study of the Legal Status of Dangerous and Severe PD (DSPD) Patients and Prisoners, and the Impact of DSPD Status on Parole Board and Mental Health Review Tribunal Decision-making*. London: Ministry of Justice.

Trebilcock, J. and Weaver, T. (2010b) *Multi-mMethod Evaluation of the Management, Organisation and Staffing (MEMOS) in High Security Treatment Services for People with Dangerous and Severe PD (DSPD)*. London: Ministry of Justice.

Tyrer, P., Barrett, B., Byford, S., Cooper, S., Crawford, M., Cicchetti, D., Duggan, C., Joyce, E., Kirkpatrick, T., Maier, M., O'Sullivan, S., Maden, T., Rogers, R., Rutter, D. and Seivewright, H. (2007) *Evaluation of the Assessment Procedure at Two Pilot Sites in the DSPD Programme. (IMPALOX Study)*. London: Ministry of Justice.

Tyrer, P., Crawford, M., Mulder, R., Blashfield, R., Farnam, A., Fossati, A. et al., Kim, Y-R., Koldobsky, N., Lecic-Tosevski, D., Ndetei, D., Swales, M., Clark, L. A. and Reed, G. M. (2011) "The Rationale for the Reclassification of PD in the 11th Revision of the International Classification of Diseases", *Personality and Mental Health*, 5, 246–259.

Tyrer, P., Duggan, C., Cooper, S., Crawford, M., Seivewright, H., Rutter, D., Maden, T., Byford, S. and Barrett, B. (2010) "The Successes and Failures of the DSPD Experiment: The Assessment and Management of Severe PD", *Medicine, Science and the Law*, 50, 95–99.

Warren, F., McGauley, G., Norton, K., Dolan, B., Preedy-Fayers, K., Pickering, A. and Geddes, J. R. (2003) *Review of Treatments for Severe PD (Home Office Online Report 30/03)*. London: Home Office.

Witharana, D., Ho, D. K. and Larkin, F. (2011) "Personality Disordered Offenders – Complex Patients Requiring More Expertise", *The Psychiatrist*, 35 (9), 355–356.

Wootton, B. (1981) *Crime and Criminal Law: Reflections of a Magistrate and Social Scientist*. London: Stevens.

Yu, R., Geddes, J.R. and Fazel, S. (2012) "Personality Disorders, Violence, and Antisocial Behavior: A Systematic Review and Meta-Regression Analysis", *Journal of Personality Disorders*, 26(5), 775–792.

Zanarini, M.C, Frankenburg, F.R, Hennen, J. and Silk, K.R. (2003) "The Longitudinal Course of Borderline Psychopathology: 6-Year Prospective Follow-Up of the Phenomenology of Borderline Personality Disorder", *American Journal of Psychiatry*, 160, 274–283.

8

THE THERAPEUTIC MANAGEMENT OF CHILD SEX OFFENDERS

Karen Harrison

Child sexual abuse (CSA) and child sex offenders have always been amongst us, but it was not until the mid-1980s that policymakers, journalists, educators and also the wider public began to be more preoccupied with their presence (Brown, 2013). This has arguably resulted in a moral panic relating to sex offenders in general but also to child sex offenders in particular (Critcher, 2003). This has been heightened further by the News of the World's naming and shaming campaign in 2002, the subsequent riots on the Paulsgrove estate in Portsmouth (Bell, 2005) and in more recent years the uncovering of a number of celebrity child sex offenders including Jimmy Saville, Rolf Harris and Max Clifford. In such circumstances, it has been common for the media to use the term paedophile to cover all those who commit sexual offences against children. The media have also contributed to a sense of insecurity and fear amongst the public with tabloids and broadsheets spreading the message that child sex offenders are dangerous and cannot be treated (Brown, 2013).

This had led to the ever-present question of how child sex offenders should be effectively managed. Many would argue that they should be sent to prison and the key thrown away or likewise that they should be indefinitely detained within mental health institutions. This chapter, however, takes a different approach. It begins by looking at the use of the term paedophile, which is nowadays synonymously used with the phrase child sex offender, and considers whether the mental health route is the most appropriate option. Concluding that it is not, it then moves on to consider three ways in which child sex offenders can be therapeutically managed, all of which aid towards reducing reoffending rates and protecting the public from serious harm.

The classification of child sex offenders

Despite the high profile nature of the term paedophile and the fact that it is now in common parlance, its precise meaning is actually quite hard to ascertain, especially if trying to find a definition which can transcend across clinical, legal and mental health spheres (Harrison, Manning, & McCarten, 2010). Having a clear multidisciplinary understanding is nevertheless crucial, especially when an individual finds themselves caught up within the criminal justice and mental health systems. When working towards a clear understanding of the term, the most obvious place to start is probably the Diagnostic and Statistical Manual of Mental Disorders (DSM) which is authored by the American Psychological Association. This makes it clear that paedophilia cannot be simply equated with CSA; indeed, in a clinical sense, there are clear demarcations made on the age of the victim with the terms hebephilia and ephebophilia also in use. DSM V, therefore, defines paedophilia as:

A   Over a period of at least six months, recurrent, intense sexually arousing fantasies, sexual urges, or behaviors involving sexual activity with a prepubescent child or children (generally age 13 years or younger).
B   The individual has acted on these sexual urges, or the sexual urges or fantasies cause marked distress or interpersonal difficulty.
C   The person is at least age 16 years and at least 5 years older than the child or children in Criterion A (American Psychiatric Association, 2013).

Hebephilia is said to refer to a sexual preference for those generally aged between 11 and 14 and ephebophilia encapsulates a preference for individuals in later adolescence (American Psychiatric Association, 2013). From this clinical perspective, it is not only the age of the victim which is taken into account, with there also being a number of different offender typologies present. An individual could, for example, be classified as a child sexual molester i.e. someone who sexually abuses a child for their own personal gratification, using the child as a sexual aid to bring them pleasure. An alternative is an incest offender, someone who has sexual contact with someone from their own family, or a paedophile, defined as someone who gains sexual gratification from contact with pre-pubescent children. While there may be crossovers between the typologies a paedophile may not necessarily be a child sexual molester and vice-versa. As acknowledged in the DSM definition above, it is not necessary for someone to commit a criminal offence, in order to be classified as a paedophile.

While such precise definitions and diagnoses may be useful in a clinical context, they can be confusing for those who work outside this field of practice and therefore are difficult to translate into, for example, a legal context. In fact, despite the growing usage of the terms paedophile and paedophilia there is no current legal definition of them, either within the United Kingdom (Hansard, 14 October 1997: Column WA113) or internationally. Rather than focusing on the clinical diagnosis, the criminal law looks at the acts of the individual and concentrates on whether that individual has committed prohibited acts mainly contained within the Sexual Offences Act 2003. This can include the contact offences of rape, sexual assault and sexual activity with a child and the non-contact offences of grooming and downloading images of CSA. For an offence to have taken place, the prosecuting authorities need to prove beyond all reasonable doubt (unless the offender pleads guilty) that the necessary actus reus (guilty act) and mens rea (guilty mind) have taken place. Defining a person as a paedophile just because they have a sexual preference towards children does not, therefore, fit in with legal constructions, owing to the fact that the law generally requires a positive act as well as the relevant mental state. This highlights the difference between clinical and legal perspectives (Harrison, Manning, & McCarten, 2010).

These differences are also significant when considering mental health provisions and the ability to detain individuals under mental health legislation. Mental health law in England and Wales is largely governed by the Mental Health Act (MHA) 2007 which updates and amends both the MHA 1983 and the Mental Capacity Act 2005. Mental disorder under the 1983 MHA covered the four classifications of mental impairment, severe mental impairment, mental illness and psychopathic disorder (section 1(2)). Under this interpretation, the term mental disorder specifically excluded sexual deviancy (Bowen, 2007) and so under the MHA 1983, you could not be considered to be suffering from a mental disorder if you were clinically classified as a paedophile. This has now changed. The MHA 2007 largely reverses this exception, and while the other previous exceptions of promiscuity, sexual orientation and dependence on alcohol and drugs remain outside the realms of mental health legislation, sexual deviancy no longer does (Bowen, 2007). This was confirmed by the House of Commons when it stated that "the amendment makes it clear that paedophilia is not within the scope of the exclusion" (Hansard, 19 June 2007: Column 1326). A clinical diagnosis of paedophilia, therefore, makes a person vulnerable to committal proceedings under mental health legislation.

Paedophilia as a mental illness

The key point for consideration is therefore whether somebody who has been classified as a paedophile is mentally ill and therefore could, in theory, be subject to detainment under mental health legislation. A point worth making here requires us to return to the DSM V. In clinical terms paedophilia is classified as a paraphilia which is a "persistent, intense, atypical sexual arousal pattern, independent of whether it causes any distress or impairment" (First, 2014, p. 192). Interestingly, the DSM V makes a difference between a paraphilia and a paraphilic disorder (when the paraphilia causes marked distress or has been acted on) with it only being the latter which requires clinical intervention. If we refer to the definition of paedophilia as outlined above, a person could, therefore, be sexually attracted to pre-pubescent children (the paraphilia) but unless they meet criterion A–C they will not be diagnosed with having the paraphilic disorder. As First rightly points out: "It is easy to imagine how the technical difference between a paraphilia and a paraphilic disorder might be lost on judges, juries, and others not well versed in the subtleties of the DSM" (First, 2014, p. 192).

There is real concern, therefore, that individuals labelled as having the paraphilia paedophilia but not actually the paraphilic disorder could still find themselves vulnerable to committal under mental health legislation.

Another point to consider is the argument that definitions of CSA are socially constructed and change across time and place. While in modern day Western societies we find all forms of CSA abhorrent, this has not always been the case. For example, in England, Scotland and Wales, the age of consent for heterosexual activities in 1285 was 10 (Thomas, 2005). This was raised in 1875 under the Offences against the Person Act to 13, and to 16 in 1885; although this was due to concerns over child prostitution and sex as a product rather than being provoked by fears of paedophilia (Green, 2002). Furthermore, Cook in the eighteenth century observed public copulation in Hawaii between an adult man and a female child – noting that there was no sense of it being improper or indecent. This was also the case in other Polynesian islands at that time (Green, 2002).

Other parts of the globe also differ from the Western World's interpretation of what CSA is. For example some non-western and traditional societies have a number of 'rites of passage' (an experience that the person has to pass through to achieve another state/stage in development) that can involve childhood sexuality – with such societies believing that these events are vital for the continuing development of the child. Examples include:

- The Siwans (North Africa) who believe that a lack of anal intercourse between men and boys is abnormal, with prominent men lending their sons to each other for this purpose.
- The Aranda Aboriginals (Australia) who hold that it is customary for men to have a 10 or 12 year old boy as a lover who will live with him as a wife, until he marries.
- The Etoro (Papa New Guinea) who believe that from the age of 10 boys should swallow the semen of older men, to aid their development into manhood (Green, 2002).

While such practices seem alien and abusive to us, does the fact that they are acceptable in other societies affect our view on whether they should automatically constitute a mental disorder under MHA 2007. If they do then as Green concludes this requires us to "declare [that] a lot of people in many cultures and in much of the past [were] mentally ill" (Green, 2002, p. 471).

The therapeutic management of child sex offenders

For all of the reasons outlined above, child sex offenders should not automatically be made subject to committal, detainment and control under mental health legislation. Notwithstanding this, there is no denying the fact that the incidence of sexual offences is problematic and that the public needs protecting from sexual offenders. For example, for the year ending March 2017, there were a total of 121,187 sexual offences reported to the police (Office for National Statistics, 2018), which while high only represents a small proportion of the actual number of sexual offences perpetrated on an annual basis. A better gauge of criminal activity is therefore the Crime Survey for England and Wales, which estimated that for the year ending March 2017 2% of all adults aged 16–59 experienced some kind of sexual assault in the previous 12 months, which equated to approximately 646,000 victims (Office for National Statistics, 2018). While such offences will range from serious contact offences to less serious non-contact offences, all offenders need to be fairly dealt with by the criminal justice system and then have a sentence imposed on them that reflects the seriousness of their crime. For those who are considered to be dangerous, which can often include child sex offenders, especially if they have similar previous convictions, the court can also extend a proportional sentence to reflect the need to detain a person for longer in custody in order to protect the public from serious harm. In many cases, this will mean that an individual will not be released from custody until the Parole Board deems it safe to do so. Despite this ability to lengthen custodial terms, the vast majority of child sex offenders will one day be released into the community, and so it is important that work is undertaken within custodial settings to ensure that such individuals become less risky in terms of reoffending. The remainder of this chapter, therefore, considers a number of therapeutic options for dealing with those offenders who have been convicted of child sexual offences. While not perfect, most have been shown to be effective in terms of trying to manage and reduce the risk which such offenders pose.

Therapeutic communities

Life in prison for a sex offender is generally not a pleasant experience. It used to be the case that sex offenders along with other vulnerable prisoners (such as those in debt, or those who had informed on others) would be kept on vulnerable prisoner wings under Prison Rule 43. This segregation was to protect them from physical and mental abuse from other mainstream prisoners. While such units still exist, more recently there has been a move to create a number of sex offender only prisons, with five such sites existing in 2017. These have been found to be effective in terms of creating a safer environment for sex offenders but can also be criticised because with so many sex offenders under one roof they can encourage the building up of sex offender networks. One way in which sex offenders can be protected and also be placed within the general prison population is through the use of therapeutic communities (TCs). This has been defined as a "structured psychologically informed environment . . . where the social relationships, structure of the day and different activities together are all deliberately designed to help people's health and well-being" (The consortium for therapeutic communities, 2018). TCs designed for the treatment of offenders have existed in England and Wales since 1962 when HMP Grendon, in Buckinghamshire, opened as a psychiatric experiment. The prison came under the control of the main prison estate in 1985 and is now run by a prison governor. Grendon is the only prison which operates TCs across all units, although in 2001 HMP Dovegate became the first purpose-built therapeutic prison which houses up to 200 men (a small local prison also exists within the main prison site which serves the needs of the local courts). TC units are also available at HMP Holme House, HMP Wymott, HMP Gartree, HMP Warren Hill and HMP Send.

The cruicial point of any therapeutic community is that it is run democratically, in the sense that the residents (not prisoners) have a say in how the communities are run. In Grendon for example twice-weekly community meetings are used to discuss any issues which are arising and any decisions which need to be made. This could involve deciding on who undertakes which jobs on the wing, what consequences should arise from misbehaviour and if the breach of the rules is severe enough whether the community still wants to work with that individual or whether they are voted out of the prison. Extraordinary wing meetings, known as 'Specials' can also be called at any time of the night or day if there has been the occurrence of a crisis which needs immediate attention. The remaining weekly mornings are used for therapy which occurs in groups of 8–10 residents. Trained prison staff facilitate these, but it is the residents who question each other and encourage residents to take responsibility for what they have done. Life on a TC, therefore, requires an individual to actively participate and if a resident is not prepared to do this and is not prepared to share their experiences with others, then there is a real risk that they will be voted out of the community and be required to return to a mainstream prison. Other therapy within a TC could involve music, art and psychodrama. In addition to organised treatment, inmates at Grendon enjoy significantly more association time when compared to other main estate prisoners, and so informal therapy takes place during these times as well. While the weekday mornings in Grendon are devoted to therapy, in the afternoons the residents are involved in work and/or education. They will also be expected to take on a voluntary job for the benefit of their wing (most wings house up to 40 residents) which could include being the chair of the community meetings or the wings research representative.

TCs often house some of the most "damaged, disturbed and dangerous" individuals who show:

> . . . high levels of psychological disturbance on psychometric assessments and often have histories of self-harm and suicide attempts. Their offending behaviour is usually serious and chronic and a substantial number have histories of pronounced institutional misconduct, sometimes severe, prior to admission. The men also show elevated scores on measures of dangerousness and often have a high risk of reconviction.
> *(Shine & Newton 2000: 33)*

There is also likely to be a real mixture of offender types including those who have committed serious violent offences and those who have been convicted of serious sexual offences including those against children. Residents who have severe mental health disorders are also commonplace. As mentioned above in other mainstream prisons, child sex offenders could not be housed with the main prison population but in a TC abuse in all of its forms is not tolerated and could once again lead to a guilty individual losing their place on the TC. In some respects, this mixture of individuals is better for sex offenders as they will be in therapy with and being questioned by non-sex offenders who are more likely to challenge and question their cognitive distortions and deviant beliefs.

Due to the nature of the offenders detained within both Grendon and Dovegate, you would expect rates of violence and incidences to be high, especially when in recent times we have seen an increase in the rates of violence in the general prison estate (HM Inspectorate of Prisons, 2018). This is not, however, the case. In 2018 it was reported that Dovegate was a "safe prison" experiencing:

> . . . little violence, and when incidents occurred, appropriate formal disciplinary action was taken, including deselection if the matter was serious. Most incidents, however, related to minor antisocial behaviour or verbal exchanges, and they were mostly managed within the communities themselves through community challenge, individual self-reflection or community sanctions.
> *(HM Chief Inspector of Prisons, 2018, p. 5)*

Similar comments have also been made concerning Grendon where:

> Incidents of violence remained infrequent. Verbal tensions were sometimes generated through the therapeutic process, but were generally dealt with through the treatment process with little need for recourse to formal procedures or interventions. The prison operated without a segregation unit and very few men were required to move to other prisons for security or disciplinary reasons.
> *(HM Chief Inspector of Prisons, 2017, p. 5)*

Due to the intensive nature of the therapy, it is perhaps unsurprising that TCs cost more than mainstream prisons. In 2018 this was estimated to be an extra £5,000 per resident per year. Despite this increase, such investment has been found to be beneficial not just because it leads to better results for the residents but also because there is significantly less damage and destruction caused to prison property and injuries caused to prison staff. In fact, it has found that for every £1 invested into Grendon there is £2.33 worth of benefits (Bennett & Shuker, 2017). Furthermore, two reconviction studies have been undertaken following men who spent time on the TC wings at Grendon (Marshall, 1997) (Taylor, 2000). Both have shown that residents who stay for 18 months or more experienced a significant reduction in their future reoffending, which in some cases was as high as 25%. It would thus appear that on all counts TCs are a useful way in which to therapeutically manage serious and high-risk child sex offenders.

Pharmacotherapy

Another way in which child sex offenders can be therapeutically managed is through the use of medication. Pharmacotherapy is the use of drugs to treat offenders, to achieve the effect of surgical castration but through less irreversible and invasive means. It is commonly referred to as chemical castration, and this is certainly how the media refers to it, although strictly speaking this is not accurate as the role of these drugs is to reduce abnormally excessive sex drives rather than to eradicate them altogether (Miller, 1998). This can be achieved through the use of either Selective Serotonin Reuptake Inhibitors (SSRIs) or more potent anti-libidinals, such as Medroxyprogesterone Acetate (MPA), Cyproterone Acetate (CPA), Luteinizing Hormone–Releasing Hormone (LHRH) inhibitors and Long-acting Gonadotropin-releasing Hormones (GnRH) agonists. In many respects, there is a hierarchy of drugs with SSRIs being the first-line drug, followed by CPA or MPA and then LHRH inhibitors/GnRH agonists, with the final line of defence being a combination of LHRH inhibitors and CPA (Briken, Hill, & Berner, 2003). It is worth noting, however, that due to the fact that the drugs reduce sexual desire and fantasies they are only likely to work for those sex offenders who offend due to uncontrollable urges – for example, child sex offenders and exhibitionists. The medication is thus unlikely to work with those who offend for reasons of power (rapists) or under the influence of alcohol or drugs.

Looking at the drugs in more detail, SSRIs work by inhibiting the reuptake of serotonin, which has the effect of increasing serotonin concentration levels in the body (Adi et al., 2002). This is useful in the therapeutic management of child sex offenders because it is thought that by enhancing central serotonin levels this reduces sexual functioning, sexual desire and associated sexual performance behaviours (Kafka, 1997). SSRIs are psychotropic medications and are often used in the treatment of depression, bulimia nervosa and obsessive compulsive disorder (OCD) (Adi et al., 2002). They were not initially designed to be used with sex offenders, but in the early 1990s, it was thought that they could be effective due to the similarities between the characteristics of OCD and sexually deviant behaviour. The foremost purpose of the drugs is to lessen the frequency and intensity of sexual fantasies which subsequently leads to a reduction in sexual urges and resulting deviant behaviour (Grubin, 2008). Other positive effects include reductions in anxiety, depression and irritability and a diminishing of low self-esteem.

The primary effect of anti-libidinal medication is to reduce testosterone levels in the body. This will have the knock-on effect of reducing an individual's sexual drive and will also decrease erotic and deviant fantasies (Hicks, 1993). Further effects include a reduction in potency, sperm production, sexual frustration and the frequency and pleasure of masturbation (Craissati, 2004). Anti-libidinals also work to reduce an offender's frustration and anger levels, making them more relaxed and thus able to concentrate on other forms of treatment such as psychotherapy. In order to achieve the most effective results, it is therefore suggested that pharmacotherapy should always be used alongside and in conjunction with psychotherapy and other treatment methods (Harrison, 2007). The main anti-libidinal used for the treatment of child sex offenders in England and Wales is CPA and although it has been seen to be effective (see below) it can produce a plethora of negative side effects. These can include fatigue, hypersomnia, lethargy, depression, a decrease in body hair, an increase in scalp hair and weight gain (Bradford & Pawlak, 1993). Other effects include liver damage, bone mineral loss, nausea, indigestion, skin rashes, galactorrhoea (abnormal production of breast milk), shortness of breath and decreased production of oil from sebaceous glands in the skin (Harrison, 2007). If the choice of drug is MPA then this additionally causes thrombophlebitis (blood clots in superficial veins), pulmonary embolism (blockages in the pulmonary arteries), hyperglycaemia, hypertension, shrinkage of the prostate vessels, diabetes and gynaecomastia (Craissati, 2004).

The effectiveness of SSRIs and anti-libidinals has been well documented, although some of the research studies have been conducted on small sample groups. Nevertheless as detailed in Table 8.1, significant reductions in deviant sexual fantasies and thus risk have been noted.

Despite positive results and bearing in mind the plethora of negative side effects associated with the use of these drugs, there are some ethical issues worth mentioning here. Perhaps one of the most contentious issues is whether pharmacotherapy should be provided on a voluntary or mandatory basis. In many states in the United States of America it is mandatory, often tied in with sentencing and/or parole arrangements. The medical suitability of the offender is therefore not always taken into account, with decisions on use often made by a lawyer (judge) rather than a health practitioner. In England and Wales, SSRIs and CPA are only given where the offender consents, but this too raises concerns, including whether that consent is valid and whether the offender truly understands what they are consenting to, including all of the possible side effects. It has therefore been argued that before voluntary treatment is allowed, the offender should be examined by at least two mental health professionals to ensure that self-hate and a desire to self-punish are not motivating them; to check that there are no mental disorders; and, to check that the offender understands all of the risks involved. A neutral party should then be appointed to ensure that the offender's consent is valid and freely given and finally, if relevant, the offender's spouse should be informed of the risks and consequences of the drugs (Harrison & Rainey, 2009).

Pharmacotherapy in England and Wales is currently available through the offender personality disorder pathway, with the national service running out of six prisons: HMP Leyhill, HMP Frankland, HMP Isle of Wight, HMP Hull, HMP Whatton and HMP North Sea Camp. In Whatton, medication is offered to those men who are sexually preoccupied and it helps them to be able to concentrate more on treatment programmes and ultimately progress through the system. Referrals are accepted by psychiatrists who are involved in the process throughout, with referrals being made by any member of prison staff. At any one time, approximately 5% of the population at Whatton will be on medication, with the majority taking

TABLE 8.1 Efficacy studies of SSRIs and anti-libidinal medication

Drug type	Study	Findings
SSRIs	(Adi et al., 2002)	A review of 9 studies involving 225 subjects. In 6 of the 9 studies levels of improvement were found to be statistically significant. Only 1 study showed insignificant improvements with only 3/13 showing positive change.
SSRIs	(Greenberg, Bradford, Curry, & O'Rourke, 1996)	Results from the study with 94 patients showed significant reductions in paraphilia fantasies.
CPA	(Bradford & Pawlak, 1993)	A study of 19 repeat sexual offenders who alternated between three months of CPA treatment and three months of placebo. Patients noted that whilst on CPA they felt calmer and less sexually preoccupied, noticing more significant reductions in sexual arousal and activity when compared to the placebo and baseline stages.
CPA	(Cooper, Ismail, Phanjoo, & Love, 1972)	Study with 1 man where the patient was unable to masturbate to orgasm.
MPA	(Maletzky, Tolan, & McFarland, 2006)	Those receiving MPA treatment were significantly less likely to sexually reoffend when compared to those receiving no treatment and in the follow-up period, none of the 79 men had returned to prison. In addition, those on treatment were more likely to keep to their parole conditions and be considered to be doing well, with any reoffending being non-sexual in nature.
LHRH	(Briken, 2002)	Study of 11 men. Sexually aggressive behaviour was eradicated and patients reported a reduction in penile erection, ejaculation, masturbation and sexually deviant impulses and fantasies, with no sexual reoffending during the treatment period.

SSRIs. Drugs are also available in the community once the offender has been released, with anecdotal evidence suggesting that the Parole Board are now willing to accept that pharmacotherapy can make a difference to risk levels. This is again provided under the offender personality disorder pathway.

Circles of Support and Accountability (COSA)

The final initiative to be considered here is COSA. Different to the other two methods, this is predominantly a means of managing child sex offenders when they are in the community; although increasingly a number of circles are now starting in prison, three months prior to release. It is included here because whatever good work has been achieved in custody, whether that is through a TC or participation in pharmacotherapy or psychotherapy, such positive gains can be lost once the child sex offender is released into the community and faces in many cases significant stigma and isolation. COSA, therefore, works to try and encourage the offender's reintegration into the community but at the same time ensures that appropriate challenge and disapproval is meted out in relation to inappropriate behaviour, thoughts and feelings. The theoretical basis of COSA arguably lies in restorative justice although instead of the offender meeting with the victim, the offender meets with volunteers from the community and is held accountable by them, arguably on behalf of the victim. Its roots can be traced to the Canadian Mennonite Church, who in 1994 agreed to mentor Charlie Taylor, a high-risk repeat child sex offender who was being released from prison into the community. A group or circle of volunteers worked with Charlie to offer him support, and despite initial pessimism from the criminal justice authorities Charlie never offended again (Wilson, McWhinnie, & Wilson, 2008). Based on the pillars of safety and support, COSA offers public protection and reintegration – with the key idea being that it is the community who accepts responsibility for its members and for addressing the child sex offender's problem (McAlinden, 2007). COSA is also linked to the Good Lives Model which looks for constructive and collaborative ways in which the offender can be helped to enhance their own capacity to live a meaningful and crime-free life (Ward & Maruna, 2007).

COSA is innovative in the sense that the majority of the supervision is carried out by trained volunteers. In most circumstances, this will be four individuals who will receive at least two full days of training. The volunteers and the core member (the offender) make up what is known as the inner circle. The outer circle is made up of those criminal justice professionals who are involved with the core member so this could be the National Probation Service, the Police, and other representatives from housing, mental health and/or social services. There is also an employed COSA co-ordinator who sets up the circles and who will, where appropriate, liaise between the inner and outer circles. The circle will start with a disclosure meeting where the core member is asked to inform the volunteers in relation to their background and offence. Meetings will then take place weekly, with mid-week telephone support if necessary and when thought appropriate dropped down to fortnightly meetings. Most circles will last for a minimum period of 12 months, although if the core member is still showing signs of risk at this stage, it can be continued. Support would include helping the offender with job applications, housing, joining appropriate clubs and societies and generally being someone whom the core member can talk to. When the volunteers may be the only people who the core member sees this is important.

Circles have existed in England and Wales since 2002. At this time the Quakers had involvement in their implementation although since 2008 it is now managed by Circles UK (see http://www.circles-uk.org.uk/). As a national body, it works to develop and co-ordinate the effectiveness and quality of circles across

England and Wales. It also works in partnership with police, probation and other relevant professionals and is funded by the Ministry of Justice, statutory agencies and a number of charitable trusts and foundations. Projects are now running in 13 areas, and in March 2017 there were 583 active volunteers and 163 circles in operation (Circles UK, 2017).

Research on the usefulness of COSA has been positive. The first evaluation in England and Wales involved a follow up of the 16 members of the original Thames Valley COSA from 2002 to 2006. No reconvictions were recorded during this time, although four were recalled to prison for breaching licence conditions, showing evidence of the accountability aspect (Bates, Saunders, & Wilson, 2007). In the latest evaluation it was held that Circles "support[ed] the Core Member, and complemented statutory supervision through supporting compliance with treatment programmes and monitoring the activities of Core Members, as well as providing a positive social network for the Core Member on release from prison" (McCarten et al., 2014, p. 9).

Conclusion

Perhaps different to many of the chapters in this volume, this contribution argues for a move away from a mental health pathway in terms of how we therapeutically manage child sex offenders. While it is freely acknowledged that such offenders have the potential to cause serious levels of harm, it is thought that there are better ways to manage and reduce this risk rather than committal under the MHA 2007 – even though the legislation clearly creates such an option. By using a combination of enabling environments such as TCs and by combining psychotherapy with pharmacotherapy and COSA, communities can in a very real way be made safer places for our children to live in.

Bibliography

Adi, Y., Ashcroft, D., Browne, K., Beech, A., Fry-Smith, A., & Hyde, C. (2002). *Clinical effectiveness and cost-consequences of SSRIs in the treatmnet of sex offenders, Health Technology Assessment 2002, Vol. 6: No. 28,* London: Home Office.

American Psychiatric Association. (2013). *Diagnostic and staistical manual of mental disorders* (5th edition). Washington, DC: American Psychiatric Association.

Bates, A., Saunders, R., & Wilson, C. (2007). Doing something about it: A follow up study of sex offenders participating in Thames Valley Circles of Support and Accountability. *British Journal of Community Justice, 5*(1), 19–42.

Bell, V. (2005). The vigilant(e) parent and the paedophile: The News of the World campaign 2000 and the contemporary governmentality of child sexual abuse. *Economy and Society, 3*(1), 83–102.

Bennett, J., & Shuker, R. (2017). The potential of prison-based democratic therapeutic communities. *International Journal of Prisoner Health, 13*(1), 19–24.

Bowen, P. (2007). *Blackstone's guide to the Mental Health Act 2007.* Oxford: Oxford University Press.

Bradford, J., & Pawlak, A. (1993). Double-blind placebo crossover study of CPA in the treatment of paraphilias. *Archives of Sexual Behavior*, 22(5), 383–402.

Briken, P. (2002). Pharmacotherapy of Paraphilias with LHRH agonists. *Archives of General Psychiatry*, 59(5), 469–470.

Briken, P., Hill, A., & Berner, W. (2003). Pharmacotherapy of paraphilias with long acting agonists of luteinizing hormine-releasing hormone: A systematic review. *Journal of Clinical Psychiatry*, 64(8), 890–897.

Brown, P. (2013). Castrate 'em!' treatments, cures and ethical considerations in UK press coverage of chemical castration. In Harrison, K. & Bernadette, B. (eds.), *The Wiley Blackweel handbook of legal and ethical aspects of sex offender treatment and management* (pp. 129–149). Chichester: John Wiley & Sons.

Circles UK. (2017). *Circles UK annual review 2016–17*. Reading: Circles UK.

Cooper, A., Ismail, A., Phanjoo, A., & Love, D. (1972). Antiandrogen therapy in deviant hypersexuality. *The British Journal of Psychiatry*, 120(554), 59–63.

Craissati, J. (2004). *Managing high risk sex offenders in the community: A psychological approach*. New York: Routledge.

Critcher, C. (2003). *Moral panics and the media*. Buckingham: Open University Press.

First, M. (2014). DSM-5 and paraphilic disorders. *The Journal of the American Academy of Psychiatry and the Law*, 42(2), 191–201.

Green, R. (2002). Is pedophilia a mental disorder? *Archives of Sexual Behavior*, 31, 467–471.

Greenberg, D., Bradford, J., Curry, S., & O'Rourke, A. (1996). A comparison of treatment of paraphilias with three SSRIs: A restrospective study. *The Bulletin of the American Academy of Psychiatry and the Law*, 24(4), 525–532.

Grubin, D. (2008). The use of medication in the treatment of sex offenders. *Prison Service Journal*, 178, 37–43.

Harrison, K. (2007). The high risk sex offender strategy in England and Wales: Is chemical castration an option. *The Howard Journal*, 46(1), 16–31.

Harrison, K., Manning, R., & McCarten, K. (2010). Multi-disciplinary definitions and understandings of paedophilia. *Social and Legal Studies*, 19(4), 481–496.

Harrison, K., & Rainey, B. (2009). Supressing human rights? A rights-based approach to the use of pharmacotherapy with sex offenders. *Legal Studies*, 29(1), 47–74.

Hicks, P. (1993). Castration of sexual offenders: Legal and ethical issues. *Journal of Legal Medicine*, 14(4), 641–667.

HM Chief Inspector of Prisons. (2017). *Report on an unannounced inspection of HMP Grendon*. London: HMIP.

HM Chief Inspector of Prisons. (2018). *Report on an unannounced inspection of HMP Dovergate therapeutic prison*. London : HMIP.

HM Inspectorate of Prisons. (2018). *HM Chief Inspector of Prisons for England and Wales annual report 2017–18*. London: HMIP.

Kafka, M. (1997). A monoamine hypothesus for the pathophysiology of paraphilic disorders. *Archives of Sexual Behaviors*, 26(4), 343–358.

Maletzky, B., Tolan, A., & McFarland, B. (2006). The oregon depo-Provera program: A five-year follow-up. *Sex Abuse*, 18(3), 303–316.

Marshall, P. (1997). *Reconviction study of HMP Grendon therapeutic community, research finding no 53*. London: Home Office.

McAlinden, A.-M. (2007). *The shaming of sexual offenders. Risk, retribution and reintegration*. Oxford: Hart.

McCarten, K., Kemshall, H., Westwood, S., Solle, J., MacKenzie, G., Cattel, J., & Pollard, A. (2014). *COSA: A case file review of two pilots*. London: Ministry of Justice.

Miller, R. (1998). Forced administrtaion of sex-drive reducing medications to sex offenders: Treatment or punishment? *Psychology, Public Policy and Law, 4*(1–2), 175–199.

Office for National Statistics. (2018). *Sexual offences in England and Wales: Year ending March 2017.* London: ONS.

Taylor, R. (2000). *Seven-year reconviction study of HMP Grendon therapeutic community, research finding no 115.* London: Home Office.

The consortium for therapeutic communities. (2018, July 18). *What is a TC.* Retrieved from The consortium of therapeutic communities: https://www.therapeuticcommunities.org/what-is-a-tc/

Thomas, T. (2005). *Sex crime: Sex offedning and society.* Cullompton: Willan Publishing.

Ward, T., & Maruna, S. (2007). *Rehabilitation: Betond the risk assessment paradigm.* London: Routledge.

Wilson, R., McWhinnie, A., & Wilson, C. (2008). Circles of support and accountability: An international partnership in reducing sexual offender recidivism. *Prison Service Journal, 178,* 26–36.

9

MENTAL HEALTH, YOUNG PEOPLE AND PUNISHMENTS

Gillian Buck and Sean Creaney

This chapter focuses upon young people who have come to the attention of criminal justice services in England and Wales and will offer a critical introduction to the ways their behaviour and mental health are constructed. The chapter begins with an overview of the young people who populate today's youth justice system, before documenting the prevalence of mental ill-health amongst this group and gaps in provision for them. We consider how diverse conceptualisations of mental health can create tensions in practice, and in doing so, ask critical questions of existing approaches, exploring the capacity for present systems to exclude key stakeholders, punish the vulnerable, and label the nonconforming. The chapter concludes by advocating for systems and approaches which do not emotionally harm young people (further) but nurture wellbeing and healthy relationships. We additionally suggest that young people be placed at the centre of these improvements so that any work done on their behalf is meaningful to them and fit for purpose.

Young people in the criminal justice system

In 1998, the Crime and Disorder Act laid the foundations for today's youth justice system in England and Wales. The Act introduced a dramatically reconfigured youth justice that "was less concerned with [welfare based approaches] and more focused on tightly managed, risk-based" activities (Case, 2018, p. 42); it also introduced multi-agency Youth Offending Teams (YOTs), "consisting of representatives from four statutory agencies: police, local authority, probation and health" (Case, 2018, p. 195). This foundation positioned young people in trouble as risks or deficits to be managed or treated, and a range of professional 'experts' as responsible for improvements to them. Rumgay (2004, p. 405) termed this "a cognitive deficit model" arguing that "within this paradigm, offenders are deficient individuals whose faulty thinking requires correction by professionals with special expertise in cognitive training" (Rumgay, 2004, p. 405). This position necessarily neglects to focus on the deprivation and disadvantage that is strongly correlated with youth crime (Yates, 2010; McAra & McVie, 2016), as behaviour is seen "as a matter of opportunity and rational choice, with young people being responsible for their actions" (Rogowski, 2014, p. 8). Correspondingly, 'punishment' becomes a valid response, "both as an expression of society's disapproval and as an individual deterrent" (Rogowski, 2014, p. 8).

The young people who occupy the youth justice system, however, destabilise the *individual deficit* rationale. Despite media and political constructions of youth crime, which often stoke public fears and fuel misconceptions (Case, 2018, pp. 41–42), there have been falls in the number of reported and recorded crimes by children (Bateman, 2017, pp. 10–11) and in the numbers of young people sentenced to immediate custody (down 74% over ten years) (YJB, 2018). While these are welcome developments, the young people who remain in the justice system often have complex needs and face a range of structural oppressions. It is of concern, for example, that young people from a Black, Asian and Minority Ethnic (BAME) background account for 45% of the custodial population, while only making up 18% of the general population of 10–17-year-olds (YJB, 2018); children who come to the attention of criminal justice agencies are also disproportionately drawn from working-class backgrounds (Yates, 2010) and live in poverty (McAra & McVie, 2016). In a recent inspection of the work of youth offending teams (HMIP, 2017, p. 16), inspectors found evidence of trauma in over 80% of cases. Such high levels of adversity have led some critics to conclude that the system for young people is punishing disadvantage (Simkins & Katz, 2002; Jacobson et al., 2010).

The prevalence of trauma in the histories of young people in trouble is receiving growing attention (Schwartz & Wingfield, 2011; Skuse & Matthew, 2015; Liddle et al., 2016), leading to increased awareness of the demands posed by correctional frameworks. Traumatised young people can struggle to form trusting relationships, due to being hyper-vigilant, constantly scanning for threats, and "misinterpreting benign events as significant threats" (YJB, 2017a, p. 6). Young people who have been abused, neglected or rejected, for example, can experience anxiety, avoidance, anger and sometimes aggression (Liddle, et al., 2016, p. 39). Such young people "are prone to emotional outbursts, frustration that escalates to fury and rage, and disappointment that descends into depression and despair" (Liddle, et al., 2016, p. 40). Moreover, young people with adverse childhood experiences may have difficulties employing abstract reasoning, controlling their impulses, or trusting that rewards will follow good behaviour and sanction bad behaviour, as they are "often not in the circumstances that teach these skills" (YJB, 2017a, p. 8). Against this backdrop, notions of rational choice and responsibility are contentious.

An additional barrier to compliance in youth justice settings is that criminalised individuals' relationships with authority figures "have often been, at worst, abusive and traumatic and, at best, inconsistent and difficult" (McNeill, 2013, p. 84). For young people,

> Having developed detrimental methods of dealing with their distress – perhaps including distrust and rejection of those in authority – these individuals tend not to engage with services. In doing so, they run the risk of further negative consequences for breaching criminal justice requirements.
> *(Liddle et al., 2016, p. 60)*

Such obstacles to trust are especially problematic, given that talking about trauma, and being accepted without judgement, is potentially transformative (Buck, 2018, p. 199; Hari, 2018, p. 243). When young people in trouble perceive their worker to be "caring" and genuinely interested in them and their life, this can be beneficial and facilitate positive outcomes (Phoenix & Kelly, 2013, p. 428; Creaney, 2018).

The mental health of young people in the criminal justice system

There is an alarming prevalence of poor mental health amongst young people in the criminal justice system (Harrington et al., 2005; Chitsabesan et al., 2006; YJB, 2017b), along with some evidence of unmet needs and inaccessible services (Chitsabesan & Bailey, 2006; Khan & Wilson, 2015; Taylor, 2016). Of the 98 children and young people who died in prison from 2003 to 2010, 51% had a history of self-harm and 48% had a history of mental health problems (Prison reform trust and INQUEST, 2012, p. 36). It is important to note that this report defines young people as 18–24 and "children" as under 18 (p. 5). The statistics presented below (and indeed the youth justice system in England and Wales) define young people as aged 17 and under (Brammer, 2010, 367; CDA 1998, s.177). These differing definitions reveal an important issue, which we do not have space to fully explore here, other than to note that the arbitrary marker of 18 as entry to adulthood is being challenged by advances in neuroimaging, which show the adolescent brain continuing to mature well into the 20s (Johnson et al., 2009, p. 216). Indeed these developments have led some "to make the case that teens should be considered less culpable for crimes they commit" (see Johnson et al., 2009, p. 216). In a mental health context, being considered 'adult' at 18 has tangible effects for young people transitioning from child to adult mental health services, both in terms of 'patchy' transitional care (Paul et al., 2015) and disagreements about responsibility for care (Swift et al., 2013). This is especially problematic given that the 'transition' ages of 16–25 are a time when young people "can be acutely vulnerable, mentally and emotionally, and are subject to a wide array of different pressures and stresses" (Theodore & Penketh, 2008, p. 130).

In 2017, the proportion of young people (under 18) in England and Wales admitted to custody with identified mental health concerns was 33%, rising to

41% for female admissions, and the proportion of custodial admissions with suicide or self-harm concerns was 31%, rising to 63% for female admissions (YJB, 2017b, pp. 13–15). Despite such prevalence, the youth custody improvement board (YCIB) recently noted that "neither the levels and type of mental illness… the impact of treatment provided, nor evidence of using specific approaches to identify the needs of this cohort seemed to be available" (YCIB, 2017, pp. 5–6); in response, they recommended that the "government should carry out a clear needs analysis of young people in custody, with a particular focus on mental health, mental and neurodevelopmental disorders" (YCIB, 2017, p. 6).

Young people subject to community justice interventions have been found to have significantly more needs than those in secure care, and these needs were often unmet (Chitsabesan et al., 2006). Primary Mental Health Workers (PMHWs) working with YOTs have noted high levels of emotional problems, self-harm and peer and family relationships difficulties (Callaghan et al., 2003). As a result, inter-agency models, which provide accessible, responsive mental health services in youth justice settings are advocated (Callaghan at al., 2003) and indeed many YOTs do have Child and Adolescent Mental Health Service (CAMHS) workers seconded to teams in an attempt to achieve this (HMIP, 2017, p. 37). It is also a strategic aim of the Youth Justice Board to "improve the safety and wellbeing of children in the youth justice system" (YJB, 2017c). Despite awareness of – and willingness to address – young people's mental health needs, a government review of the youth justice system (Taylor, 2016, p. 9) highlighted that youth offending teams "consistently report difficulties in getting support to those… who need it most [and that] thresholds for [CAMHS involvement] appear to be impossibly high in some areas". A mapping exercise of community-based forensic child and adolescent mental health services also found "patchy geographical provision… across England, Scotland and Wales" and heterogeneous commissioning arrangements (Peto et al., 2015).

It is relevant to note that understandings of 'mental health' vary, encompassing biochemical, emotional, structural and social explanations (Sayce, 2000). However, biochemical and medicalised notions of 'disorder' dominate in both mental health and youth justice settings. The term 'mental disorder' denotes a range of medically defined disorders, which include:

> [D]epression, bipolar affective disorder, schizophrenia, anxiety disorders… substance use disorders, intellectual disabilities, and developmental and behavioural disorders with onset usually occurring in childhood and adolescence, including autism.
>
> *(WHO, 2013, p. 6)*

Contemporary services (including youth justice) are, therefore "dominated by an understanding of poor mental health as something that has physically gone wrong in the body. Mental illness is deemed to be a medical problem [and] treatments are overwhelmingly medication-based" (Golightley & Goemans, 2017, p. 47). Such a "pathologisation of madness" (Spandler & Anderson, 2015, p. 20) has the claimed advantage of reducing stigma and blame, given mental illness is no longer seen as a moral weakness, the fault of parents, or caused by the environment, but a physiological problem (Sayce, 2000, p. 87). However, such pathologisation can be problematic in terms of people achieving full citizenship (Sayce, 2000, p. 99). Those perceived to be

> at the mercy of neurochemistry may appear more, rather than less, frightening to others [whereas social explanations] would result in less stigma and discrimination, because they enable people to understand, empathise [with] and relate to a person's behaviour in the context of their life.
> *(Spandler & Anderson, 2015, p. 21)*

A further consequence of pathologising distress is that the 'individual deficit' approach is as prevalent in mental health as criminal justice. Young people's interventions include individualised diversionary programmes (e.g. teaching emotional resilience in schools), cognitive behavioural therapy, community mental health therapy and in-patient care (Longfield, 2017, p. 4). In forensic contexts, young people's mental wellbeing is quantified by standardised screening tools (see YJB, 2003, 2014) and categorised through "tiered" interventions, which assign responsible specialists and enable stratified management (Khan & Wilson, 2010, p. 29). Young people with lower levels of distress are designated to 'Tier 1' universal services (such as GPs, health visitors and teachers); those with more significant problems to Tier 2 or 3 CAMHS specialists (who offer consultation, training or outpatient service delivery); those presenting in most significant distress to Tier 4 specialist day/ inpatient units. While interventions are allocated based on the level of medical specialism required, the diagnosis of disorders and complex needs "are beset with difficult challenges including: inconsistent definitions of cognitive impairments; a lack of standardised assessment processes [and] a shortage of culturally sensitive, appropriate and validated screening tools" (Baldry et al., 2018, p. 18).

Medicalising and categorising the wellbeing of young people is further problematised by a consideration of the 'factors' which can place young people at risk of poor mental health, including parental factors, abuse and neglect, illness or bereavement (Claveirole, 2011). These overwhelmingly social factors have led to calls for more psychosocial 'responses', which help people to understand how "life and circumstances have brought them to this point, [and work] with individuals and families to promote well-being and control over their lives" (Golightley & Goemans, 2017, p. 49). Such approaches recognise that good mental health is more than the absence of diagnosable problems, it also involves the capacity to develop physically, emotionally, intellectually and spiritually; intra-personally (in terms of mastery, confidence, self-esteem and belonging); and inter-personally (being aware of others, empathising and sustaining mutually satisfying relationships) (Claveirole, 2011, p. 13).

The diverse understandings of 'mental health' are reflected in the multiple systems working with young people in trouble. Criminal justice, mental health, education and social care all have "different fundamental aims and approaches" which can be complementary or contradictory (Rogers et al., 2015, p. 6). In practice, this can result in young people being shunted between services which construct them in different ways:

> [E]ducation may view the difficulty as a learning problem, CAMHS... as a mental health difficulty, and social care and criminal justice... as 'behavioural' – often because no one system has the 'answers' or intervention on their own to treat the presenting concerns.
>
> *(Rogers et al., 2015, p. 6)*

There is, therefore, a need for stakeholders to work together and not compound the young person's distress. Cooper et al., (2016) reviewed factors facilitating inter-agency collaboration in children's mental health settings and found 'facilitating factors' to be good interagency communication, joint training, good understandings across agencies, mutual valuing across agencies, senior management support, protocols on interagency collaboration and a named link person. Ideally, in youth justice settings, this link person should be co-located in YOT premises (HMIP, 2017, p. 37). Perceived barriers to interagency collaboration included: poor interagency communication, lack of valuing across agencies, differing perspectives, poor understandings across agencies, confidentiality issues and inadequate resourcing (Cooper et al., 2016). Resourcing is not just vital for collaboration, but also to the provision of early interventions, which can be especially important to facilitate diversion above criminalisation (Baldry et al., 2018, p. 9). However, broader "austerity measures have reduced...services that protect and fulfil children's rights including [CAMHS]; education; early years; preventative and early intervention services; and youth services" (UK Children's Commissioners, 2015, p. 2). While it is encouraging, therefore, that the UK government is increasing Liaison and Diversion services[2] and has pledged to commit £1.4 billion for young people's mental health, to recruit therapists and deliver treatments (DoH & DfE, 2017), it is equally important that universal services are resourced to provide spaces in young people's communities that promote and maintain wellbeing (Tickle, 2016).

The 'expert' informed landscapes of criminal justice and mental health, which each primarily responds to the *bad/mad* young person as an individual in deficit, make it likely that young people become passive stakeholders in their own mental wellbeing, particularly while subject to punishments. The fractured conceptualisations of 'mental health' across professions and contexts additionally mean that young people are subject to multiple external constructions of their lived experiences and identities, which may not match their own. This is problematic because a sense of control over one's life has been found to be important in terms of both recovery from mental illness (Tew, 2015, pp. 76–77) and desisting from crime (Maruna, 2001). In the following section, we, therefore, argue that there is a need to supplement existing youth justice/mental health practices with approaches which *minimise harm* to young people and facilitate their *active* engagement.

Minimising harm: promoting 'well' systems

There is an urgent need to promote wellbeing *within* criminal justice. Imprisonment has been identified as having "a significant negative impact on mental health", not least because bullying is frequently rife in young offender institutions (Rogers et al., 2015, p. 5). Moreover, mental disorder, cognitive disabilities and complex needs have been found to be "especially high within remand populations [and] the uncertainties invoked by the status of penal remand are known to exacerbate such conditions" (Baldry et al., 2018, p. 18). Further to the general unsuitability of custody for promoting wellbeing, there is a specific concern about the growing practice of isolating imprisoned young people for long periods. In May 2018, UK Member of Parliament Seema Malhotra highlighted that the use of solitary confinement is much more widespread than we might realise, with almost four in ten boys in detention spending some time in solitary confinement – some for periods of almost three months. Young people are increasingly being kept in cells or rooms for up to 22 hours a day amid reports of staff shortages and increased violence (Malhotra, 2018). The use of this strategy raises concerns about profound negative impacts on children, such as paranoia, anxiety and depression, along with barriers to social reintegration (Singh Dhesi, 2018). The British Medical Association has also highlighted the unsuitability of solitary confinement for managing children and young people at risk of self-harm or suicide, or experiencing other mental health crises (2018, p. 5), particularly as Lord Carlile's inquiry (2006) described solitary confinement conditions as 'inducements to suicide'. Writing in *the Lancet*, Alcorn (2014) highlighted the strong associations between solitary confinement, severe mental illness and suicide attempts, advocating instead a secure residential treatment facility model, wherein young people (who have committed serious crimes and suffer severe mental illness) are housed in small units, supervised by childcare workers, attend classes on the outside to keep up with their peers, and are not physically restrained or asked to leave. The aim is to offer "a sense of security they might have never felt in the past" (Alcorn, 2014, p. 1284). This is argued to be vital for children experiencing emotional distress, given "... a grim backdrop of emotional need... is inescapable, unless it is addressed by positive nurturing" (Grimshaw, et al., 2011, p. 8, cited in Liddle et al., 2016, p. 24). However, such an 'attachment' informed (Bowlby, 1988), nurturing approach to wellness and behaviour regulation contrasts sharply with the UK youth secure estate, wherein, for the year ending March 2017, the number of Restrictive Physical Interventions of young people increased (5% to just over 4,500) and there was a marked increase in self-harm injuries requiring medical treatment, with rates of self-harm being much higher for females than males (YJB, 2018, p. 37).

In addition to minimising potential harm, there is a need to *bridge the gaps* between young people in trouble and the support they may need. The first of these gaps is language. For example, young people often "conceptualise 'mental illness' in highly stereotyped, negative and limited terms… and tend not to relate it to their own identities or experiences" (Apland et al., 2017, p. 7). 'Disorder' is also a term many young people dislike because of its psychiatric connotations and stigmatising effect (Claveirole, 2011, pp. 17–18). Indeed, 'mentally disordered offenders' are doubly stigmatised – "their offending places them apart from other psychiatric patients, and major mental disorder separates them from most offenders" (McInerny & Minne, 2004, p. 43). Labels such as 'offender', 'victim' or even 'young person with a mental health problem', wherein the primary association is deficit, are unlikely to be embraced by young people; rather, young people often strive to construct their own identities. The "sense of power, experienced through control of one's identity, is so important [to well-being] that powerful identities are sometimes chosen in contradiction to social norms" (Ungar & Teram, 2000, p. 246). This suggests that utilising definitions and language which young people are comfortable identifying with, is a necessary prerequisite to meaningful engagement. In order to do this, adults need to listen carefully to young people and *learn their language*.

A participatory approach to wellbeing and justice: promoting 'well' agents

While formal language and paternalistic authority can obstruct meaningful engagement, when service users are included in shaping design and delivery, it can "enhance the credibility, meaning or legitimacy of those interventions" (Weaver & McCulloch, 2012, p. 4) and shed new light on the experience of minority groups within disciplinary systems (Dumbrill, 2006; Buck, 2019). This is especially important for young people from black and minority ethnic (BME) groups, given that psychiatry has tended to "disregard narratives about how racism hurts and how it can cause mental distress despite the fact that racialised experiences have been linked with mental illness" (Keating, 2015, p. 129). We, therefore, need to understand the *unique experiences and identities of BME service users*, who have not only been marginalised in other participatory movements but are also hugely over-represented in detention settings across health and justice (Keating, 2015, emphasis in original; YJB, 2018). User participation in youth justice is claimed to increase levels of engagement and increase self-esteem, "making 'motivation to change' more likely" (Creaney, 2014, p. 126). There is also an ethical imperative, given that the UN convention on the rights of the child outlines a child's right to express their views in matters affecting them and to have due weight given to those views (see YJB, 2016). In a mental health context, including young people in service design and delivery can help them to feel 'empowered'; offer them specialised knowledge; influence organisational change; raise awareness of the issues facing young people; and enable young people to give something back

(Theodore & Penketh, 2008). These benefits are particularly useful in forensic contexts, given that self-belief and generativity – or giving back – are positively associated with desistance from crime (Maruna, 2001; LeBel, 2007). Crucially, the participation projects that Theodore & Penketh (2008) focused upon, also reported improved communication: "young people educated professionals on how to use language that young people could understand, while simultaneously learning the different styles of language and terminology used by professionals" (2008, p. 137). Participation, therefore, became a conduit for staff and young people to learn one another's language.

In 2016, the Youth Justice Board published a 'participation strategy', outlining a commitment to young people having a voice in the planning, delivery and evaluation of activities across the youth justice system. The strategy aims to prioritise advocacy for young people; to value young people's feedback from inspections; to engage young people in service improvement; to encourage all services to have a named champion for the voice of the young person; to share the views of young people with government ministers, and to make written resources accessible to young people. *Consultation* also featured strongly in plans for practice development, service commissioning and governance. While these are welcome developments, what remains to be seen is whether the solutions young people call for are invested in, particularly as their perspectives can often challenge an individual deficit approach. Buck et al. (2017, p. 1759), for example, studied a peer-led, 'gang' intervention project, their teenaged respondents suggested workable interventions, which included resource-building in communities and with families, alongside groups to facilitate healthy relationships. In other words, they proposed interventions which encompassed social, structural and interpersonal solutions, using their own local assets.

Similarly, a recent peer-led study of youth 'Liaison and Diversion' services (Zumu et al., 2016), illustrated the value that young people placed on their own networks. When researchers asked: "who can help you have good emotional health and wellbeing?", 75% of participating young people chose family members, 50% chose themselves, but none of the young people identified doctors or CAMHS (Zumu et al., 2016, p. 30). Interestingly, in answer to the same question, 50% of adults (in the young people's lives) chose doctors and CAMHS, 30% chose family, and 34% chose young people themselves. This (albeit small scale) study indicates that there may be a vital disconnect between young people's and adults' perspectives of what constitutes a support network. Taken together, both studies make a case for recognising and building upon the strengths present within young people's families and local support networks, but for such a shift from a *retributive* to *strength based* orientation to occur, Artello (2014, p. 391) argues that a paradigm shift needs to take place. Drawing upon a project for 'juvenile offenders' diagnosed with severe mental illness, which "emphasizes youth's strengths and assets and strives to keep them in their home communities" (Artello, 2014, p. 385), she details how family members, front line workers and the wider community need to be 'indoctrinated' into a strength-based approach. This involves training justice professionals to see young people and families as resources, rather than challenges and highlighting the favourable cost of such approaches in comparison with expensive residential or inpatient approaches (Artello, 2014, pp. 386–390).

There are also more substantive ways of involving young people, including peer to peer work. While research into such approaches is limited, there is evidence that as they move away from crime, young people aim to shed "offending identities", and that prosocial opportunities can offer young people a "hook for change" (Creaney, 2018; McMahon & Jump, 2018, p. 8). Weaver and McCulloch (2012, p. 7) noted that "helping or advocating on behalf of others may help maintain a person's pro-social identity and facilitate the maintenance of desistance". Providing criminalised (young) people with opportunities to adopt helping roles can also "send a message to the wider community that an individual is worthy of further support and investment in their reintegration" (Maruna & LeBel, 2009, p. 69). Peer mentors can also be "instrumental for combatting trust issues [in service users]… and for instilling hope through the example of a positive role model who has overcome similar challenges" (DuBois & Felner, 2016, p. 9). Indeed, in young people's experience, "those who most easily 'get it right' are peers who have lived a similar life and come through it" (Peer Power, 2018, p. 6). It is relevant to note, however, that peer to peer work is beset with a diversity of goals and roles, which makes 'outcomes' difficult to quantify, there are also ethical issues such as boundaries and safeguarding to consider (Devilly et al., 2005). There is, therefore, a need for more evaluations of the potentially inimitable impact of youth peer support services (Buck et al., 2017; Gopalan et al., 2017).

Despite the unique potential of participatory approaches in this field, and a strategic commitment at a national level, young people in trouble face numerous barriers to 'participation', not least because so much of their lives are outside their influence:

> Young people cannot change where they live in order to move to areas that are less heavily policed. They cannot leave Local Authority Care or abusive families in order to create a more stable life for themselves… They have little or no choice about the circumstances in which they are raised, including their schooling […and they] cannot vote for politicians whose political policies might address key issues shaping their lives.
>
> *(Phoenix, 2016, p. 135)*

Young people are punished for actions, which are shaped by conditions they cannot affect (Phoenix, 2016, p. 135) and become 'objects' of concern (Case, et al., 2015) "on which mechanisms and technologies of control operate, and whose liberties and rights can be justifiably curtailed or dispensed with in the presumed public interest" (Weaver & Barry, 2014, p. 279). This is true regardless of whether young people are viewed as *sad, bad or mad*:

> The *sad* victims of circumstances are not to blame for their behaviour, and the *mad* require medication… Although the *bad* are held 'responsible' for

their behaviour, this construes into them being irresponsible and thus not able to affect positive change.

(Macleod, 2006, p. 162)

In any of the above scenarios, the "agency ascribed" to young people is limited (Macleod, 2006, p. 162). The risk of introducing participatory approaches in such an environment is that children are *merely consulted* (and potentially ignored), as opposed to *meaningfully included* in the decision-making process (Haines & Case, 2015). A further challenge is the involuntary nature of supervision (and some mental health 'treatment'). Young people subject to court orders are 'involuntary clients' (Trotter, 1999), and as such, may be reluctant to engage. For example, a report on desistance and young people found patterns of *compliance*, rather than *active engagement*:

> The YOT just make you go on these courses to show that you've done victim work. Then they say well done, you nod, smile and move on. I was just playing with them.
>
> *(former service user, HMIP, 2016, p. 21)*

Such "inauthentic transactions" (Buck, 2018, p. 198) hinder children's active participation and engagement. However, when young people are engaged through nurturing, relational approaches, which privilege their world view, their experience and expertise, this may make services more "fit for purpose and thus effective" (Weaver & McCulloch, 2012, p. 4). This is likely to be especially significant with older children, for whom a sense of autonomy and independence is vital (Patton et al., 2016; Apland et al., 2017).

Conclusion

The majority of young people now subject to formal punishment in England and Wales have experienced adversity, trauma and/or structural discrimination. Despite this, their problematic behaviours are primarily understood and responded to as personal deficit. They are positioned by criminal justice legislation, medical discourse and cultural practices (in both health and justice settings) as flawed subjects, requiring expert intervention at an inter-personal level. While there is value in work which seeks to build individual resilience; medically assist young people in crisis; and positively nurture emotional regulation, to *only* work at the level of the individual, neglects a focus on forms of structural and social disadvantage, which are strongly correlated with both 'offending' and poor mental health. Furthermore, to intervene *upon* young people, through formal, hierarchical structures, using language they are not invested in, may undermine the credibility of interventions and create non-compliance or passive compliance as opposed to meaningful engagement. A way forward is to include young people more centrally in defining both the problems they face and possible solutions.

In order to build the trust and skills needed for such collaborative working, there is a need for staff in both justice and mental health settings to prioritise relational and nurturing approaches above bureaucratic or correctional ones. Doing so may not only help young people to feel safe when working with adults and inspire their investment in interventions, but it may also increase their confidence and feelings of autonomy, enabling them to paint a fuller picture of their world, including possible strengths and supports.

References

Alcorn, T. (2014). Rethinking mental health care for young offenders. *The Lancet*, *383*(9925), 1283–1284. doi: 10.1016/S0140-6736(14)60449-9

Apland, K., Lawrence, H., Mesie, J., & Yarrow, E. (2017). *Children's voices: A review of evidence on the subjective wellbeing of children with mental health needs in England*. London, UK: Children's Commissioner for England.

Artello, K. (2014). Shifting "tough on crime" to keeping kids out of jail: Exploring organizational adaptability and sustainability at a mental health agency serving adjudicated children living with severe mental illness. *Criminal Justice Policy Review*, *25*(3), 378–396. doi: 10.1177/0887403412473473

Baldry, E., Briggs, D. B., Goldson, B., & Russell, S. (2018). 'Cruel and unusual punishment': An inter-jurisdictional study of the criminalisation of young people with complex support needs. *Journal of Youth Studies*, *21*(5), 636–652. doi: 10.1080/13676261.2017.1406072

Bateman, T. (2017). *The State of youth justice 2017: An overview of trends and developments*. London, UK: National Association for Youth Justice.

Bowlby, J. (1988) *A secure base*. Oxon, UK: Routledge. (2012 Edition).

Brammer, A. (2010). *Social work law* (3rd ed.). Harlow: Pearson Education.

Buck, G. (2018). The core conditions of peer mentoring. *Criminology & Criminal Justice*, *18*(2), 190–206. doi: 10.1177/1748895817699659

Buck, G. (2019). Politicisation or professionalisation? Exploring divergent aims within UK voluntary sector peer mentoring. *The Howard Journal of Crime and Justice*, *58*(3), 349–365. doi: 10.1111/hojo.12305

Buck, G., Lawrence, A., & Ragonese, E. (2017). Exploring peer mentoring as a form of innovative practice with young people at risk of child sexual exploitation. *The British Journal of Social Work*, *47*(6), 1745–1763. doi: 10.1093/bjsw/bcx089

Callaghan, J., Pace, F., Young, B., & Vostanis, P. (2003). Primary mental health workers within youth offending teams: A new service model. *Journal of Adolescence*, *26*(2), 185–199. doi: 10.1016/S0140-1971(02)00131-8

Carlile, A. (2006). *An independent inquiry into the use of physical restraint, solitary confinement and forcible strip searching of children in prisons, secure training centres and local authority secure children's homes*. London: Howard League for Penal Reform.

Case, S. (2018). *Youth justice: A critical introduction*. Oxon, UK: Routledge.

Case, S., Creaney, S., Deakin, J., & Haines, K. (2015). Youth justice past present and future. *British Journal of Community Justice*, *13*(2), 99–110.

Chitsabesan, P., & Bailey, S. (2006). Mental health, educational and social needs of young offenders in custody and in the community. *Current Opinion in Psychiatry*, *19*(4), 355. doi: 10.1097/01.yco.0000228753.87613.01

Chitsabesan, P., Kroll, L., Bailey, S., Kenning, C., Sneider, S., MacDonald, W., & Theodosiou, L. (2006). Mental health needs of young offenders in custody and in the community. *The British Journal of Psychiatry, 188*(6), 534–540. doi: 10.1192/bjp.bp.105.010116

Claveirole, A. (2011) Setting the scene. In A. Claveirole & M. Gaughan (Eds.). *Understanding children and young people's mental health* (pp. 4–28). West Sussex, UK: John Wiley & Sons.

Cooper, M., Evans, Y., & Pybis, J. (2016). Interagency collaboration in children and young people's mental health: A systematic review of outcomes, facilitating factors and inhibiting factors. *Child: Care, Health and Development, 42*(3), 325–342. doi: 10.1111/cch.12322

Creaney, S. (2014). The benefits of participation for young offenders. *Safer Communities, 13*(3), 126–132. doi: 10.1108/SC-02-2014-0003

Creaney, S. (2018) Children's voices—are we listening? Progressing peer mentoring in the youth justice system. *Child Care in Practice,* 26(1), 22–37.

Department of Health & Department for Education (2017) *Transforming children and young people's mental health provision: A Green paper*. London, UK.

Devilly, G. J., Sorbello, L., Eccleston, L., & Ward, T. (2005). Prison-based peer-education schemes. *Aggression and Violent Behavior, 10*(2), 219–240. doi: 10.1016/j.avb.2003.12.001

DuBois, D. L., & Felner, J. K. (2016). *Mentoring for youth with backgrounds of involvement in commercial sex activity: National Mentoring Resource Center Population Review*. Chicago, IL: National Mentoring Resource Centre.

Dumbrill, G. C. (2006). Parental experience of child protection intervention: A qualitative study. *Child Abuse & Neglect, 30*(1), 27–37. doi: 10.1016/j.chiabu.2005.08.012

Golightley, M., & Goemans, R. (2017). *Social work and mental health*. Exeter, UK: Learning Matters.

Gopalan, G., Lee, S. J., Harris, R., Acri, M. C., & Munson, M. R. (2017). Utilization of peers in services for youth with emotional and behavioral challenges: A scoping review. *Journal of Adolescence, 55*, 88–115. doi: 10.1016/j.adolescence.2016.12.011 Haines, K., & Case, S. (2015) *Positive youth justice: Children first, offenders second*. Bristol, UK: Policy Press.

Hari, J. (2018). *Lost connections: Uncovering the real causes of depression–and the unexpected solutions*. London, UK: Bloomsbury Publishing.

Harrington, R., Bailey, S., Chitsabesan, P., Kroll, L., Macdonald, W., Sneider, S.,... & Barrett, B. (2005). *Mental health needs and effectiveness of provision for young offenders in custody and in the community*. London, UK: Youth Justice Board.

Her Majesty's Inspectorate of Probation (2016) *Desistance and young people: An inspection by HM Inspectorate of Probation*. Retrieved from: https://www.justiceinspectorates.gov.uk/hmiprobation/wp-content/uploads/sites/5/2016/05/Desistance_and_young_people.pdf

Her Majesty's Inspectorate of Probation (2017) *The work of youth offending teams to protect the public*. Manchester, UK: Her Majesty's Inspectorate of Probation.

Jacobson, J., Bhardwa, B., Gyateng, T., Hunter, G., & Hough, M. (2010). *Punishing disadvantage-A profile of children in custody*. London, UK: Prison Reform Trust.

Johnson, S. B., Blum, R. W., & Giedd, J. N. (2009). Adolescent maturity and the brain: The promise and pitfalls of neuroscience research in adolescent health policy. *Journal of Adolescent Health, 45*(3), 216–221. doi: 10.1016/j.jadohealth.2009.05.016

Keating, F. (2015). Linking 'race', mental health and a social model of disability: What are the possibilities? In H. Spandler, J. Anderson, & B. Sapey (Eds.), *Madness, distress and the politics of disablement* (pp. 127–138). London, UK: Policy Press.

Khan, L., & Wilson, J. (2010). *You just get on and do it: Healthcare provision in Youth Offending Teams*. London, UK: Centre for Mental health.

LeBel, T.P., (2007). Examination of the impact of formerly incarcerated persons helping others. *Journal of Offender Rehabilitation*, 46(1–2), 1–24. doi: 10.1080/10509670802071485

Liddle, M., Boswell, G., Wright, S., & Francis, V. with Perry, R. (2016). *Trauma and young offenders: A review of the research and practice literature*. London, UK: Beyond Youth Custody.

Longfield, A. (2017). *Briefing: Children's mental healthcare in England*. London, UK: Children's Commissioner for England.

Macleod, G. (2006). Bad, mad or sad: Constructions of young people in trouble and implications for interventions. *Emotional and Behavioural Difficulties*, 11(3), 155–167. doi: 10.1080/13632750600833791

Malhotra, S. (2018). Solitary confinement: Children and young people. *Hansard* HC Deb vol 640 col 95WH (1 May 2018) [Electronic version].

Maruna, S., (2001). *Making good; how ex-convicts reform and rebuild their lives*. Washington, DC: American Psychological Association.

Maruna S., & LeBel, T.P (2009). Strengths-based approaches to reentry: Extra mileage toward reintegration and destigmatization. *Japanese Journal of Sociological Criminology*, 34, 58–80.

McAra, L., & McVie, S. (2016). Understanding youth violence: The mediating effects of gender, poverty and vulnerability. *Journal of Criminal Justice*, 45, 71–77. doi: 10.1016/j.jcrimjus.2016.02.011

McInerny, T., & Minne, C. (2004). Principles of treatment for mentally disordered offenders. *Criminal Behaviour and Mental Health*, 14(S1), S43–S47.

McMahon, G., & Jump, D. (2018). Starting to stop: Young offenders' desistance from crime. *Youth Justice*, 18(1), 3–17. doi: 10.1177/1473225417741223

McNeill, F. (2013), 'Transforming rehabilitation: Evidence, values and ideology'. *British Journal of Community Justice*, 11(2/3), 83–87.

Patton, G. C., Sawyer, S. M., Santelli, J. S., Ross, D. A., Afifi, R., Allen, N. B., … Viner, R. M. (2016). Our future: A Lancet commission on adolescent health and wellbeing. *The Lancet*, 387(10036), 2423–2478. doi: 10.1016/S0140-6736(16)00579-1

Paul, M., Street, C., Wheeler, N., & Singh, S. P. (2015). Transition to adult services for young people with mental health needs: A systematic review. *Clinical Child Psychology and Psychiatry*, 20(3), 436–457. doi: 10.1177/1359104514526603

Peer Power (2018) *Getting it right young people's vision for Liaison and diversion services*. London, UK: Peer Power and Young Minds.

Peto, L. M., Dent, M., Griffin, M., & Hindley, N. (2015). Community-based forensic child and adolescent mental health services in England, Scotland and Wales: A national mapping exercise. *The Journal of Forensic Psychiatry & Psychology*, 26(3), 283–296. doi: 10.1080/14789949.2015.1004635

Phoenix, J. (2016). Against youth justice and youth governance, for youth penality. *The British Journal of Criminology*, 56(1), 123–140. doi: 10.1093/bjc/azv031

Phoenix, J., & Kelly, L. (2013). 'You have to do it for yourself' responsibilization in youth justice and young people's situated knowledge of youth justice practice. *The British Journal of Criminology*, 53(3), 419–437. doi: 10.1093/bjc/azs078

Prison Reform Trust and Inquest (2012). *Fatally flawed: Has the state learned lessons from the deaths of children and young people in prison?* London, UK: Prison Reform Trust.

Rogers, A., Harvey, J., Law, H., & Taylor, J. (2015) Introduction. In A. Rogers, J. Harvey, & H. Law (Eds.). *Young people in forensic mental health settings* (pp. 1–19). Hampshire, UK: Palgrave Macmillan.

Rogowski, S. (2014). Radical/critical social work with young offenders: Challenges and possibilities. *Journal of Social Work Practice, 28*(1), 7–21. doi: 10.1080/02650533.2013.828280

Rumgay, J. (2004). Scripts for safer survival: Pathways out of female crime. *The Howard Journal of Criminal Justice, 43*(4), 405–419. doi: 10.1111/j.1468-2311.2004.00338.x

Sayce, L. (2000). *From psychiatric patient to citizen: Overcoming discrimination and social exclusion*. London, UK: Macmillan Press.

Schwartz, J., & Wingfield, R. (2011). *My story: Young people talk about the trauma and violence in their lives*. In R. Grimshaw (Ed.), London: Centre for Crime and Justice Studies. Retrieved from: http://www.crimeandjustice.org.uk/publications/my-story-young-people-talk-abouttrauma-and-violence-their-lives

Simkins, S., & Katz, S. (2002). Criminalizing abused girls. *Violence against Women, 8*(12), 1474–1499. doi.: 10.1177/107780102237966

Singh Dhesi, T. (2018) Solitary confinement: Children and young people. *Hansard* HC Deb vol 640 col 95WH (1 May 2018) [Electronic version].

Skuse, T., & Matthew, J. (2015). The Trauma Recovery Model: Sequencing youth justice interventions for young people with complex needs. *Prison Service Journal, 220*, 16–24.

Spandler, H., & Anderson, J. (2015) Unreasonable adjustments? Applying disability policy to madness and distress. In H. Spandler, J. Anderson & B. Sapey (Eds.). *Madness, distress and the politics of disablement* (pp. 13–26). London, UK: Policy Press.

Swift, K. D., Hall, C. L., Marimuttu, V., Redstone, L., Sayal, K., & Hollis, C. (2013). Transition to adult mental health services for young people with Attention Deficit/Hyperactivity Disorder (ADHD): A qualitative analysis of their experiences. *BMC Psychiatry, 13*(1), 74. doi: 10.1186/1471-244X-13-74

Taylor, C. (2016). *Review of the youth justice system in England and Wales*. London, UK: Ministry of Justice.

Tew, J. (2015). Towards a socially situated model of distress. In H. Spandler, J. Anderson, & B. Sapey (Eds.). *Madness, distress and the politics of disablement* (pp. 69–82). Bristol, UK: Policy Press.

Theodore, C. V., & Penketh, K. (2008) Listen up! Young people's participation in service design and delivery. In C. Jackson, K. Hill, & P. Lavis (Eds.) *Child and adolescent mental health today: A handbook* (pp. 129–139). Brighton, UK: Pavilion Publishing.

Tickle, S. J. (2016). *The youth centre as a 'sanctuary' in aiding safer communities for young people.* Early Career Academics Network Bulletin, 1.

Trotter, C. (1999). *Working with involuntary clients: A guide to practice*. London, UK, Thousand Oaks, CA and New Delhi, India: Sage.

UK Children's commissioners (joint report) (2015) *Report of the UK Children's Commissioners UN Committee on the Rights of the Child Examination of the Fifth Periodic Report of the United Kingdom of Great Britain and Northern Ireland*. Retrieved from: https://www.childcomwales.org.uk/wp-content/uploads/2016/04/Report-of-the-UK-CCs-UN-CRC-Examination-of-the-Fifth-Periodic-Report.pdf

Ungar, M., & Teram, E. (2000). Drifting toward mental health: High-risk adolescents and the process of empowerment. *Youth & Society, 32*(2), 228–252. doi: 10.1177/0044118X00032002005

Weaver, B., & Barry, M. (2014). Managing high risk offenders in the community: Compliance, cooperation and consent in a climate of concern. *European Journal of Probation, 6*(3), 278–295. doi: 10.1177/2066220314549526

Weaver, B., & McCulloch, T. (2012) *Co-producing criminal justice*. Glasgow, UK: Scottish Centre for Crime and Justice Research.

World Health Organisation (WHO) (2013). *Mental health action plan 2013–2020.* Geneva, Switzerland: World Health Organisation.

Yates, J. (2010) Structural disadvantage, youth, class, crime and poverty. In W. Taylor, R. Earle & R. Hester (Eds.). *Youth justice handbook: Theory, policy and practice* (pp. 5–23). Cullompton, UK: Willan.

Youth custody improvement board (YCIB) (2017) *Findings and recommendations of the youth custody improvement board.* Retrieved from: https://assets.publishing.service.gov.uk/government/uploads/system/uploads/attachment_data/file/594448/findings-and-recommendations-of-the-ycib.pdf

Youth Justice Board (2003). *Screening for mental disorder in the youth justice system: Supporting notes.* London, UK: Youth Justice Board.

Youth Justice Board (2014). *Asset plus physical and mental health screening tools: Supporting guidance.* London, UK: Youth Justice Board.

Youth Justice Board (2016). *Participation strategy: Giving young people a voice in youth justice.* London, UK: Youth Justice Board.

Youth Justice Board (2017a). *In brief: Trauma informed youth justice.* London, UK: Youth Justice Board.

Youth Justice Board (2017b). *Key characteristics of admissions to youth custody April 2014 to March 2016.* London, UK: Youth Justice Board and Ministry of Justice.

Youth Justice Board (YJB) (2017c). *Business plan 2017/18.* Retrieved from: https://assets.publishing.service.gov.uk/government/uploads/system/uploads/attachment_data/file/660018/yjb-business-plan-2017-18.pdf

Youth Justice Board (2018) *Youth justice statistics 2016/2017 England and Wales.* London, UK: Youth Justice Board and Ministry of Justice.

Zumu, B., Imafidon, K., Bellio, L., Douglas, A. M., & Dossett, C. (2016) *Just health: An enquiry into the emotional health and wellbeing of young people in the youth justice system.* London, UK: Clearview research and Peer Power.

10

'SECURING' TREATMENT FOR FEMALE PRISONERS WITH MENTAL HEALTH ISSUES

Sharon Morley

Prison has consistently been shown to be a brutalising and inhumane environment, and this is particularly so for women (Corston, 2007). The harmful effects of imprisonment have been continuously and continue to be acknowledged via a range of official reports and inquiries as well as academic research and third sector organisations. Women in prison experience higher levels of mental and physical illness than men and the general population. This higher level of mental illness is frequently a result of a history of violence and sexual abuse. Thus, women represent a particularly vulnerable population as a predominant stress for women is sexual victimisation. This includes the severity of injuries and also the prolonged nature of the violence. This trauma, Pilgrim (2017) argues, can lead to anxiety, depression and panic disorders.

The focus of this chapter is women who have come into contact with the criminal justice system in England and Wales. It is concerned with those women who have mental health issues and how their behaviour is constructed within a narrative of individualisation and responsibilisation – mad, bad or sad. It will also highlight the specific needs of Black, Asian and minority ethnic women who are serving a prison sentence and who have mental health issues. This work is not suggesting that there is no place for women's prisons or secure residences. There may be a time when prison is the only recourse for violent female offenders. These should be small custodial units rather than the current large, overcrowded and inhumane prisons (Commission on Women Offenders, 2012; All-Party Parliamentary Group on Women in the Penal System, 2015). However, we should urgently consider alternatives to prison for the majority of female offenders who commit non-violent, petty offences. These alternatives should focus on providing the appropriate support required for women who offend and addressing the reasons why they offend as well as their mental health issues. These alternatives include, but are not restricted to, a more concerted use of community sentences, rehabilitation programmes which focus on the unique circumstances and needs of women offenders and Criminal Justice centres.

Research (for example, Corston, 2007; McIvor, 2001; McIvor & Burman, 2011; Cox & Sacks-Jones, 2017; Prison Reform Trust, 2017a) continues to find that government, policymakers and criminal justice system professionals neglect to consider women's circumstances. Research consistently highlights the link between gender-based violence and women's offending (Prison Reform Trust, 2017b). The Prison Reform Trust (2017b) found that women who experience domestic violence are over-represented in the Criminal Justice System. Indeed, the experiences of women who offend are often ignored in favour of a more punitive sentencing approach. Gelsthorpe et al. (2007) contend that this is in part due to the lack of alternatives to prison. Economic inequality, poverty, unemployment, racism, sexism and all forms of violence and abuse which are often ignored in pursuit of solutions that reside within the individual.

The Department of Health requested that NICE (2017) provide guidance on improving the mental health of people in prison. This guidance is to ensure that there is equivalence between mental health care provided in prisons with that provided in the community. This policy on mental health services in prison was generally welcomed by many, including health care professionals. This policy stated that mental health services in prison should be provided as they are within the community and in line with national policy. It also states that there should be continuity of care between custody and community. However, this questions the assumed equivalence of mental health services in the prison setting. As Forrester et al. (2014) contend, prisoners, particularly women prisoners, who have a variety of specific mental health needs, are a particularly vulnerable group. Additionally, this policy on providing mental health care in the prison setting is made more difficult by the lack of appropriate data on mental health in prisons. This lack of data makes it difficult to plan services and monitor the effectiveness of these services. In meeting the needs of prisoners with mental health issues, prison mental health in-reach teams (MHIRTs) were introduced to ensure the 'equivalence of care' with that of the general public as well as providing continuity of care from the community to the prison using the Care Programme Approach (CPA). Although these measures have been introduced, research conducted by Brooker and Gojkovic (2009) found that not all prisoners were being managed under the CPA. So, although this system is meant to operate nationally irrespective of location, there continue to be disparities between institutions. Thus, there continues to be a concern with the ability to provide this care in an environment which prioritises security and control over care and rehabilitation. These contradictory values and goals create tensions between care versus custody and, challenges the ideas and attitudes of some prison staff and members of the general public that prisoners are undeserving of care. This, together with the idea of 'less eligibility', in terms of provision of care available to prisoners and, hostile prison environments, provides barriers to appropriate and/or adequate care.

Women's offending behaviour and imprisonment

Despite continued calls for the reduction of prison as a punishment or the abolition of the prison, current statistics demonstrate that the prison population is still increasing. As of March 2019, the total prison population was 82,634 with female numbers at 3,832. A breakdown of these statistics shows that 520 females were on remand and 3,284 females were sentenced to prison (Ministry of Justice, 2019). Nine hundred forty-eight females were sentenced for violence against the person, 125 for sexual offences, 590 for theft offences and 436 for drug offences (Ministry of Justice, 2019). Prison population figures ranked by ethnic group and sex show that Asian and Asian British women account for a total of 164 prisoners, Black and Black British women account for 276 prisoners, Mixed 173, other ethnic groups 22 prisoners respectively, and white females account for 3,181 prisoners (Ministry of Justice, 2019).

Eighty-four per cent of women serving a prison sentence committed a non-violent offence (Women in Prison, 2011). The majority of these offences are for petty crimes. As the Ministry of Justice (2018a) highlights, the majority of female offenders are assessed as low or medium risk and commit non-violent and low-level offences. The petty nature of much of women's offending provided some optimism that there would be a reduction in the rates of women's imprisonment. Sadly, this has not come to fruition. Rather, what we are witnessing is women receiving more severe sentences for what remain petty offences (Home Office, 2004; McIvor & Burman, 2011). Those women who have committed petty crimes are serving a prison sentence of 12 months or less. Thus what we are seeing is a sharp rise in the number of women serving short sentences for lesser offences. Over the last 23 years, the number of women serving short sentences has nearly doubled, resulting in a sharp increase – in 1993 only a third of women were given a custodial sentence of fewer than six months, and in 2017 it was nearly double this, 62% (Offender Management Statistics 2017; Prison Reform Trust 2018). What has resulted since 1993 is a reduction in community sentences for women, having halved in a decade, the use of short prison sentences remaining stable since this time and, a sharp increase in the number of short custodial sentences of less than six months.

Women sentenced to imprisonment typically come from low-income communities with high rates of unemployment, poverty and drug use and mental illness. These women typically have weak social networks and are particularly vulnerable to negative social forces. Those women with mental illness and who find themselves in contact with the criminal justice system are often socially excluded. The Ministry of Justice found that 50% of female prisoners need help with their mental health. Nearly 50% suffer from anxiety or depression and 25% show symptoms which are indicative of psychosis (Ministry of Justice, 2019). The Nursing Times (2013) found that one in four women account for incidents of self-harm. Female prisoners are more than twice as likely as male prisoners to report needing help for mental health problems, 49% and 18% respectively.

Forty-one per cent of young women admitted to custody have identifiable mental health problems, with 68% of female custodial admissions showing concern over self-harm (Youth Justice Board, 2017, pp. 13–15). Depression, psychotic illness and substance misuse are reported to be the most common mental illnesses in prisons (Fazel et al., 2016).

History of abuse and trauma

The Prison Reform Trust (2017a) found that women who experience domestic violence are over-represented in the Criminal Justice System. Additionally, those women who experience domestic violence suffer from mental health issues. Research consistently highlights the link between gender-based violence and women's offending (Prison Reform Trust, 2017b). Fifty-seven per cent of female prisoners have suffered domestic violence prior to being sent to prison, while 53% have experienced abuse as a child (Bromley Report, 2017). Crook (cited in Labhart & Wright, 2018) highlights how '[Women] typically have more complex needs than men. They are more likely to be victims of abuse, and more likely to have been sentenced for offending related to their exploitation by a partner'. Thus, many female offenders are vulnerable and have experienced chaotic lifestyles including mental health issues often as a result of being the victims of abuse and trauma. This indicates that a female prisoner might already be entering prison with mental health issues. NACRO found that 26% of women received treatment for a mental health issue in the year preceding entry into prison (NACRO, n.d.).

Prison as a possible re-traumatising environment

Imprisonment has been identified as having "a significant negative impact on mental health" (Valamuri & Stillman, 2007, p. 18). It often leaves women worse off than when they were sentenced. This is in part due to women being contained in institutions that fail to rehabilitate and support them often due to a lack of appropriate resources. Often rehabilitation programmes are inappropriate – lack of training for staff, the trauma of children being taken into care or adopted, high levels of self-harm which in some cases require hospitalisation due to injuries inflicted. In 2017, the Bromley Report found that rates of self-harm among women are at the highest level for six years. Also, levels of self-harm for women were 19% despite only making up 5% of the total prison population.

In addition to an increase in mental illness among female prisoners, there has also been an increase in women's deaths in custody. These are related to several factors. Many of which are gender-specific and include geographical dislocation, separation from children and family, bullying, loss of experienced staff, female prisoners are spending increased time in their cells, reduced contact with personal officers, unmet mental health needs and substance misuse needs (Independent Advisory Panel in Deaths in Custody, 2017).

Despite a growing understanding of the impact of prison on female prisoners, there is a lack of knowledge about additional vulnerabilities women face in prison. These include a lack of social support both internal and external to the prison environment, intellectual disability, autism and illiteracy, threats of deportation and language difficulties that contribute to mental ill-health and affect access to healthcare, including mental health care (Bartlett & Hollins, 2018, p. 135). In order to address many of these shortcomings, both policy and legislation are in place; this includes the Equality Act 2010, which includes physical, educational and mental disability. However, in order for support for these disabilities to be accommodated, they need to be diagnosed correctly. For this assistance to be accessible, prisoners must be able to read in order to understand their legal rights. Unfortunately, however, high-levels of female illiteracy in prisons mean this is not always the case. This is exacerbated by the fact that a high percentage of female prisoners come from deprived backgrounds, meaning they do not have the finances to access appropriate legal advice and support.

The Prison Reform Trust (2017a) estimates that more than 17,000 children a year are separated from their mothers, with just 5% of these children remaining in their own homes while their mothers are serving a prison sentence. Separation from children has a profound impact on some women, and it can cause distress and anxiety (Luke, 2002). Women who experience traumatic separation from their children are more likely to re-offend (Missina et al., 2006). Although it is acknowledged that contact and visits with children help to maintain women's mental well-being, due to the small number of women's prisons contact with children can be limited or non-existent. On average, female prisoners were imprisoned 60 miles away from their home and families, making prison visits and maintaining family relationships more difficult (Prison Reform Trust, 2015). Additionally, a lack of information about children and their welfare when in prison can exacerbate mental illness in women.

The normal practices and regime of the prison can trigger emotional and psychological harm for women. For example, learning disabilities, language barriers, illiteracy may make it hard for women to comply with prison rules. O'Brien, et al. (2001) found that women with mental health problems are more likely to be disciplined. This discipline can include confinement to their cell. Such punishment/discipline can have a detrimental impact on women's mental health. O'Brien et al. found that women who were disciplined had higher rates of self-harm and suicide attempts than the general prison population. These forms of discipline are often utilised to control women who have mental health problems. Thus, mental health problems and high levels of distress can make it difficult for women to cope with prison routines and rules.

Additionally, the practices and regimes of prison can trigger emotional and psychological harm for women who have experienced traumatic events. The constant monitoring, restricted movements, contact with male prison officers and abuse by prison staff and inmates can re-traumatic and/or exacerbate trauma for women who have a history of abuse and violence. As Mollard and Brage

Hudson (2016) assert, the experience of imprisonment can trigger mental health illness. This can include anxiety and depression. This anxiety and depression can also be exacerbated by the lack of cleanliness, privacy and dignity which can affect women's physical and emotional well-being. These are compounded by a lack of access to adequate mental health support and/or treatment.

As discussed, the prison environment exacerbates the poor mental health of prisoners in a number of ways. Importantly, the current neo-liberal approach to crime and punishment, with its focus on risk reduction and responsibilisation fails to consider the circumstances of many female offenders' lives, including poverty, gender-based violence including domestic violence. This neo-liberal approach and recent austerity measures, including a reduction in welfare support, have had and, continue to have a disproportionate impact on women from disadvantaged communities (Wacquant, 2008). Furthermore, Wacquant (2009) has illustrated how welfare and penal interventions are increasingly merged; he argues how this merging has disproportionately impacted women in the 'double regulation of the poor'. Despite these insurmountable odds, women face stigma and shame of accusations that they only have themselves to blame. As Skotnicki states, this neo-liberal approach fails to acknowledge "the organising principle that honours human life as scared" (2019, p. 14) has caused harm to those imprisoned.

Barriers to securing mental health support

Research (Reed, 2003; McKenzie & Sales, 2008; Prisons and Probation Ombudsman, 2016) consistently finds that there are long waiting lists for treatment for acute mental health problems, with some prisoners waiting longer than the 14-day target set by the Department of Health, while those who require a transfer to a secure hospital waiting over a year (House of Commons, 2016). As Forrester et al. (2009) contend, many prisons are waiting rooms for those prisoners with acute mental health needs who require hospitalisation or hospital treatment. The under-staffing of prison health care systems and lack of other essential resources is hampering the delivery of appropriate health care in prison (HM Inspectorate of Prisons, 2018; House of Commons, 2018). Good relationships between staff and prisoners based on trust and understanding cannot be made and sustained which is essential for accessing support and rehabilitation. The issue of under-staffing is compounded by the lack of appropriate training of staff who are not always receiving appropriate or timely training in order to provide adequate care. This lack of training reduces the ability to effectively support prisoners with mental health needs (Forrester et al., 2013). Under-staffing and lack of training impacts not only on support and treatment for prisoners but also on the welfare of prison staff, with staff feeling unsupported which impacts on levels of staff morale and continuity of service (Morse et al., 2012). This, in turn, has an impact on the multidisciplinary nature of mental health care within prisons, which undermines the 'equivalence of care' within prisons. Even for those women who can access support and treatment, they may face irregular or interrupted counselling and/or therapeutic sessions due to prison transfers, shortage of prison staff to escort prisoners to hospital or clinic appointments and sessions (House of Commons, 2016).

Revolving Doors Agency asserts that female prisoner may have low levels of help-seeking behaviour as a result of distrust in statutory services, for example, being taken into care as a child/adolescent, disbelief when reporting being a victim of abuse. Fear of stigmatisation may also prevent female prisoners from accessing support, for example, being labelled 'mentally ill' or 'mad'. The pathologising of female mental health and women's fear of being perceived as 'mad' can impact them achieving full citizenship and on their autonomy; they may be labelled as being more problematic. These labels may still have a negative impact after release from prison where public and official perceptions are evident; these include perceptions such as a woman's inability to parent, which in turn can result in increased stigma, discrimination and isolation.

Further difficulties women may face in accessing mental health support when serving a prison sentence includes lack of resources including funding and staff knowledge in identifying prisoners with mental health needs; lack of specialist psychiatric doctors along with a shortage of mental health trained nursing staff. Thus the services for prisoners with mental health issues fall below the standard of the National Health Service (NHS). For seriously mentally ill female prisoners who need to be transferred to appropriate NHS facilities face delays in finding suitable beds in the NHS, meaning that very ill women are sometimes contained in settings without adequate qualified care and treatment. Accommodating these women in prison health care centres while awaiting an available NHS bed generates additional distress not only for the female prisoner herself but also for prison staff and other prisoners. The standards set for the NHS and the practice of prison mental health care can highlight numerous gaps for, as previously evidenced, female prisoners have much higher rates of mental disorder, drug misuse, and histories of abuse and self-harm than women with mental health issues in the community. As the Prison Reform Trust (2001, p. 36) argued, "The NHS needs to develop an integrated service to ensure that a woman in prison with a given mental health problem receives the same range and standards of care as would apply to someone with the same problem outside". However, this gap still exists today with disparities between institutions, and institutions and the NHS.

Moreover, there is a lack of access to prisoners' full medical records when they arrive in custody resulting in no or partial knowledge of their mental health needs. Given that a significant number of women entering prison have a mental health issue and have been proscribed medication such as anti-depressants, hypnotics or anxiolytics, and anti-psychotic medication it is important that prison and medical staff have access to full medical records. The cellular confinement of prisoners with mental health issues impacts on counselling and/or rehabilitation session. This confinement is often used in order to secure the safety of mentally ill prisoners. However, women with evidence of anti-social or other personality disorders were three times more likely to be punished with cellular confinement

(O'Brien et al., 2001). Upon release from prison, women may face a lack of continuity of care. These difficulties severely limit women's access to mental health care and to living a healthy and stable life while serving a prison sentence. Furthermore, the lack of appropriate support, rehabilitation programmes, accommodation, employment and, family contact can also severely limit a woman's ability to lead a healthy and stable life upon release from prison.

Black, Asian and minority ethnic women in the criminal justice system

Ethnic minority women's experiences extend beyond those of the majority of white women who come into contact with criminal justice system. For example, Muslim women not only experience domestic violence, including abusive and controlling behaviour by their husband or partner, but they also face cultural ideals and expectations that the majority of white women may not. For instance, Muslim women may be expected to act in what is deemed appropriate female behaviour to maintain family honour, and not bring shame to their family. Although cultural ideals and norms about appropriate female behaviour are not unique to Asian women, they are of a particular significance for Asian women. Strong cultural and value-based beliefs about appropriate female behaviour combined with patriarchal beliefs can result in unrealistic expectations of women. This can create tensions for all women but it highlights the double standards Asian women can face concerning certain behaviours of men and women. These cultural stereotypes are not only evident in mainstream society, but are also evident within the criminal justice system. For example, there is an assumption that Asian women are more likely to have support from family when they come into contact with the criminal justice system, from arrest through to release from prison. However, research (Muslim Hand, 2018, p. 3) found that "prison resettlement teams misjudged the extent of family support". Furthermore, Asian women offenders may find that they lose contact with family due to their offending behaviour, arrest and imprisonment being perceived to have disgraced the family and disrupting family honour (Muslim Hand, 2018).

In addition to Black, Asian, and ethnic minority people (BAME) women facing a number of these specific family and cultural difficulties, they may face discrimination by prison staff and inmates (Cox & Sacks-Jones, 2017) and; faith-based discrimination (Muslim Hand, 2018). There is also a lack of tailored support for women generally, but these are more profound for BAME women. This has led Muslim Hand (2018) to highlight the lack of appropriate support for Muslim female prisoners. Where there has been this support it is usually the first to face financial cost cuts; research (Said, 2011) found that rehabilitation services including BAME specific and women's services have been some of the first to face cuts. This lack of support can be more profound for BAME women, especially those whose first language is not English; this can impact on their understanding of the processes and rules of the prison.

The difficulties mentioned above faced by BAME women serving a prison sentence can have a profound impact if they also have mental health issues. For example, if English is not a woman's first language, they may not be able to understand a diagnosis of mental illness. A diagnosis of mental illness along with serving a prison sentence, may make a woman feel that she has brought further shame on her family. Additionally, a lack of contact with family members may exacerbate a mental health illness as the woman may lack support from her family or community upon release. This highlights the importance of the research conduct by Muslim Hand discussed previously, that cultural stereotypes must be challenged as some BAME particularly Asian women will not have family support on release from prison and this can have a detrimental impact on resettlement and subsequently a woman's mental health and, reoffending. These stereotypes can impact on BAME women's willingness to seek help and support for their mental health needs. This lack of engagement with support services impacts on the continued stigma of mental health within BAME communities and impacts on programmes/interventions/support, etc.

Women face extreme difficulties upon release from prison, with non-accommodation, delayed benefits, lack of support upon release related to mental health issues, unemployment and access to children. This often results in many women living in temporary accommodation, unemployed and lacking financial support. Additionally, many women are likely to return to the same communities, same deprivations, abuses, without receiving any help to address their underlying problems. There are limited resources available to support women on and after release. Many women find themselves living in temporary accommodation which contributes to their already chaotic lifestyles. In addition to these barriers very little progress is being made by the criminal justice system to respond to the specific mental health needs of BAME prisoners.

Moving forward

Historically there has been a lack of tailored support for female prisoners generally but more profound for female prisoners with mental health issues and BAME women who have mental health issues. The Corston Report (2007) recommended a holistic woman-centred approach to responding to the needs of women who have offended or who are at risk of offending. A holistic approach should make connections between the criminal justice system and 'community' ensuring that there is the integration of mental health, drugs and alcohol. Additionally, this approach should address the effects of social isolation and victimisation that many female offenders face and which have a profound impact on their lives. The benefits of a holistic approach aim to ensure that individual interventions are treated with caution to ensure that the approaches implemented do not result in holding women accountable for their behaviour without taking into account the structural context of their lives including poverty, unemployment, history of previous abuse and trauma. As asserted by McIntosh (2008), the criminal justice system often neglects the importance of connections to the community even though there has been an acknowledgement of the significance of engagement between service users and providers.

Custodial sentences exacerbate mental health issues and already difficult family circumstances. In acknowledging the negative impact of serving a prison sentence, the Government are changing their approach to addressing the offending behaviour of women. This is evident in The Female Offender Strategy which aims to divert the most vulnerable women in criminal justice system away from custody by providing through tailored support which recognises "their unique and complex circumstances" (Gauke, 2018b). This strategy recognises that many women who come into contact with the criminal justice system are amongst the most vulnerable within society. It is acknowledged that many of these women face issues with substance misuse and have mental health issues which are often the result of a history of abuse and violence, "almost 60% of female offenders have experienced domestic abuse" (Gauke, 2018a, p. 3, Forward: Female Offender Strategy).

The strategy focused on a shift towards community services to support the needs of women who find themselves in contact with the criminal justice system and help address their offending behaviour. This shift from imprisonment to support outside the prison environment was intended to include the introduction of five women's residential centres across England and Wales. It was argued this approach will "help us deliver the best possible outcomes for women, placing greater emphasis on community provision and cutting of female offending" (Ministry of Justice, 2018a). It was envisioned that this would be achieved by providing a range of support services to reduce rates of self-harm and self-inflicted deaths, supported transition back into the community including appropriate mental health support and drug misuse support and, tackling the underlying causes of offending and re-offending by women. However, the recommendations of the Female Offender Strategy (2018a) and the recommendation of introducing smaller custodial centres have had little impact on changing the female prison estate. This is despite evidence from Scotland which appears to support the move from large prisons to small custodial centres that are more geographically dispersed (see Malloch et. al., 2014; Malloch, 2016). Optimism was high that England would follow this approach with plans to build five new community centres for women. However, the Ministry of Justice (2018a) has scrapped these plans and instead increased the use of non-custodial sentences. In order for this approach to be effective further funding is required (All-Party Parliamentary Group on Women in the Penal System, 2016). In order for 'treatment' in the community to be effective there needs to be a consideration of the environment into which the offender will return upon release. This includes accessing how offenders "are equipped with necessary skills, provide the required support and establish the conditions needed to maintain attitudinal and behavioural change following transition to the community" (Shuker & Bates, 2014, p. 213).

Webster (2001, cited in Shuker & Bates, 2014, p. 214) also contents that "any treatment or rehabilitation programme needs to be attentive to the wider systemic contextual factors", including family, community and peer groups. Without this attention, any treatment or rehabilitation will be undermined. This is also important for women upon release from prison, and particularly so for BAME women who may find that they are not accepted back into the family or community due to the shame and dishonour they have brought upon the family and/or the community In order to achieve this, the lack of knowledge about successful interventions, rehabilitation and diversion strategies need to be addressed.

Conclusion

"Reforming the prison system for women and developing more 'appropriate' community punishments may have little impact while the problems that need to be addressed require deep and radical transformative change" (Malloch, 2016, p. 3). England and Wales should consider the approach suggested by Commission on Women Offenders (2012) which includes "the establishment of Community Justice Centres; intensive mentoring, these mentoring services should provide effective support for the reintegration of women". These services are better able to address marginalisation, isolation and exclusion. They are also able to provide alternative relationships as many of the women's key relationships have become fragmented. This is particularly important for BAME women who as we have seen may lose family and community relationships due to bringing shame and dishonour on the family and community. Alternatives to prison should include a focus on welfare issues as this will help to address and alleviate many of the contributing factors of women's offending behaviour. These include financial issues, poverty, high rates of domestic violence, addiction, distress, trauma and violence.

On release, there is a need for gender-specific support (Aday & Dye, 2019), for example, child care, protection from further sexual and/or violent abuse including domestic violence. More importantly, any approach should acknowledge that expert knowledge dominates the field, which impacts on women as passive recipients who are worked on rather than worked with. This 'expert' approach impacts on constructions of women's lived experiences which depart from women's realities. This lack of control over one's life needs addressing, women need to have control over and work with experts in order to recover from mental illness and to desist from crime. Therefore, no one approach is effective; rather, there is a need for multiple approaches which draw on women's realities, providing a personalised approach. However, as previously argued, these personalised/individual approaches should ensure avoiding holding women responsible for their behaviour without due consideration to the structural context of their lives.

References

Aday, R. H., & Dye, M. H. (2019). Examining predictors of depression among older incarcerated women. *Women & Criminal Justice*, *29*(1), 32–51. doi: 10.1080/08974454.2018.1443870

All-party Parliamentary Group on Women in the Penal System, (2015). Report on the inquiry into preventing unnecessary criminalisation of women. The Howard League for Penal Reform. https://howardleague.org/wp-content/uploads/2016/02/APPG_final.pdf

All Party Parliamentary Group on Women in the Penal System, (2016). Report on the inquiry into preventing unnecessary criminalisation of women. The Howard League for Penal Reform. http://howardleague.org/ wp-content/uploads/2016/02/APPG_final.pdf

Bartlett, A., & Hollins, S. (2018). Challenges and mental health needs of women in prison. *The British Journal of Psychiatry, 212*(3), 134–136. doi: 10.1192/bjp.2017.42.

Bromley Report. (2017). *Bromley briefings prison fact file*. Prison Reform Trust, August 2017. London: PRT.

Brooker, C., & Gojkovic, D. (2009). The second national survey of mental health in-reach services in prisons. *The Journal of Forensic Psychiatry & Psychology, 20*(sup 1), S11–S28. doi: 10.1080/14789940802638325

Commission on Women Offenders (2012). Report of the Commission on women offenders, http://www.scotland.gov.uk/Resource/0039/00391828.pdf

Corston, J. (2007). The Corston report: A report by Baroness Jean Corston of a review of women with particular vulnerablilities in the criminal justice system. London: Home Office.

Cox, J., & Sacks-Jones, K. (2017). *"Double disadvantage": The experiences of Black, Asian and minority ethnic women in the Criminal Justice System*. London: Agenda, Women in Prison.

National Institute for Health and Care Excellence. (2017). http://www.nice.org/guidance/indevelopment/gid-cgwave0726

Fazel, S., Hayes, A. J., Bartellas, K., Clerici, M., & Trestman, R. (2016). Mental health of prisoners: Prevalence, adverse outcomes, and interventions. *The Lancet Psychiatry, 3*(9), 871–881. doi: 10.1016/S2215-0366(16)30142-0

Forrester, A., Exworthy, T., Olumoroti, O., Sessay, M., Parrott, J., Spencer, S. J., & Whyte, S. (2013). Variations in prison mental health services in England and Wales. *International Journal of Law and Psychiatry, 36*(3), 326–332. doi: 10.1016/j.ijlp.2013.04.007

Forrester, A., Henderson, C., Wilson, S., Cumming, I., Spyrou, M., & Parrott, J. (2009). A suitable waiting room? Hospital transfer outcomes and delays from two London prisons. *Psychiatric Bulletin, 33*(11), 409–412. doi: 10.1192/pb.bp.108.022780

Forrester, A., MacLennan, F., Slade, K., Brown, P., & Exworthy, T. (2014). Improving access to psychological therapies in prisons. *Criminal Behaviour and Mental Health, 24*, 163.

Gauke, D. (2018a). Forward: Female offender strategy. Perth: Ministry of Justice. HM Stationary Office.

Gauke, D. (2018b). Press release: Secretary of state launches dedicated strategy to 'break the cycle' of female offending. Ministry of Justice, 27 June 2018.

Gelsthorpe, L., Sharpe, G., & Roberts, J. (2007). *Provision for women offenders in the community*. London: Fawcett Society and Nuffield Foundation.

HM Inspectorate of Prisons. (2018). Report on an unannounced inspection of HMP Liverpool by HM Chief Inspector of Prisons, 4–15 September 2017. HM Inspectorate of Prisons, 2018. https://www. justiceinspectorates.gov.uk/%0bhmiprisons/wp-content/uploads/ sites/4/2018/01/HMP-Liverpool-Web-2017.pdf.

Home Office (2004). *Statistics on women in the Criminal Justice System, 2003*. London: Stationary Office.

House of Commons Committee of Public Accounts. Mental health in prisons: Eighth report of session 2017–2019. 3 House of Commons Committee of Public Accounts, 2016. https://publications. parliament.uk/pa/cm201719/cmselect/cmpubacc/400/400.pdf

House of Commons Justice Committee (2018). *HM Inspectorate of Prisons report on HMP Liverpool: Fifth Report of Session 2017–2019*. House of Commons Justice Committee. https://publications.parliament.uk/pa/cm201719/cmselect/cmjust/751/751. Pdf.

Independent Advisory Panel on Deaths in Custody (2017). *Preventing the deaths of women in prison – Initial results of a rapid information gathering exercise by the independent advisory panel on deaths in custody.* IAPDIC, 2017. http:// iapdeathsincustody.independent.gov.uk/wp-content/uploads/2017/04/IAPrapid-evidence-collection-v0.2.pdf.

Labhart, J., & Wright, L. (2018) Why doesn't prison work for women? BBC News, 29 September 2018. bbc.co.uk/news/uk-england.45627845

Luke, K. P. (2002). Mitigating the ill effects of maternal incarceration on women in prison and their children. *Child Welfare, 81*(6), 929–948.

Malloch, M. (2016). Justice for women: A penal Utopia? *Justice, Power and Resistance, Foundation Volume.* http://dspace.stir.ac.uk/handle/1893/23308

Malloch, M., McIvor, G., & Burgess, C. (2014). 'Holistic' community punishment and criminal justice interventions for women. *The Howard Journal of Criminal Justice, 53*(4), 395–410. doi: 10.1111/hojo.12077

McIntosh, A. (2008). *Rekindling community.* Devon: Green Books for the Schumacher Society.

McIvor, G. (2001) Treatment in the community. In C. R. Hollin (ed), *Offender assessment and treatment.* London: Wily.

McIvor, G., & Burman, M. (2011). *Understanding the drivers of female imprisonment in Scotland.* http://dspace.stir.ac.uk/handle/1893/13057

McKenzie, N., & Sales, B. (2008). New procedures to cut delays in transfer of mentally ill prisoners to hospital. *Psychiatric Bulletin, 32*(1), 20–22. doi: 10.1192/pb.bp.107.015958

Missina, N., Burdon, W., Hagopian, G., & Prendergast, M. (2006). Predictors of prison-based treatment outcomes: A comparison of men and women participants. *The American Journal of Drug and Alcohol Abuse, 32*(1), 7–28. doi: 10.1080/00952990500328463

Ministry of Justice (2018a). Female offender strategy. MJ, London https://assets.publishing.service.gov.uk/government/uploads/system/uploads/attachment_data/file/719819/female-offender-strategy.pdf

Ministry of Justice (2018b). Vulnerable offenders steered towards treatment. http://www.gov.uk/government/news/vulnerable-offenders-steered-towards-treatment

Ministry of Justice (2019). Prison population statistics. https://www.gov.uk/government/collections/prison-population-statistics

Mollard, E. & Bradge Hudson, D. (2016). Nurse-led trauma-informed correctional care for women. *Perspectives in Psychiatric Care, 52*(3), 224–230.

Morse, G., Salyers, M. P., Rollins, A. L., Monroe-DeVita, M., & Pfahler, C. (2012). Burnout in mental health services: A review of the problem and its remediation. *Administration and Policy in Mental Health and Mental Health Services Research, 39*(5), 341–352. doi: 10.1007/s10488-011-0352-1

Muslim Hand (2018). (In)visibility: Female, Muslim, imprisoned. https://muslimhands.org.uk/latest/2018/02/in-visibility-female-muslim-imprisoned

NACRO (n.d.). People with mental health issues. https://www.nacro.org.uk/about-us/who-we-support/people-mental-health-issues/

Nursing Times (2013) Women prisoners more likely to self-harm. nursingtimes.net/clinical-archive/womens-health/women-prisoners-more-likely-to-self-harm/5066473.article

O'Brien, M., Mortimer, L., Singleton, N., & Meltzer, H. (2001). *Psychiatric morbidity among women in prison in England and Wales.* London: Office of National Statistics.

Offender Management Statistics (2017). Ministry of Justice, https://www.gov.uk/government/statistics/offender-management-statistics-quarterly-july-to-september-2017

Pilgrim, D. (2017). *Key concepts in mental health.* London: Sage.

Prison Reform Trust (2001) *Justice for women: The need for reform* (The Wedderburn Report). London: PRT.
Prison Reform Trust (2015). *Transforming lives: reducing women's imprisonment*. London: PRT.
Prison Reform Trust (2017a). Why focus on reducing women's imprisonment? http://www.prisonreformtrust.org.uk/Portals/0/Documents/Women/whywomen.pdf
Prison Reform Trust (2017b). *"There's a reason we're in trouble": Domestic violence as a driver to women's offending*. London: Prison Reform Trust.
Prison Reform Trust (2018). Bromley briefings prison factfile. http://www.prisonreformtrust.org.uk/Portals/0/Documents/Bromley%20Briefings/Autumn%202018%20Factfile.pdf
Prisons and Probation Ombudsman (2016). Learning from PPO investigations: Prisoner mental health. London: Crown copyright http://www.ppo.gov.uk/wp-content/uploads/2016/01/PPO-thematic-prisoners-mental-health-web-final.pdf .
Reed, J. (2003). Mental health care in prisons. *The British Journal of Psychiatry, 182*(4), 287–288. doi: 10.1192/bjp.182.4.287
Revolving doors agency (n.d). Rebalancing act: A resource for directors of public health, police and crime commissioners, the police service and other health and justice commissioners, service providers and users. http://www.revolving-doors.org.uk/file/2049/download?token=4WZPsE8I
Said, L. (2011). *Young British muslims: Ex-offenders and resettlement needs*. London: Muslim Youth Helpline.
Shuker, R., & Bates, A. (2014). 'Offending behaviour programmes: Managing the transition from prison into the community'. In Z. Ashmore & R Shuker (eds), *Forensic Practice in the community* (pp. 213–229). Oxon: Routledge.
Skotnicki, A. (2019). *Conversion and the rehabilitation of the penal system: A theological rereading of criminal justice*. Oxford: Oxford University Press.
Valamuri, M. R. & Stillman, S. (2007). Longitudinal evidence on the impact of incarceration on labour market outcomes and general well being. Researchgate. https://www.researchgate.net/publication/228873587_Longitudinal_Evidence_on_the_Impact_of_Incarceration_on_Labour_Market_Outcomes_and_General_Well-Being.
Wacquant, L. (2008). *Urban outcasts*. Cambridge: Polity.
Wacquant, L. (2009). *Punishing the poor*. Durham: Duke University Press.
Women in Prison (2011). *Breaking the cycle for women*. London: WIP.
Youth Justice Board for England and Wales Business Plan (2017). assets.publishing.services.gov/government/uploads/systems/uploads/attachments_data/file/660018/yjb-business-plan-2017-18/pdf

11

INTELLECTUAL DISABILITY AND PUNISHMENTS

Andrew Lovell

This chapter seeks to examine the relationship between intellectual disability and punishment, primarily though not exclusively in the United Kingdom (UK), with a historical frame of reference, and in terms of the implications for this population in contemporary society. The chapter begins by looking at how offending behaviour has been associated with intelligence, particularly the notion of intelligence quotient (IQ), and the consequences in terms of the institutional movement over the course of the twentieth century. The role of language, such as moral defective and degeneracy, is drawn upon to demonstrate how the societal response of segregation and incarceration was legitimised, a punitive response to having a low IQ, below 70, rather than offending behaviour. The focus of the chapter then changes to examine community care as policy, essentially since the 1980s, which coincided with the development of fairly comprehensive secure services, low, medium and high, specialising in caring for people with intellectual disabilities, yet within a mental health framework. The chapter analyses how the relationship between intellectual disability and crime was subject to a changed lens during the 1990s, the idealism of community care much diminished, and a greater emphasis emerged on punishment responses identifying this population as a discrete group. The chapter ends with an examination of current concerns, from diversion from prison following over-representation in this context, critique of the risk framework, and understanding intellectual disability in terms of complexity, such as in association with personal history, issues of substance misuse, and with additional concerns around personality disorder and autistic spectrum disorder.

Intellectual disability and intelligence quotient (IQ): the initial construction of a problem group

The relationship between intellectual disability and criminal behaviour has a long problematic history, which has served to facilitate the production of powerful inaccurate information, mythology and subsequent structural prejudice and stigma with regard to this population (Johnston, 2005). The impact of the early twentieth century Eugenics movement has been enormous, with its basic premise that society was being contaminated and degraded by people with an intellectual disability having children, but lacking the capacity to effectively care and produce contributing community members. The policy of segregation and construction of the asylum system was geared towards the protection and welfare of the general population, though it was also underpinned by the ideological belief that this was for the safety of the most vulnerable members of society (Reynolds, Zupanick, & Dombeck, 2013). Intellectual disability was essentially defined as being detrimental to the health of the society, a clinical truth was constructed, and seemingly robust evidence about the dangerousness of this group and the threat they posed to the societal gene pool became real. The institutional movement, though, perhaps not initially designed as a punitive response, became so over the course of time. The construction of the asylum system, with the high walls, bloc treatment approaches to care, means of depersonalisation, and established punishment devices, such as isolation rooms, locked wards, mechanical restraining apparatus, and increasing reliance on psychotropic and other medication, gave rise by the middle of the century to an intellectual critique (Barton, 1959; Goffman, 1961; Morris, 1969) and a series of hospital scandals at Ely, Farleigh, Normansfield, amongst others, which ultimately signalled their demise. The asylum system had become a means of warehousing segments of the population (e.g. the mentally ill, those with epilepsy, people with intellectual disabilities) and controlling their behaviour and movements through an elaborate framework of intrinsically punitive responses.

The over-arching punitive approach to people with an intellectual disability required that they were viewed a particular way, as a deviant population, and this was supported by the use of language designed to regard them through a particular lens. Many specific labels were applied over the course of the twentieth century, beginning with the separation of intellectual disability from mental health within the Mental Deficiency Act (1913), with its sub-groups of idiot, imbecile, feeble-minded, and moral defective. During the course of the century, the language altered, with mental providing the basic descriptive platform then linked to terms such as deficient, defective, subnormality, retardation and handicap. The most powerful, perhaps, was mental subnormality, the term of choice in relation to the nursing qualification for caring for this group until the mid-1980s, and suggestive of people being below normal, constituting part of Goffman's 'less than human' (1963). The employment of such language within a particular discourse justifies a particular policy approach towards a segment of the population, which can include a series of discriminative practices but can also contribute to much more punitive strategies, such as compulsory sterilisation and the genocidal policies of Nazi Germany. More progressive language, however, such as the contemporary use of intellectual, learning, cognitive or developmental, in conjunction with disability, have not necessarily eradicated stigmatising and other discriminatory practices. Continuing difficulties, such as in Cornwall, Suffolk, and most recently, Winterbourne (DH, 2012), along with reports accentuating that people with an intellectual disability live on average nearly 30 years less than those without an intellectual disability, suggest that the relationship with this population and society remains problematic (Social Care, Local Government and Care Partnerships, 2014). The emphasis has altered from uncertainty in describing the nature of the 'mental' problem towards debate around the processes within the mind, but to an extent, this is a question of societal preference.

The IQ approach to intellectual disability remains problematic, primarily, in the context of criminal activity, in relation to this population, because the vast majority of offences are committed by those in the mild range (IQ: 50–70), and also because adaptive functioning is the key diagnostic criteria (American Psychiatric Association, 2013). Furthermore, people with an IQ below 80 were historically excluded from offence-specific treatment in the prison and probation service (Langdon, Clare, & Murphy, 2010), which includes, therefore, a number of people, who would not meet the strict criteria for intellectual disability (below 70). Consequently, there is provision within current mental health legislation for those with an IQ of 70–75, who may have other developmental disabilities, such as Autistic Spectrum Disorder (ASD), Fragile X Syndrome or Acquired Brain Injury, to receive treatment on the basis of having a mental disorder, the key legal category of the last decade (Mental Health Act, 2007). Talbot (2009) made the point over a decade ago now, though it remains strikingly pertinent, that, given a prison population of 82,000, there will be 5,740 with an IQ below 70 and 20,500 70–80. The increasing complexity of people with intellectual disabilities and an offending background is something I will return to later in the chapter, the point here is an historical one really, yet one that continues to resonate. Society might be more inclusive now in its relationship with people with intellectual disabilities, they might be more visible and have their human rights protected by legislation, but part of the punitive back story has been the opposite of these factors, their exclusion from the mainstream, their invisibility, and the lack of recognition of their human rights. Punishment can take many forms, but perhaps the most powerful action that a society can adopt is one that fails to recognise the humanity of a vulnerable group ('subnormal'), discriminating simply through exclusion from all participation, even sometimes from offending behaviour.

Intellectual disability and offending behaviour

The relationship between intellectual disability and criminal behaviour remains fraught with difficulty, with some evidence that people with intellectual disabilities are over-represented within the criminal justice system, but acknowledged concerns over what we understand by offending (Holland, 2004). Many more crimes are committed, for example, than are reported to the police, and people with an intellectual disability, in particular, may benefit from the police choosing not to pursue behaviour that might be regarded more harshly were it perpetrated by those not affected by intellectual disability (Clare & Murphy, 1998). This is due to a number of factors, the legal necessity for a guilty state of mind (*mens rea*) or recklessness by the perpetrator, concern by those in receipt of the act as to whether to press charges (Lyall, Holland, & Collins, 1995), and the victims also being likely to have an intellectual disability, and the associated concerns around giving evidence and conviction (Crichton, 1995). There are, nonetheless, certain areas of offending behaviour that are complicated through association with intellectual disability, and others where this population are much less likely to be represented. The vast majority of people with intellectual disabilities, for example, who do require interventions, particularly legal detention through mental health legislation, relating to their offending behaviour, have difficulties around serious violence and aggression, sex offences, damage to property and/or fire-setting (O'Brien et al., 2010). There is no doubt, however, that association with some criminal behaviour differs according to societal context and general perceptions, with certain offending behaviours being viewed more punitively than others at any given moment in time. The association of a specific area of offending behaviour with the general societal response is also significant in terms of determining how punitively the legal system should respond. Violent crime, for example, provokes a fear in many people in society, particularly when associated with those perceived as more vulnerable, such as the elderly or young women, and is sometimes associated with 'moral panics'. Frequently, though, it is this toxic mix of violence, public fear and media response, that propels crimes, such as mugging (Waddington, 1986), or, more recently, knife crime (Younge, 2017) onto a different level, altering the way in which a group, young black men, for example, or indeed people with intellectual disabilities, are perceived.

The emergence of sex offending as a contemporary area of concern goes back at least a few decades, with Lindsay observing that "prurient interest" had increased markedly since the late 1990s (2004, p. 163), and referring, somewhat depressingly, to Pfaefflin's comment a couple of years earlier that such interest constituted "lust without guilt" (cited In Lindsay, 2004, p. 163). There is some evidence that sex offending rates amongst people with intellectual disabilities are slightly higher than in the general population (Borthwick-Duffy, 1994), though, in the main, similarities in offending between those with and those without intellectual disabilities are much greater than the differences (Craig & Hutchinson, 2005). Nevertheless, one prospective study of 62 intellectually disabled men, not specific to sex offending, found that they did begin offending early, had a history of multiple offences, were over-represented in the areas of sex offending and fire setting, and were more likely to re-offend (Barron, Hassiotis, & Banes, 2004). The role of the individual with an intellectual disability's own abusive history in contributing to engagement in sexual offending remains a little nebulous, though, in conjunction with social circumstances, appears to be significant (Read & Read, 2009); people with intellectual disabilities might be more likely to replicate their own experiences of abuse, rather than apply abstract concepts to further understanding of one's own experiences and feelings (Lindsay et al., 2001). The role of 'counterfeit deviance', whereby sexual offending behaviour might be precipitated by a lack of sexual knowledge, poor social skills, reduced opportunities to build healthy sexual relationships, and sexual naivety, has been forwarded as an explanation for some men's failure to differentiate between sexually appropriate and unacceptable behaviour (Luiselli, 2000), though Lindsay (2008) suggests such individuals to be very few and for most sex offenders to have greater sexual knowledge than other service users. It is abundantly clear, nonetheless, that this is a complicated area for analysis, and any such association between intellectual disability and sex offending has serious implications in relation to the impact on the lives of this already stigmatised group.

The increased availability of treatment approaches to combat the violent and offending behaviour of people with intellectual disabilities has been a relatively recent development, only a few decades ago services having been characterised by the absence of any such approaches. This is primarily due to a growing recognition that the previous discourse, necessitating a certain amount of intellectual understanding as a prerequisite for treatment, was misguided at best and dismissive at worst. This was similar to the denial of the application of diagnoses such as personality disorder to people with intellectual disabilities on the basis that a certain amount of intelligence was fundamental to suffering from the condition. The approach towards treatment availability began to change as services and individual professionals started to successfully alter the way in which we perceived our expectations of how people should engage with therapy. A significant proportion of treatments are based on the principles of Cognitive Behaviour Therapy (CBT), wherein individuals are encouraged to alter their relationship with offending behaviour primarily through cognitive restructuring, fundamentally altering one's thought processes around the initiation, commission and personal mitigation of sexual offences. The central tenet of the argument relates to challenging "pre-existing attitudes, initial planning and misinterpretation of a victim's interaction with the offender, as well as post-offence evaluations and expectations" (Ward et al., 1997, p. 498). The breakthrough came with the application of CBT principles to people with intellectual disabilities, particularly in the context of sex offending, through the development of the Adapted Sex Offending Treatment Programme (ASOTP), based on the innovative work done over a number of years with sex offenders at the Brooklands unit (Hill & Hordell, 1999). This subsequently altered the previous reliance on punishment alone, based on the notion that if people with intellectual disabilities couldn't engage with CBT principles, and were thereby unable to benefit from treatment, then restrictively orientated responses, including suppression of sexual desire, were the only option. Other approaches, such as Dialectical Behavioural Therapy and more psychotherapeutically orientated talking treatments, such as problem-solving treatment (Nezu, Fiore, & Nezu, 2006), have similarly become more accessible, addressing offending behaviour sometimes more obliquely than the directness of the step approach of the SOTP, but essentially focusing on facilitating change in the decisions people make rather than solely punishment. One small-scale study indicated that the ASOTP had some impact on factors such as motivation to stop offending, increasing knowledge and risk disclosure (Large & Thomas, 2011), but there is an absence of research indicating the overall effectiveness of therapeutic approaches, other than confirming that CBT is the most dominant (Marotta, 2017). The whole arena of treating sex offenders, furthermore, is shrouded in mystique, with an ongoing emphasis on separation of offenders from other offenders, both in penal and secure systems, uncertainty around effectiveness, and a lack of consensus in relation to the usefulness of punishment. Hutchinson, Lovell and Mason (2012) argue that there is such pressure on the need for professionals to appear to frame their investigations in the science of objective assessment, and similarly in the need to contain and maintain the individual rather than challenge the offending behaviour, that, in effect, everything becomes subsumed within the therapeutic performance, whereby the desire to demonstrate the logic of the approach adopted, and how it leads seamlessly on from structured assessment, outweighs everything else. The likely consequences of perceived failure, such as an individual continuing to offend, are so pronounced, based around containment, punishment, marginalisation, that it becomes preferable to always steer a low profile course towards low-risk failure.

Forensic intellectual disability services

The tripartite relationship between intellectual disability, crime and society is fundamental to our understanding of the shape and development of the service response to the issue. The changing ideology, for example, of social role valorisation (formerly normalisation) (Wolfensberger et al., 1972; Wolfensberger, 1983), which underpins our contemporary understanding of people with intellectual disabilities as contributing members of society, and accompanying concepts, such as self-advocacy, empowerment, integration and inclusion, reflects the need for forensic services to be humane, therapeutic and tailored to the specific offending population. Despite the evidence of continuing abusive practice, the general emphasis on hospital services to provide long-term residential accommodation for people with intellectual disabilities many miles from their homes and families has declined exponentially over recent decades. Institutional critique, furthermore, has not only been influential in the demise of the old institutional network, which had generally been achieved by the mid to late 1990s but has infiltrated the provision of services for offenders with intellectual disabilities, accentuating the need for more creative, community-orientated approaches to caring for people with an offending background. Nevertheless, some sort of institutional framework in the provision of therapeutically orientated care for some individuals with intellectual disabilities, whether through the state or via the private and independent sector, has been central to services over the course of the last century, and will continue to be important, especially for those whose offending is most severe. This is why the Mental Health Act (2007) ensures that people with intellectual disabilities requiring secure residential care should only be detained when there is an established relationship between the intellectual disability and the offending behaviour. Learning disability/intellectual disability does not fulfil the criteria for a mental disorder unless, according to Section 1(2A), there is an association with "abnormally aggressive or seriously irresponsible behaviour".

The move towards a more sophisticated model of secure provision had begun in the early 1970s with the establishment of the Butler committee to examine future needs around 'mentally abnormal offenders' (Department of Health and Social Security [DHSS], 1975). The reliance on high secure hospitals at Broadmoor, Rampton, Moss Side and Park Lane (the last two later amalgamated to form Ashworth) meant that offenders with intellectual disabilities were either cared for alongside those with mental health problems or within a designated setting (Moss Side), which was essentially an exceptionally secure version of a regular hospital for the 'mentally subnormal'. One of the main recommendations of the committee was to emphasise the need (following the recommendations of The Glancy Report the previous year [DHSS, 1974]) for more regionally based secure provision for those requiring higher security than an open hospital but less than that within high security. The subsequent two decades, as the general institutional system retracted, placed an onus on a more varied secure system, both in mental health and intellectual disability, wherein different types of units were developed, albeit without being fully realised within a coordinated, national strategy. Intensive support units, medium secure, low secure, the increasing influence of the more mixed economy of care, hospital closure, these were all influential in determining the secure environmental landscape by the end of the twentieth century. The basic emerging framework, however, began to revolve around the notion of different levels of security geared towards people with intellectual disabilities requiring a graduated response towards the type and severity of the threat that they presented. The concepts of physical, relational and procedural security increasingly came to be entrenched as the primary ways in which those directly employed in this secure system framework, primarily intellectual/learning disability nurses with forensic experience, understood their roles (Allen, 2015). Similarly, the concept of risk emerged and became consolidated as the primary mechanism in which decision-making apparatus around safety, contact with the public, and level of dangerousness were approached (Quinsey, 2004).

The emerging secure service framework for people with intellectual disabilities, therefore, in the early years of the current century relied on the identification of an individual's intellectual disability and subsequent determination of the level of security (high, medium or low) in accordance with the danger to self, others and society more generally. There are currently around 48 high secure in-patient beds, 604 medium secure and 1,741 low secure, with a further 345 forensic rehabilitation beds for people with intellectual disabilities in

England (Alexander et al., 2014). This is a period of significant change, though, and the last few years have witnessed organisational activity in the relationship between intellectual disability and secure care, which is yet to be entirely resolved. The emphasis remains, however, on upholding individual rights, developing a therapeutic relationship within the particular environment, provision of the minimal level of security required, and creating a non-custodial, non-punitive care system. Some secure units, for example, re-negotiated the level of security designated, moving from medium to low, a transition not without consequences, with some staff struggling to adapt to vicissitudes, their professional identity having been related to the higher level of security (Astbury et al., 2011). These authors go on to investigate how more punitive care practices are associated with the particular culture of a secure facility, and how strong leadership, in particular, can prevent, what they refer to as the 'toggle' group, the main group of staff within a service, from attaching themselves to the most negative workers, those who fundamentally believe in the value of punishment as the most effective strategy. This is punishment through general lethargy, reluctance to be accountable, emphasis on security above all other unit activity; the 'toggle' would adopt a contradictory posture so that they might be evidently agreeable to innovation, but then resistant through an ultimate alliance with the most negative unit elements. The dominance of such a punitive culture could only be avoided through the pervasive working of the more progressive nursing staff, those in positions of authority, in conjunction with policies, procedures and practices to reinforce innovation and progress. The establishment of the Community Treatment Order (CTO) as part of mental health legislation, in addition to the under-utilised Guardianship order, and comprehensive after-care arrangements helped to promote the development of community options, even for those presenting significant challenges. A cultural change had taken place, in terms of the negotiated balance between security and therapy, what Mason (2007) referred to as 'pendulum', whereby care tends to swing between the two extremes depending on the social and political climate. In relation to intellectual disability, a population with such a problematic secure institutional history (e.g. Bowden, 1980), it was clear that a hugely significant change had occurred throughout the service, so that, despite the continuing complex relationship between this population and society, the therapeutic context of care was clearly in the ascendancy. The difficulties, however, of developing a service to accommodate people with intellectual disabilities and an offending background, by the early years of the twenty-first century, had become extremely complicated. The structural approach to care delivery, revolving around the type of secure services available, levels of security, and the role of prison, became bound up in debates around agency, the extent to which offenders with intellectual disabilities could engage with treatment programmes, and issues of additional diagnoses, such as Borderline Personality Disorder (BPD), Autism Spectrum Disorder (ASD), Attention Deficit Hyperactive Disorder (ADHD), and the ubiquity of other mental health issues.

Diversion

The publication of the Bradley Report (2009) followed the publication of a couple of investigations identifying a number of people with intellectual disabilities being incarcerated, perhaps wrongly, and almost certainly problematically, within the penal system (Mottram, 2007; Talbot & Riley, 2007). The consequence was considerable discussion as to the pertinence of imprisonment to many people with intellectual disabilities, particularly around the appropriateness of punishment for those who may be subject to bullying, exploitation, and have a poor understanding of the purpose of the system. There was an evident tension, which was challenging to resolve and reflected the broader ongoing debate, which, if anything, has deepened in an ensuing couple of decades, around the political decision to incarcerate more people and for more extended periods of time. This is coupled with an increased sense of comfort around labelling societal reactions to offending behaviour as punitive, following a period of time when those in positions of power sought to place less emphasis on punishment and more on rehabilitation. The "punitive turn" had been first applied to societal responses to juvenile offending behaviour (Muncie, 2008, p. 107), but has resonance with other groups in society too, such as people with mental health problems, personality disorders and those with intellectual disabilities. The demise of the old asylum system, somewhat inevitably, had a number of unintended consequences, one of which, according to the analysis of the United States context, was an increase in numbers within the prison population of those who might previously have been accommodated within the hospital system (Harcourt, 2006). The tension revolves around the notion of culpability of people with intellectual disabilities, their capacity for understanding the nature of the offence and thereby participating in their own defence. The role of mental health legislation is to support decisions with regard to this central tension, but context is important and recent years have witnessed a reluctance to relieve individuals of accountability because of mitigating circumstances, such as the role of the intellectual disability in influencing offending behaviour. The situation is complicated further by the absence of consensus around the way in which they are held accountable (Hayes, 2004), which "should not mean that they are denied due process in the courts, housed in settings where they face high risks of victimisation, or denied access to work and treatment" (Petersilia, 2000, p. 41).

The current focus within secure intellectual disability care is on reducing the number of beds and developing community service models to replace the emphasis on hospitalised care, a reasonable premise since some individuals are subject to a greater level of security than necessary (Lovell, 2010). This has been the overt national policy since Winterbourne, embodied in the Building the Right Support plan, which sought to provide alternative care for people who "display behaviour that challenges" (NHS England, 2015, p. 4). The goal is for a 50% reduction in inpatient admissions and for considerably less emphasis on larger institutional structures, with secure units more integrated into the overall diversity of services.

A fundamental dimension of the plan, though, is for new community services to be in place prior to hospital closure, and some observers have voiced considerable reservations about current progress and the absence of a vision with regard to what these community service models might look like (Taylor et al., 2017). Perhaps the most significant aspect of the approach and one that makes it particularly problematic is the association by policymakers of the specific group likely to require services of this type, as we have seen, primarily those with mild/borderline intellectual disabilities, with the notion of challenging behaviour, which is most associated with the self-injurious and aggressive behaviours of those with much more severe intellectual disabilities. Challenging behaviour has been defined specifically in relation to its measurability, in terms of severity, frequency and duration, its consequences with regard to both the individual and others, and the potential for exclusion from mainstream services (Emerson et al., 1987; Emerson, 2001). The difficulty is that it was designed for people with quite severe intellectual disabilities, yet was subsequently associated with individuals who might present a much greater degree of dangerousness, including the use of weapons. This has resulted in significant confusion between people with intellectual disabilities, where their primary issues revolve around challenging behaviours, such as lashing out at others, headbanging and spitting, and those with intellectual disabilities, with whom this chapter is centrally concerned, where violence and offending behaviour have resulted in engagement with the criminal justice system. There is a clear need for separation between these two issues by those in positions of responsibility in relation to future policy and subsequent service responses.

Intellectually disabled offenders: complexity

Current developments within the intellectual disability secure system have become complicated over the last few years by association with the transforming care agenda, and the consequences of these changes are difficult to determine accurately at the time of writing. There is emerging evidence, furthermore, that the presentation of people with intellectual disabilities, who need support because of their offending, is becoming more complex, with considerable evidence of multiple diagnoses, such as borderline personality disorder, autism, ADHD, and significant mental health issues, in conjunction with a problematic personal history (Lovell et al., 2014). These authors suggest that those caring for such individuals consequently need to alter the knowledge base to accommodate such increased complexity and ensure that other core competencies, around communication and team working, use such knowledge as a platform to enhance decision making. The alternative, of course, is to respond to enhanced complexity in a more punitive way, concealing uncertainties relating to knowledge deficits by an increased emphasis on issues such as control and reliance on risk management. The ubiquity of risk assessment alongside policies like zero tolerance has become entrenched within the delivery of forensic services over recent years, and have sought to combat concerns relating to violence against staff and decision making being more evidence-based, though such strategies are not without consequence. The critique of zero tolerance has gathered force over the last 20 years (Rowe & Bendesky, 2003; Bennet et al., 2017), based on growing recognition that a primarily punitive policy inculcates a punitive culture with no corresponding amelioration of the problem, whether violence, crime or any other sphere of human behaviour. The difficulty, of course, is that the policy of minimising restrictive practice, which surrounds and underpins service approaches to risk-taking and progressive care practices, is inconsistent with the dominance of fears around litigation, minimising risks, and punishment through negative decision-making. There is a tension between promoting the inclusion and integration of people with intellectual disabilities, particularly those with an offending background, and reducing the likelihood of recidivism.

Transforming care necessarily involves a continued move from an emphasis on institutional services towards a more community-orientated approach, and despite contemporary concerns around the absence of the latter as the former decline, the history of the move from hospital-based to community services for people with intellectual disabilities, more generally, has been one of considerable success, with many now living fruitful and inclusive lives. Services for offenders with intellectual disabilities will take shape over the coming decade, and will probably be best informed by the recovery-orientated model now prevalent in mental health services, which is perhaps particularly pertinent for those with intellectual disabilities and an offending background (Lovell, 2017). Many, maybe most, people with intellectual disabilities, who come into contact with the law and become subject to mental health legislation, have extremely difficult backgrounds. They frequently struggle with knowing how to lead healthy lives and come from circumstances of chaos and uncertainty. Care approaches often revolve around having decent role models, learning how to take responsibility, and, maybe most importantly, learning how to apply a given structure to their lives. This means that those working with such individuals in less structured circumstances, primarily individualised community packages rather than the group-orientated approach of secure facilities, need to learn to work in a different way, one less reliant on the observation of rules, regulations and policies alone. There is an increasing recognition that trauma-informed care has much to offer in terms of therapeutic responses to people exposed to events and experiences, which have significantly altered their relationship with the social world (Sweeney et al., 2016). Many people with intellectual disabilities and a background of offending behaviour, furthermore, have histories of abuse, neglect, rejection, substance misuse and homelessness. Such personal history is then complicated further by combinations of diagnoses relating to intellectual disability, ASD, BPD, ADHD, and numerous other conditions. Lovell and Bailey (2017) argue the need for professionals, particularly direct care staff, such as nurses, to utilise a variety of attributes in order to understand such individual complexity, how it manifests in everyday interactions, and how this knowledge can inform the development of therapeutic relationships which serve to facilitate individual growth and progress. The challenge for services during this period of service transformation relates to unlocking the potential of individual professionals, in order to make it possible for people with intellectual disabilities and an offending background to function effectively without recourse to secure institutional structures. This will require the development of community-orientated services to accommodate such change, and, as with the closure of the hospitals in the mid-1990s, will take some time for good service models to be developed and become successful. The development of interpersonal and other skills by nurses and other professionals, especially around working with complexity, understanding how trauma and diagnostic criteria inter-relate in the manifestation of individual behaviour, will be critical to policy success. The most innovative community care schemes have been those where the emphasis has been on relationship-building, the anticipation of some difficulties, and individualised resource packages; this is further complicated by offending behaviour, differentiated from challenging behaviour, which necessitates highly skilled individuals building strong therapeutic relationships. Individuals with intellectual disabilities and an offending background can thrive in community settings, but only through non-punitive relationships, which utilise risk as a means of promoting growth and development.

References

Alexander, R. T., Devapriam, J., Forrester, A., Jones, G., Phillips, N., deSouza, D., & Sukhural, S. (2014). *Forensic care pathways for adults with intellectual disability involved with the criminal justice system*. London: Royal College of Psychiatrists.

Allen, E. (2015). *Your guide to relational security: See, think, act*. London: Royal College of Psychiatrists Quality Network for Forensic Mental Health Services.

American Psychiatric Association (APA). (2013). *Diagnostic and statistical manual of mental disorders: DSM-5* (5th edition). Arlington, VA: APA.

Astbury, G., Lovell, A., Mason, T., & Froom, K. (2011). Cultural change in a learning disability secure service: The role of the 'toggle' group. *Journal of Psychiatric and Mental Health Nursing, 18*(9), 804–812. https://doi.org/10.1111/j.1365-2850.2011.01725.x

Barron, P., Hassiotis, A., & Banes, J. (2004). Offenders with intellectual disability: A prospective comparative study. *Journal of Intellectual Disability Research: JIDR, 48*(1), 69–76. https://doi.org/10.1111/j.1365-2788.2004.00581.x

Barton, R. (1959). *Institutional neurosis*. Bristol: John Wright and Sons.

Bennet, J., Kingsbury, K., Fox, N., Bajaj, V., Gay, M., Giacomo, C., Schmemann, S., Stayles, B., Wegman, J., Broder, J., & Kelley, L. (2017). The legacy of zero tolerance policy. *The New York Times* 20/2/17.

Borthwick-Duffy, S. A. (1994). Epidemiology and prevalence of psychopathology in people with mental retardation. *Journal of Consulting and Clinical Psychology, 62*(1), 17–27. https://doi.org/10.1037//0022-006x.62.1.17

Bowden, P. (1980). *Report of the review of Rampton Hospital. DHSS, Cmnd. 8703. 11 1980*. London: HMSO.

Clare, I. C. H., & Murphy, G. H. (1998). Working with offenders or alleged offenders with intellectual disabilities. In E. Emerson, A. Caine, J. Bromley & C. Hatton (Eds.), *Clinical psychology and people with intellectual disabilities*. Retrieved from https://kar.kent.ac.uk/32092/

Craig, D. L. A., & Hutchinson, R. B. (2005). Sexual offenders with learning disabilities: Risk, recidivism and treatment. *Journal of Sexual Aggression, 11*(3), 289–304. https://doi.org/10.1080/13552600500273919

Crichton, J. (1995). *Psychiatric patient violence: Risk and response.* London: Gerald Duckworth & Co.

Department of Health. (2012). *Transforming care: A national response to Winterbourne View Hospital.* London: Department of Health.

DHSS. (1974). *Revised report of the working party on security in NHS psychiatric hospitals: The Glancy report.* London: HMSO.

DHSS. (1975). *The Butler report: The committee on mentally abnormal offenders.* London: HMSO.

Emerson. E, Toogood. A, Mansell. J, Barrett. S, Bell. C, Cummings. R & McCool. C (1987) Challenging Behaviour and Community Services:1. Introduction and overview. *British Journal of Learning Disabilities, 15*(4), 166–169.

Emerson, E. (2001). *Challenging Behaviour: Analysis and Intervention in People with Severe Intellectual Disabilities* (2nd edn.). Cambridge: Cambridge University Press.

Goffman, E. (1961). *Asylums: Essays on the social situations of mental patients and other inmates.* Oxford: Doubleday (Anchor).

Goffman, E. (1963). *Stigma: Notes on the management of spoiled identity.* New York: Prentice Hall.

Harcourt, B. E. (2006). *From the asylum to the prison: Rethinking the incarceration revolution* (SSRN Scholarly Paper No. ID 881865). Retrieved from Social Science Research Network website: https://papers.ssrn.com/abstract=881865

Hayes, S. (2004). Pathways for offenders with intellectual disabilities. In W. L. Lindsay, J. L. Taylor, & P. Sturmey (Eds.), *Offenders with developmental disabilities* (pp. 68–89). Chichester, UK: Wiley.

Hill, J., & Hordell, A. (1999). The Brooklands sex-offender treatment programme. *Learning Disability Practice, 1,* 16–21.

Holland, A. J. (2008). Criminal behaviour and developmental disability: An epidemiological perspective. In W. R. Lindsay, J. L. Taylor & P. Sturmey (Eds.), *Offenders with developmental disabilities* (pp. 23–34). https://doi.org/10.1002/9780470713440.ch2

Hutchinson, J., Lovell, A., & Mason, T. (2012). Managing risk: A qualitative study of community-based professionals working with learning-disabled sex offenders. *Journal of Psychiatric and Mental Health Nursing, 19*(1), 53–61. https://doi.org/10.1111/j.1365-2850.2011.01754.x

Johnston, S. J. (2005). *Epidemiology of offending in learning disability.* Retrieved from https://repository.nottinghamshirehealthcare.nhs.uk/handle/123456789/2880

Langdon, P. E., Clare, I. C. H., & Murphy, G. H. (2010). Developing an understanding of the literature relating to the moral development of people with intellectual disabilities. *Developmental Review, 30*(3), 273–293. https://doi.org/10.1016/j.dr.2010.01.001

Large, J., & Thomas, C. (2011). Redesigning and evaluating an adapted sex offender treatment programme for offenders with an intellectual disability in a secure setting: Preliminary findings. *Journal of Learning Disabilities and Offending Behaviour, 2*(2), 72–83. https://doi.org/10.1108/20420921111152450

Lindsay, W. R. (2004). Sex offenders: Conceptualisation of the issues, services, treatment and management. *Offenders with Developmental Disabilities,* 163–185. https://doi.org/10.1002/9780470713440.ch9

Lindsay, W. R., Law, J., Quinn, K., Smart, N., & Smith, A. H. (2001). A comparison of physical and sexual abuse: Histories of sexual and non-sexual offenders with intellectual disability. *Child Abuse & Neglect, 25*(7), 989–995. https://doi.org/10.1016/s0145-2134(01)00251-4

Lovell, A. (2010). Forensic services. In P. Talbot, G. Astbury & T. Mason (Eds.), *Key concepts in learning disabilities* (pp.112–116). London: Sage.

Lovell, A. (2017). Learning disability nursing in secure settings: Working with complexity. *Journal of Psychiatric and Mental Health Nursing*, 24(1), 1–3. https://doi.org/10.1111/jpm.12364

Lovell, A., & Bailey, J. (2017). Nurses' perceptions of personal attributes required when working with people with a learning disability and an offending background: A qualitative study. *Journal of Psychiatric and Mental Health Nursing*, 24(1), 4–14. https://doi.org/10.1111/jpm.12326

Lovell, A., Bailey, J., Kingdon, A., & Gentile, D. (2014). Working with people with learning disabilities in varying degrees of security: Nurses' perceptions of competencies. *Journal of Advanced Nursing*, 70(9), 2041–2050. https://doi.org/10.1111/jan.12362

Luiselli, J. K. (2000) Cueing, demand fading and positive reinforcement to establish self-feeding and oral consumption in a child with chronic food refusal. *Behaviour Modification,* 24(3), 348–358

Lyall, I., Holland, A. J., & Collins, S. (1995). Offending by adults with learning disabilities: Identifying need in one health district. *Mental Handicap Research*, 8(2), 99–109. https://doi.org/10.1111/j.1468-3148.1995.tb00148.x

Marotta, P. L. (2017). A systematic review of behavioral health interventions for sex offenders with intellectual disabilities. *Sexual Abuse: A Journal of Research and Treatment*, 29(2), 148–185. https://doi.org/10.1177/1079063215569546

Mason, T. (2007). Pendulum. In D. Pilgrim (Ed.), *Inside Ashworth: Professional reflections of institutional life* (pp.23-38). London: Radcliffe.

Morris, P. (1969). *Put away: Sociological study of institutions for the mentally retarded* (First edition). London: Routledge & Kegan Paul Books.

Mottram, P. G. (2007). *HMP Liverpool, Styal and Hindley study report*. Liverpool: University of Liverpool.

Muncie, J. (2008). The punitive turn in juvenile justice: Cultures of control and rights compliance in Western Europe and the USA. *Youth Justice,* 8(2), 107–121.

Nezu, M. C., Fiore, A. A., & Nezu, A. M. (2006). Problem solving treatment for intellectually disabled offenders. *International Journal of Behavioral Consultation and Therapy*, 2(2), 266–276.

NHS England. (2015). Building the right support. Retrieved from https://www.england.nhs.uk/wp-content/uploads/2015/10/ld-nat-imp-planoct15. pdf

O'Brien, G., Taylor, J., Lindsay, W., Holland, A., Carson, D., Steptoe, L., Price.K., Middleton, C., & Wheeler, J. (2010). A multi-centre study of adults with learning disabilities referred to services for antisocial or offending behaviour: Demographic, individual, offending and service characteristics. *Journal of Learning Disabilities and Offending Behaviour*, 1(2), 5–15. http://dx.doi.org/10.5042/jldob.2010.0415

Petersilia, J. (2000). *Doing justice? Criminal offenders with developmental disabilities*. Berkeley, CA: California Policy Research Centre.

Quinsey, V. L. (2004). Risk assessment and management in community settings. In W. R. Lindsay, J. L. Taylor & P. Sturmey (Eds.), *Offenders with developmental disabilities* (pp. 131–141). Chichester: Wiley.

Read, F., & Read, E. (2009). Learning disabilities and serious crime – Sex offences. *Mental Health and Learning Disabilities Research and Practice, 6*, 37–51.

Reynolds, T., Zupanick, C. E., & Dombeck, M. (2013). Historical and contemporary perspectives on intellectual disabilities. *MentalHelp.net*. Retrieved from https://www.mentalhelp.net/articles/historical-and-contemporary-perspectives-on-intellectual-disabilities/ (accessed 18th May 2018)

Rowe, M., & Bendersky, C. (2003). Workplace justice, zero tolerance and zero barriers, in T.A. Kochan and D. Lipsky (Eds), *Negotiations and change: from the Workplace to Society* (pp. 117–140). Ithaca: Cornell University Press

Social Care, Local Government and Care Partnerships/Mental Health and Disability/Learning Disability and Autism. (2014). *Premature deaths of people with learning disabilities: Progress update.* London: Department of Health.

Sweeney, A., Clement, S., Filson, B., & Kennedy, A. (2016). Trauma-informed mental healthcare in the UK: What is it and how can we further its development? *Mental Health Review Journal, 21*(3), 174–192.

Talbot, J. (2009). No one knows: Offenders with learning disabilities and learning difficulties. *International Journal of Prisoner Health, 5*(3), 141–152. https://doi.org/10.1080/17449200903115797

Talbot, J., & Riley, C. (2007). No one knows: Offenders with learning difficulties and learning disabilities. *British Journal of Learning Disabilities, 35*(3), 154–161.

Taylor, J. L., McKinnon, I., Thorpe, I., & Gillmer, B. T. (2017). The impact of transforming care on the care and safety of patients with intellectual disabilities and forensic needs. *BJPsych Bulletin, 41*(4), 205–208. https://doi.org/10.1192/pb.bp.116.055095

Waddington, P. A. J. (1986). Mugging as a moral panic: A question of proportion. *The British Journal of Sociology, 37*(2), 245–259. https://doi.org/10.2307/590356

Ward, T., Hudson, S. M., Johnston, L., & Marshall, W. L. (1997). Cognitive distortions in sex offenders: An integrative review. *Clinical Psychology Review, 17*(5), 479–507. https://doi.org/10.1016/s0272-7358(97)81034-3

Wolfensberger, W. (1983). Social role valorization: A proposed new term for the principle of normalization. *Mental Retardation, 21*(6), 234–239.

Wolfensberger, W., Nirje, B., Olshansky, S., Perske, R., & Roos, P. (1972). The principle of normalization in human services. *Books: Wolfensberger Collection.* Retrieved from https://digitalcommons.unmc.edu/wolf_books/1

Younge, G. (2017). Beyond the blade: The truth about knife crime in Britain. *The Guardian* 28/3/17. Retrieved from https://www.theguardian.com/uk-news/2017/mar/28/beyond-the-blade-the-truth-about-knife-in-britain (accessed 16 July 2018)

INDEX

accountability 89, 138, 181
actuarial 45, 73, 110
actus reus 23, 131
addiction 37, 169
adversarial justice 20
advocacy 151
aftercare 90
alcohol 33, 39, 74, 96, 110, 136
anti-libidinal medication 136, 137
asylum 9, 13, 42, 51
autism 28, 163, 180, 182

Bedlam 7
bio-power 53, 55

capitalism 45, 57
castration 136
Clunis, Christopher 14
coercion 17, 123
consent 75, 137
counselling 75, 164
criminalisation 148
criminogenic 47, 73, 93
custody 23, 34, 42, 71, 87, 121, 133, 144, 145, 162

dangerousness 52, 72, 73, 109, 134, 174, 182
deinstitutionalisation 33, 41
dementia 95
deviance 41, 177
discretion 22, 112

diversion 23, 35, 74, 92, 148, 151, 181
DSPD 46, 79, 111

epilepsy 8, 174
ethnicity 93, 166
eugenics 174
exploitation 162, 181

Fallon Inquiry 113
fire-setting 176

gender 7, 15, 162
grooming 131
Guardianship 180

Hare, Robert 45, 109
homelessness 99, 111, 183
homicide 25, 100

incarceration *see* custody
inequality 160
intermediary 23

jury 20, 27, 28, 37

labelling 6, 45
learning disability 27, 179
lunacy 11, 88

media representation 55, 109, 112, 136, 144, 176
medicalisation 7

mens rea, 23, 28, 131, 176
military 96
mitigation 21, 37

narcissism 79, 108
neoliberalism 51, 57
non-compliance 77, 81

paedophilia 130, 131
personality disorder 58, 81, 91, 108, 165, 177
probation 49, 73, 81, 100
proportionality 73, 133
psychopath 45, 79, 109, 131

race 38, 40, 150, 160, 166
recall 22, 100
reconviction 135
recovery 110, 148, 183
rehabilitation 81, 160

remand 90, 108, 149
restraint 12
risk management 80, 182

self-harm 40, 92, 120, 134, 145, 161
stigmatisation 71, 165, 174
suicide 39, 72, 88, 92, 101, 149, 163
supervision 22, 74, 81, 100, 112

transinstitutionalisation 42
trauma 80, 110, 144, 162, 183

victimisation 40, 159, 181
vulnerability 23, 71, 97

welfare 35, 143, 163

York Retreat 9, 11

Zito, Jonathan 14